LMS
BRANCH LINES
IN
NORTH WALES

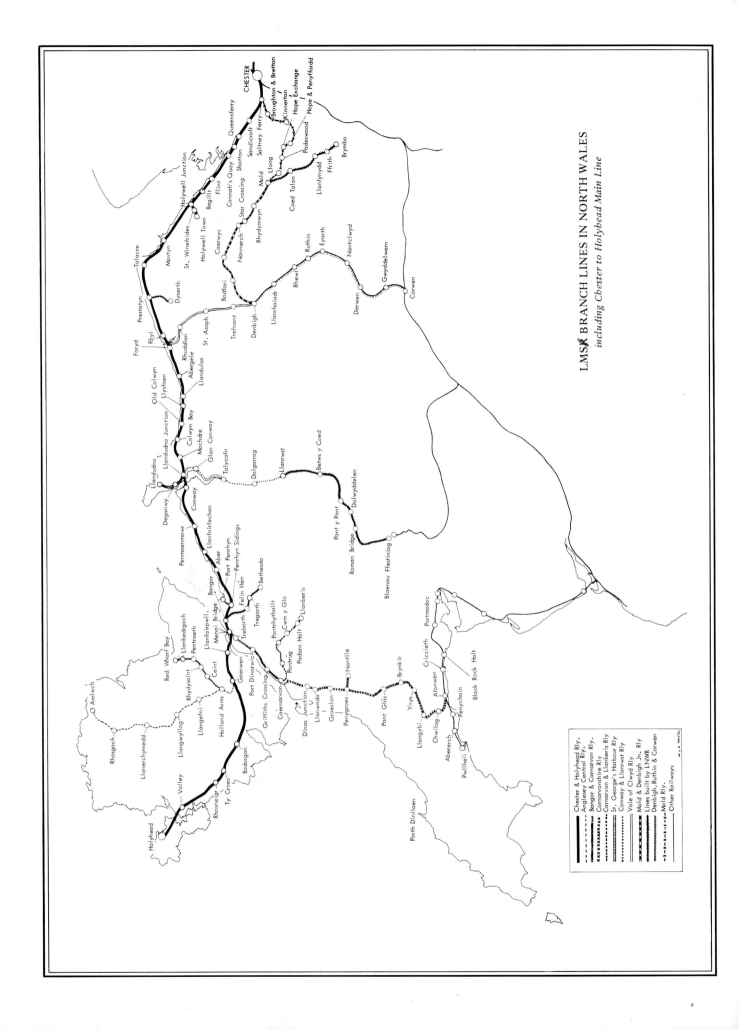

LMSR BRANCH LINES IN NORTH WALES
including Chester to Holyhead Main Line

CHESTER

Broughton & Bretton
Kinnerton
Hope Exchange
Hope & Penyffordd
Padeswood
Llong
Coed Talon
Llanfynydd
Ffrith
Brymbo

Queensferry
Sandicroft
Saltney Ferry
Shotton
Connah's Quay
Star Crossing
Mold
Flint
Bagillt
Rhydymwyn
Caerwys
Nannerch
Holywell Town
Holywell Junction
St. Winefrides
Mostyn

Talacre
Prestatyn
Dyserth
Bodfari
Trefnant
Denbigh
Llanrhaiadr
Rhewl
Ruthin
Eyarth
Nantclwyd
Derwen
Gwyddelwern
Corwen

Foryd
Rhyl
Rhuddlan
Abergele
Llandulas
St. Asaph

Old Colwyn
Llysfaen
Llandudno Junction
Colwyn Bay
Mochdre
Glan Conway
Talycafn
Dolgarrog
Llanrwst
Betws y Coed

Llandudno
Deganwy
Conway
Penmaenmawr
Llanfairfechan
Aber
Port Penrhyn
Penrhyn Sidings
Bethesda
Felin Hen
Tregarth
Bangor
Dolwyddelan
Pont y Pant
Roman Bridge
Blaenau Ffestiniog

Red Wharf Bay
Pentraeth
Llanbedrgoch
Llanfairpwll
Menai Bridge
Treborth
Pontrhythallt
Cwm y Glo
Llanberis
Pont Dinorwic
Padarn Halt
Pontrug

Rhosgoch
Amlwch
Llanerchymedd
Rhydysaint
Llangefni
Llangwyllog
Ceint
Holland Arms
Goerwen
Griffiths Crossing
Dinas Junction
Caernarvon
Llanwnda
Groeslon
Penygroes
Nantlle
Pont Glàs
Brynkir
Ynys

Valley
Rhosneigr
Ty Croes
Bodorgan

Holyhead

Porth Dinllaen

Portmadoc
Criccieth
Afonwen
Penychain
Black Rock Halt
Llangybi
Chwilog
Abererch
Pwllheli

Legend:
— Chester & Holyhead Rly.
--- Anglesey Central Rly.
×××× Bangor & Carnarvon Rly.
∙∙∙∙ Carnarvonshire Rly.
∙∙∙∙ Carnarvon & Llanberis Rly.
∙∙∙∙ St. George's Harbour Rly.
∙∙∙∙ Conway & Llanrwst Rly.
— Vale of Clwyd Rly.
▬▬ Mold & Denbigh Jn. Rly.
⟡⟡⟡ Lines built by LNWR
—•—• Denbigh, Ruthin & Corwen
—∙∙— Mold Rly.
—•—• Other Railways

L M S
BRANCH LINES
IN
NORTH WALES
VOLUME ONE

W. G. Rear

WILD SWAN PUBLICATIONS LTD.

*This work is dedicated to Geoffrey H. Platt, scholar and gentleman.
He was the prime mover in getting this work started, and gave
inspiration and encouragement as well as sound informed opinion.
His methodical approach to railways and life in general was an
object lesson to all who had the privilege to meet him. He is
sadly missed but never forgotten.*

Designed by Paul Karau
Typesetting by Berkshire Publishing Services
Printed and bound by Butler & Tanner Ltd., Frome

Published by
WILD SWAN PUBLICATIONS LTD.
Hopgoods Farm Cottage, Upper Bucklebury, Berks.

Contents

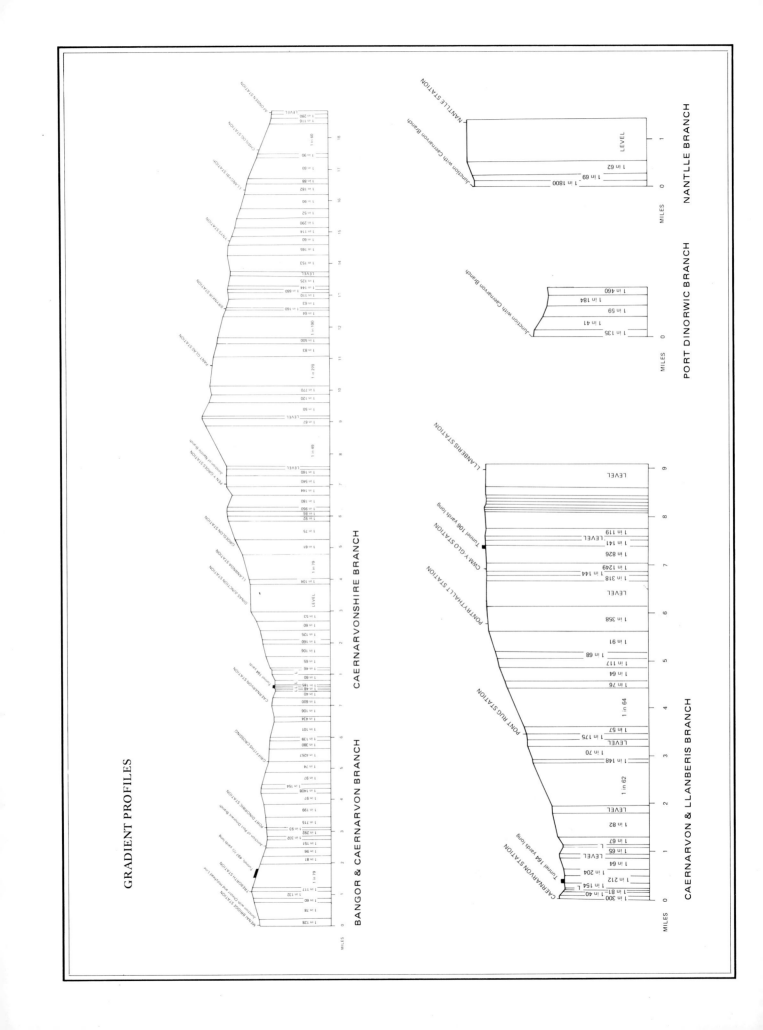

GRADIENT PROFILES

BANGOR TO AFONWEN

THE Bangor to Afonwen line was formed by the amalgamation of the Bangor & Carnarvon Railway, from Menai Bridge on the Chester & Holyhead main line to Caernarvon, and the Carnarvonshire Railway, from Pant station on the outskirts of Caernarvon to Afonwen, on the Cambrian Railways line from Dovey Junction to Pwllheli. The two lines were separate with their own terminal stations at Caernarvon, about a mile and a half apart. Ultimately they were joined to form a through line.

The Bangor & Carnarvon Railway was incorporated on 20th May 1851. The contractors for the construction were McCormack and Holme who also provided finance in return for tolls when the line commenced operating, until the debt was cleared. The line was initially constructed to Port Dinorwic quay, and was a single track from Menai Bridge where a junction with the Chester & Holyhead was made. Sufficient land was acquired to enable a double track to be laid.

The line was leased to the Chester & Holyhead from about the time of opening, the C & H in its turn being worked by the LNWR. Freight and passenger traffic between Bangor and Port Dinorwic commenced on 1st March and 10th March 1852 respectively. The remaining section to Caernarvon was also completed as a single line from Port Siding, about a mile north of Port Dinorwic, leaving the line to the quayside as a branch. The first station at Port Dinorwic was located on the Bangor side of its successor, about half a mile towards Bangor. Stations were opened at Griffiths' Crossing in 1854 and Treborth in 1855 although the latter closed for a brief period in 1858.

Initially, traffic was limited to four trains each way on weekdays and two on Sundays. By 1860 this had been increased to six in each direction with three trains each way on Sundays. As constructed, there was no direct access for 'down' trains from Bangor to the Caernarvon line at Menai Bridge, 'down' trains having to draw past the station and set back into the branch platform before continuing the journey to Caernarvon. 'Up' trains were able to make a straight connection from the platform face on to the 'up' main line. This track layout remained in use until 1872 when it was altered to provide a direct double junction, and an additional platform face was built on the Caernarvon line 'down' side.

The B & CR Caernarvon station was originally constructed as a terminus with a single platform face, goods sidings and a small locomotive depot, but with the Carnarvonshire Railway and the Carnarvon & Llanberis Railway coming under the operating control of the LNWR, it was inevitable that a physical connection between the three concerns was made. The southern termini at Pant and Morfa were some distance from the town centre although the two lines eventually met and ran side by side along the harbour.

The Carnarvon Town Line, authorised on 5th July 1865, was built to connect the three railways. It was jointly proposed by the Carnarvon & Llanberis and the Carnarvonshire companies, although the LNWR as operators of the two concerns was also directly involved. The town line burrowed under Castle Square, from the back of the harbour, and climbed behind Pool Street and Bangor Street to connect with the Bangor & Carnarvon line. The tunnel under Castle Square was 163 yards long with a double track bore which bridged the Afon Cadnant just inside the Bangor end. The combination of the restricted space and gradient caused flooding problems throughout the line's history and was never resolved. Under the Act the LNWR was obliged to provide a station at the south end of the tunnel, with offices at street level. However, Caernarvon Corporation agreed to waive this condition in return for a contribution towards works in Bridge Street, where the line passed under Turf Square.

The Carnarvon Town Line opened for freight on 5th July 1870, five years after its authorisation. In the same month, the C & L was vested in the LNWR. In August orders were given to remove Morfa station, and the remainder of the Nantlle line was converted to standard gauge. At the same time, and by the same orders, Pant station, its goods shed and turntable were removed. Through traffic from the C & L, and the Carnarvonshire lines to Caernarvon and Bangor, was not permitted until January 1871, powers to double the B & CR being granted the same year. This entailed the construction of a second bore to the Vaynol tunnel, south of Treborth.

In May of that year the combination of gradient and tunnel at Caernarvon contributed towards an accident, when an Afonwen train, which had been shunting, was required to place stock in the south bay prior to returning to Afonwen. In order that he might get the stock into the bay and avoid stalling on the 1 in 40 gradient, the driver took it through the tunnel and up the bank towards Seiont bridge, to get a run up the bank and into the bay. A Llanberis train had arrived on the 'up' line, and after running round, was cleared to leave by the signalman who had forgotten about the Afonwen train which was now being propelled up the incline.

At the site of the proposed station, at the south end of the tunnel, where space was very restricted, a scissors crossover was located, controlled by a signal box known as Carnarvon No. 3 box. When Caernarvon station was rebuilt in 1894, the scissors crossover from which the single lines for Llanberis and Afonwen commenced, was removed to the south end of the station, just south of No. 2 signal box. The two branches ran side by side with no physical connection until they went their separate ways by Seiont bridge. It is interesting to note that the proposal to erect a halt south of Caernarvon tunnel reappeared twice, after the First and Second World Wars, and, although investigation showed that it would have been well used by the public, the LNWR and LMS did not consider the cost would have been justified.

The Carnarvonshire Railway had been incorporated by an Act of 29th July 1862 with powers to construct a line from the Bangor & Carnarvon Railway at Caernarvon to Portmadoc. In the event, neither terminal point was reached by the company and only the section between Penygroes and Afonwen was built. An Afonwen to Portmadoc line was also included in Cambrian Railways schemes and by joint arrangement it was decided on 13th December 1865 to leave that section to the Cambrian.

The authorised line between Penygroes and Caernarvon was abandoned with the Carnarvonshire Railway (Nantlle Transfer) Act of 25th July 1867 when the existing 3' 6" gauge Nantlle Railway was absorbed into the Carnarvonshire.

The Nantlle Railway had opened in 1828 as a tramroad to carry minerals from copper mines and slate quarries in the Nantlle valley to Penygroes and then in a northerly direction to the quayside at Caernarvon. The engineers were George and Robert Stephenson. Disagreements between directors delayed the construction of the Carnarvonshire Railway until 1864 when Thomas Savin undertook to construct the line. North of Penygroes the line was to be on the Nantlle Railway trackbed, re-aligned and modified at certain points to ease curves and gradients. By February 1866 construction of standard gauge track had progressed sufficiently that an engine was able to run between Afonwen and Penygroes, whilst the narrow gauge track between Penygroes and the Seiont bridge at Caernarvon had been converted to standard gauge.

The Carnarvonshire Railway suffered its first accident before the line had been officially inspected when an excursion from Portmadoc to Caernarvon was derailed at Brynkir on 6th September 1866, with a loss of six lives.

The formal inspection of the line took place in October 1866. The northern terminus was at Pant, about one and a half miles south of Caernarvon, and south of the Afon Seiont. Intermediate stations were provided at Pwllheli Road, later named Llanwnda, Groeslon, Penygroes and Brynkir. The official consent to open the line was withheld due to incomplete works.

The Carnarvonshire Railway eventually opened to traffic on 2nd September 1867 between Pant and Afonwen and until 10th October, when the Cambrian commenced working to Pwllheli, the company exercised its running powers over the Cambrian and extended its services from Afonwen to Penrhyndeudraeth. Cambrian Railways locomotives were hired until the Carnarvonshire's own locomotives were delivered in 1868. A new station was opened at Chwilog shortly after services commenced in 1868 and others were authorised at Pant Glâs and Llangybi in 1869 and at Ynys in 1872.

With the transfer of ownership to the LNWR in March 1869, the reciprocal running powers with the Cambrian were cancelled, although through running was arranged with the Cambrian and the Great Western at various dates. Cambrian locomotives, trains and crews worked into Caernarvon for the Investiture in 1911 and Cambrian men are believed to have undertaken some workings as far as Bangor for a limited period in 1917, when the LNWR experienced locomotive shortages. There is also an unconfirmed but reliable report that GWR locomotives worked excursions from Chwilog on two occasions in the late 1930s and that some GWR crews from Portmadoc and Pwllheli sheds commenced route learning during the Second World War, with the possibility of working some trains through to Caernarvon. It is believed that '22XX' class 0–6–0s were envisaged but there is no evidence to support the rumour that such a working ever took place. It was only when demolition of the Carnarvonshire commenced from Llanwnda that Western region men from Pwllheli worked over the line regularly, although it must not be forgotten that for several summer seasons, the Radio Land Cruise train from Criccieth, to Barmouth, Corwen, Denbigh, Rhyl, Llandudno Junction, Bangor and Caernarvon ran on three days a week for the high summer season, worked by Pwllheli locomotives and crews. It has not yet been confirmed whether the train crews signed for the route, or whether pilotmen were used for the various sections. Photographs of the train passing through Denbigh indicate two men on the footplate, although this is not conclusive evidence.

Following the closure of the Afonwen branch, the line between Caernarvon and Menai Bridge was singled. Traffic was regulated by miniature electric train staff, with the instruments located in Caernarvon No. 2 cabin and Menai Bridge box. The whole line was operated as one single section. Certain modifications were made to this arrangement for the Investiture of Prince Charles when the section was split at Felin Heli level crossing, east of Port Dinorwic. The instruments were located in a 6' x 4' shed on the 'down' side of the track, underneath the footbridge. This 'signal box' lasted for the one day, and was disconnected shortly afterwards, although the 'cabin' remained on site until the line closed.

When the Bangor & Caernarvon closed to passengers in 1970, the signalling and other re-usable equipment was removed but when the Britannia Bridge was out of action the branch was given a new temporary lease of life as a freightliner terminus. All train movements were under the control of the signal box at Menai Bridge, and public telephone to Caernarvon No. 2 signal box covered traffic movements, an arrangement which persisted until final closure on 5th February 1972.

General view of Bangor MPD in the late 1940s, with LNW coal tank, Stanier class '5' 4–6–0, Watford tank, L & Y Aspinall 0–6–0 and LMS 0–6–0 on shed. In those days it was known as 7B. *D. Chaplin*

'Bangor Loco'

The rostered turns for Bangor are based on one specific period, namely May 1955, as the information for this month can be verified from the daily working diary in the author's possession. This diary covers the period from March to May 1955, and there were some slight variations in the early weeks. This was also before the introduction of DMUs into regular working. There are two other diaries to hand, for May-July 1957, and May-July 1961. These include the summer duties, but the Saturday rosters are not included, hence the selection of the earlier record.

In 1955 there were eight links working. The turn number refers to the duty to which the driver is rostered, and the destination of the first trip only is listed, together with the time of that trip. Rest days are also included. The driver on the spare week would normally cover work in his own link, although it was not uncommon for passed firemen with the required route knowledge to cover turns in the case of absenteeism. Some duties differed from day to day, and to give the complete picture would add pages of detail to the work. No. 1 link was the senior and drivers rose through the links when a vacancy arose. It was

the normal practice for the senior driver in each link to be offered the opportunity to move up but not all drivers chose to; indeed some preferred to remain in lower links for health reasons or personal preferences, foregoing the chance of mileage turns.

Other points of note are as follows: 'P' shunt refers to passenger shunting duties on the station 'up' side at Bangor. In many cases the duty covered only a short period and the crew would possibly work a trip elsewhere, being relieved by another crew. 'F' shunt referred to the freight shunt and the permanent way yard shunt at Bangor, and the same notes apply as for the 'P' shunt. Menai Bridge shunt was different and the crew could spend most or all of their time shunting the yard at Menai Bridge. Some freight workings, such as the Llanberis or Nantlle goods, did not depart from Bangor but ran light engine to Menai Bridge where they took up their train from the yard. No. 6 and 7 links were generally reserved for drivers recovering from sickness or on light work. The firemen allocated to these were invariably passed firemen waiting their opportunity to become regular drivers. They would expect to start regular driving duties in No. 5 link. Apart from the turning links, which were also regarded as light work, there was only one regular Sunday turn, the crew from which usually worked turn 111 on Monday afternoon. This arrange-

This view was taken from above Belmont tunnel, to the west of Bangor station, before the 'up' side loop and station offices were added in 1924. Local trains to Caernarvon, Afonwen, Llanberis and the Anglesey branch lines commenced and terminated in the bay platforms.

Author's collection

The eastern end of Bangor, about 1924, when work on rebuilding and enlarging the station had just commenced. The Bethesda bay is shown under construction behind the smaller No. 1 box.

Author's collection

Bangor shed, viewed from the west end of the 'down' platform. The carriage sidings are to the extreme right of the photograph.   *J. H. Moss*

ment was by the decision of the locomotive shed committee.

Before 1949, information is less dependable, being based on the memories of drivers who were inclined to offer conflicting statements. Nevertheless after much talking and cross-checking the following is believed to be accurate, although someone might have conflicting evidence for a specific period. Driver Eric Lynn has been the chief source of information. He transferred to Bangor in 1937 from Annersley, as a passed cleaner, and worked through the links as a fireman and latterly a driver, eventually becoming the last one to be based at Bangor shed. Much of his recollections has been supported by driver W. Jones, known as 'Will Bach Bob Shunt'. He commenced his footplate work at Chester before being transferred back to his home town of Caernarvon as a cleaner.

Before the Second War, the No. 1 link comprised four sets of men. They worked the Euston turns on alternate days. These were lodging and mileage trips, the regular working being the 8.30 a.m. Bangor-Euston, returning with the 8.45 a.m. Blackpool train as far as Crewe, then working back to Bangor with local work. In the summer season the link was increased by four extra sets of men providing the crew of the 11.00 a.m. Holyhead-Euston. 'The Welshman' from Bangor, returned the following day with the down 'Welshman'.

The No. 2 link had more workings along the coast, including two daily trips. The first started with the 11.30 a.m. Bangor to Liverpool Lime Street. From there the men worked to Manchester Exchange, returning with a Manchester to Bangor train, which arrived at Bangor at 6.30 p.m.

The second trip was the 12.10 p.m. Bangor to Manchester Exchange, Manchester to Liverpool Lime Street, and returning with a Liverpool to Bangor train, arriving at Bangor at 7.10 p.m.

There was a Saturdays only working in this link to Birmingham, departing from Bangor at 9.50 a.m. and booking off in Monument Lane. This was a lodging turn, the crew working the 9.00 a.m. empty coach stock to Llandudno, arriving at approximately 1.30 p.m. on the Sunday. The final stage, Llandudno to Bangor, was worked light engine.

No 3 link was responsible for the Chwilog to Broad Green 'milk', again a lodging turn, working the empty vans to Chwilog at 5.30 p.m., assisting the service train to Afonwen, returning to Bangor with loaded vans and departing for Broad Green at 8.45 p.m., where they arrived at Hanson's dairy sidings after midnight. After shunting the crew worked light engine to Edge Hill, booking off at 2.30 a.m. They booked on again at 1.30 p.m. and, after preparing the loco, returned to Broad Green to pick up the empty vans, departing there at 3.30 p.m. It was a lightly loaded train from Chwilog and the locomotive was usually a class '2P' 4–4–0 No. 446 or No. 625. The train re-formed and picked up additional vans at Chester. The working moved to No. 2 link when the work at Bangor contracted and the traffic was transferred elsewhere, probably to road, in 1950 or early 1951. It is possible that the through working was lost to Bangor by the winter duties of 1950 as I cannot recall seeing the working on the list of rostered turns in November of that year. The London duties were also lost to Bangor about this time, and the Manchester and Liverpool three-cornered working was transferred to Llandudno Junction and worked as straight trips to Liverpool and return, and Manchester and return. The junction men were not familiar, as far as I know, with the Lime Street to Manchester Exchange road.

No. 3 link was also responsible for the passenger trips to Bethesda, which were covered by two turns working four trips each way until the service was withdrawn. Latterly the Red Wharf Bay line freight service ran as a 'Q' trip, or 'run as required'. The regular service had been attached to No. 5 link but, as odd trips were withdrawn, the link structure at Bangor altered, and the pattern was continually changing. The eight links in existence from 1951 to 1961 were

probably the most stable pattern to have existed in recent years, and the period chosen, 1955, was a typical example. By 1957 there were three regular diesel duties, and these had increased to six by 1961. By 1964, when the shed closed, the link system had disappeared and crews worked around the board in turn. After the shed closed, there were several duties that signed on at the station platform, but these were gradually whittled away.

Details of Bangor loco depot are somewhat sketchy in the early days, but the pattern of work for both men and machines probably did not change significantly over the years, until the run down of steam and the closure of branch lines.

An evening scene inside the shed with a fireman drawing his lamps from the stores. The usual clutter of equipment includes an assortment of shovels, coal picks, and reporting number boards. The wall cabinets contain management and trades union notices.   *E. N. Kneale*

TRAIN CREWS, PAY NUMBER AND LINK
5th August 1950

Driver	No.	Fireman	No.
No. 1 link			
Williams, R.E.	8	Jones, J.T.	103
Williams, D.	5	Williams, J.	102
Smith, W.	23	Pritchard, G.	110
Jones, G.Ll.	11	Jones, J. R.	106
Davies, W. H.	17	Baston, F. M.	108
Williams, H. O.	10	Williams, R. H.	105
Parry, T.	24	Roberts, A.	111
Owen, J.	9	Williams, J. H.	104
Owen, E.	19	Parry, J. R.	109
Williams, R.	2	Blain, H.	112
No. 2 link			
Hughes, J.	39	Humphries, W. E.	83
Williams, A. V.	29	Williams, G.	73
Williams, R. J.	27	Jones, J. E.	72
Davies, W. J.	32	Evans, O. T.	85
Jones, W.	58	Roberts, O. G.	76
Caulfield, H.	38	Williams, J. M.	82
Roberts, W.	40	Hughes, F. S.	84
Davies, W.	36	Williams, W. J.	80
Davies, B. E.	60	Jones, S. V.	79
Edwards, V. N. B.	25	Hughes, H. O.	71
Roberts, H.	37	Jones, W. N.	81
Hughes, R. R.	31	Lynn, E.	74
No. 3 link			
Davies, E.	42	Hughes, L.	115
Jones, H.	47	Mooney, J.	91
Jones, E. J.	44	Parry, W. P.	88
Jones, W.	49	Hughes, A. W.	93
Roberts, C. S.	50	Pritchard, R. C.	117
Hughes, H.	46	Owen, D. L.	90
Jones, R.	45	Humpries, D.	89
Price, R. E.	61	Williams, J. O.	95
Roberts, D.	48	Jones, J. T.	116
Griffiths, Ll.	43	Edwards, R.	87
No. 4 link			
Lewis, B.	51	Owen, E. G.	119
Kelly, I. S.	62	Jones, J. R.	101
Jones, G.	22	Davies, G.	98
Jones, H.	16	Hughes, R. N.	97
Williams, A. W.	13	Jones, J. I.	96
Morgan, F. W.	63	Humphries, R.	99
No. 5 link			
Edwards, O.	21	Griffiths, W. A.	69
Roberts, R. J.	26	Jones, D. L.	70
Graham, W. J.	53	Williams, H. H.	121
Dean, W. S.	64	Davies, J. N.	68
Read, W. R. J.	14	Edwards, M.	66
Jones, W.	18	Williams, T. J.	122
No. 6 link			
Williams, T.	20	Hughes, O. E.	78
Williams, P.	12	Williams, G. E.	124
Williams, W.	7	Williams, G. R.	123
Roberts, W. T.	28	Johnson, F.	125
No. 7 link			
Ellis, C.	65	Owen, T.	77
Williams, G.	33	Davies, W. E.	114
Roberts, J. J.	54	Davies, E. W.	126

ROSTERED TURNS — MAY 1955

Turn	Time	Destination of 1st trip	Rest Days
No. 1 link			
108	4.35 a.m.	Afonwen	Sun + Sat
81	1.32 p.m.	Llandudno Jctn	Sun
80	6.45 a.m.	Llandudno Jctn	Sun + Mon
117	9.20 a.m.	'P' Shunt	Sun
70	7.42 a.m.	Holyhead	Sun + Tues
112	11.50 a.m.	Afonwen	Sun
73	9.12 a.m.	Holyhead	Sun + Wed
95	12.10 p.m.	Chester. Mon. only	Sun
96	3.50 p.m.	Crewe. Mon. excepted	
78	7.45 a.m.	Llandudno Jctn	Sun + Thurs
84	3.10 p.m.	Llandudno Jctn	Sun
		spare week covering rest days	Sun + Fri
111	4.04 p.m.	Afonwen	—
No. 2 link			
225	5.15 a.m.	'F' Shunt	Sun + Tues
114	2.52 p.m.	Pwllheli	Sun
107	5.30 a.m.	Pwllheli	Sun + Mon
85	2.40 p.m.	Llandudno Jctn	—
69	6.58 a.m.	Holyhead	Sun + Wed
248	10.40 a.m.	'F' Shunt	Sun
208	7.30 a.m.	Nantlle	Sun + Sat
236	11.50 a.m.	Llandudno Jctn	Sun
241	6.25 a.m.	Llanberis	Sun + Fri
237	7.20 p.m.	Llandudno Jctn	Sun
		spare week covering rest days	Sun + Thurs
231	7.10 a.m.	Amlwch	Sun
No. 3 link			
105	1.24 p.m.	Afonwen	Sun
239	9.30 p.m.	Llandudno Jctn	Sun + Sat
222	8.50 a.m.	Amlwch	Sun
		spare week covering rest days	Sun + Tues
140	1.25 p.m.	'P' Shunt	Sun
100	6.00 a.m.	Caernarvon	Sun + Sat
235	4.28 p.m.	Llandudno Jctn	Sun
75	3.42 p.m.	Holyhead	Sun + Tues
240	12.55 p.m.	Menai Bridge shunt	Sun
110	11.30 a.m.	Pwllheli	Sun + Fri
No. 4 link			
211	11.45 a.m.	Llangefni	Sun
50	6.45 a.m.	Amlwch	Sun + Sat
132	12.40 p.m.	Amlwch	Sun
40	5.25 p.m.	Amlwch	Sun + Fri
No. 5 link			
210	3.00 a.m.	Menai Bridge shunt	Sun
223	5.52 p.m.	Menai Bridge shunt	Sun + Sat
125	7.35 a.m.	'P' shunt	Sun
No. 6 link			
227	4.50 a.m.	Caernarvon shunt	Sun
228	2.15 p.m.	Caernarvon shunt	Sun + Wed
No. 7 link			
242	12.55 p.m.	Llanfair goods	Sun
Turning Link			
	12.01 a.m.	Monday only	
	10.00 p.m.	Monday-Saturday	Sun
	6.00 a.m.		Sun
	2.00 p.m.		Thurs

WORKING ARRANGEMENTS — MAY 1955

Day	Time	Destination	Loco type	Shed	Turn	Link
Sunday	6.00 am	Turning	–	–	–	–
	8.00 am	Crewe	5	6H	62	1
	3.00 pm	Turning	–	–	–	–
Monday	12.01 am	Turning	–	–	–	– M.O.
	1.24 am	Afonwen goods	4	6H	105	3 M.O.
	3.00 am	Menai Bridge	2	6H	210	5
	3.40 am	Afonwen Goods	4	6H	106	3 MX
	4.35 am	Afonwen	4	6H	108	1
	4.50 am	Caernarvon shunt	4	6H	227	6
	5.15 am	'F' shunt	2	6H	225	2
	5.25 am	Amlwch	2	6H	40	4
	5.30 am	Pwllheli	4	6H	107	2
	6.00 am	Turning	–	–	–	–
	6.00 am	Caernarvon	4	6H	100	3
	6.25 am	Llanberis goods	4	6H	241	2
	6.45 am	Amlwch	2	6H	50	4
	6.45 am	Llan. Jctn.	4	6H	80	1
	6.58 am	Holyhead	5	6H	69	2
	7.10 am	Amlwch	2	6H	231	2
	7.30 am	Nantlle goods	5	6H	208	2
	7.35 am	'P' shunt	–	6H	125	5
	7.42 am	Holyhead	5	6H	70	1
	7.45 am	Llan. Jctn.	4	6H	78	1
	8.50 am	Amlwch	2	6H	222	3
	9.12 am	Holyhead	rel.	5A	73	1
	9.20 am	'P' shunt	–	6H	117	1
	10.40 am	'F' shunt	–	6H	248	2
	10.50 am	Port Siding	by turn 125			5
	11.30 am	Pwllheli	4	6H	110	3
	11.45 am	Llangefni	2	6H	211	4 SX
	11.50 am	Afonwen goods	4	6H	112	1
	12.10 pm	Chester	5	6J	95	1 M.O.
	12.15 pm	Menai Bridge	4	6H	240	3
	12.20 pm	Afonwen	by turn 117			1
	12.40 pm	Amlwch	2	6H	132	4
	12.55 pm	Llanfair	8	6B	242	7
	1.25 pm	'P' shunt	2	6H	140	3
	1.32 pm	Llan. Jctn.	rel.	–	81	1
	2.00 pm	Turning	–	–	–	–
	2.15 pm	Caernarvon shunt	4	6H	228	6
	2.40 pm	Llan. Jctn. goods	8	6B	85	2
	2.52 pm	Pwllheli	4	6H	114	2
	3.10 pm	Llan. Jctn.	4	6H	84	1
	3.42 pm	Holyhead	rel.	–	75	3 M.O.
	3.50 pm	Crewe	6	5A	96	1 MSX
	4.04 pm	Afonwen	4	6H	111	1
	4.38 pm	Llan. Jctn.	5	6B	235	3 M.O.
	5.25 pm	Menai Bridge	2	6H	223	5
	7.20 pm	Llan. Jctn. goods	8	6B	237	2
	9.30 pm	Llan. Jctn. goods	8	6B	239	3
	10.00 pm	Turning	–	–	–	–
	10.30 pm	Menai Bridge	by turn 237			2 M.O.
	11.50 pm	Llan. Jctn.	5	6H	236	2
Saturday	3.00 am	Menai Bridge	4	6H	212	5
	4.35 am	Afonwen	4	6H	108	1
	4.45 am	Afonwen Goods	4	6H	106	3 SO
	4.50 am	Caernarvon shunt	4	6H	229	6
	5.15 am	'F' shunt	4	6H	225	2
	5.25 am	Amlwch	2	6H	40	4
	5.30 am	Pwllheli	4	6H	107	2
	6.00 am	Turning	–	–	–	–
	6.00 am	Caernarvon	4	6H	101	3
	6.25 am	Llanberis goods	4	6H	241	2
	6.45 am	Amlwch	2	6H	50	3
	6.45 am	Llan. Jctn.	4	6H	80	1
	6.58 am	Holyhead	5	6H	69	2
	7.10 am	Amlwch	2	6H	231	2
	7.30 am	Nantlle goods	5	6H	209	2
	7.35 am	'P' shunt	4	6H	141	5
	7.42 am	Holyhead	5	6H	60	1
	7.45 am	Llan. Jctn.	4	6H	79	1
	8.40 am	Amlwch	2	6H	224	3
	9.00 am	Caernarvon	rel.	–	230	3
	9.12 am	Holyhead	rel.	–	74	1
	11.25 am	'F' shunt	rel.	–	115	2
	11.30 am	Pwllheli	4	6H	110	2
	11.40 am	Amlwch	2	6H	130	3
	11.50 am	Afonwen goods	4	6H	112	1
	11.55 am	Llangefni	2	6H	213	4
	12.20 pm	Afonwen	4	6H	113	1
	12.40 pm	Amlwch	2	6H	131	4
	12.55 pm	Menai Bridge	2	6H	249	6
	12.55 pm	Llanfair	8	6B	242	7
	1.30 pm	'F' shunt	–	–	116	1
	1.32 pm	Llan. Jctn.	5	6J	82	1
	2.00 pm	Turning	–	–	–	–
	2.40 pm	Llan. Jctn. goods	8	6B	87	2
	2.52 pm	Pwllheli	by turn 115			2
	3.00 pm	'P' shunt	–	–	86	2
	3.50 pm	Chester	6	5A	97	1
	3.55 pm	Amlwch	2	6H	133	3
	4.38 pm	Llan. Jctn. goods	8	6B	83	1
	5.39 am	Afonwen	by turn 116			1
	5.48 pm	Llan. Jctn.	4	6H	77	3
	6.20 pm	Llan. Jctn. goods	by turn 86			2
	10.00 pm	Turning	–	–	–	–

Ex-LNWR 0–6–2Ts were used extensively at Bangor until replaced by newer machines. Here a 'Watford' tank, still bearing its LMS livery, albeit somewhat faded, is shunting the goods yard on the duty referred to as 'F' shunt on the listed turns. The small cabs were very cramped and, as these engines were usually in run-down condition, life was uncomfortable for their crews. *D. Chaplin*

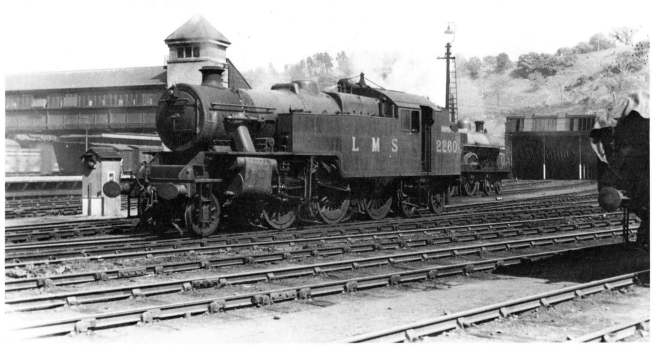

2–6–4T No. 2260 on shed awaiting its next turn of duty in 1947. *J. M. Dunn*

LOCOMOTIVE ROSTERING — MAY 1955

As with other sheds, Bangor diagrammed its locomotives to work with more than one duty in the working day. The pattern was adhered to for convenience and at Bangor was as follows. Some duties had built in differences and the starting time might vary on some days. There might also be differences within the duties even when the starting times remained the same.

MONDAYS TO FRIDAYS

Time	Destination	Turn No.
1.24 am	Afonwen Goods M.O.	105
3.40 am	Afonwen Goods M.X.	106
12.15 pm	Menai Bridge	240
3.00 am	Menai Bridge shunt	210
11.45 am	Llangefni	211
4.35 am	Afonwen	108
3.10 pm	Llan. Jctn.	84
4.50 am	Caernarvon shunt	227
2.15 pm	Caernarvon shunt	228
5.25 am	Amlwch	40
12.40 pm	Amlwch	132
5.30 am	Pwllheli	107
11.30 am	Pwllheli	110
6.00 am	Caernarvon	100
2.52 pm	Pwllheli	114
6.25 am	Llanberis goods	241
4.04 pm	Afonwen	111
6.45 am	Amlwch	50
1.25 pm	'P' shunt M.X.	140
6.45 am	Llan. Jctn.	80
12.20 pm	Afonwen	117
6.58 am	Holyhead	69
1.32 pm	Llan. Jctn.	81
11.50 pm	Llan. Jctn.	236

Time	Destination	Turn No.
7.10 am	Amlwch	231
7.30 am	Nantlle	209
7.35 am	'P' shunt	125
11.50 am	Afonwen goods	112
10.30 pm	Menai Bridge shunt	237
7.42 am	Holyhead (M.P. turn 70)	71
7.45 am	Llan. Jctn.	78
8.50 am	Amlwch	222
5.52 pm	Menai Bridge shunt	223

SATURDAYS

Time	Destination	Turn No.
3.00 am	Menai Bridge shunt	212
11.45 pm	Llangefni	213
3.40 am	Afonwen goods	106
2.52 pm	Pwllheli	115
4.35 am	Afonwen	108
9.00 am	Afonwen	230
5.39 pm	Afonwen	116
4.50 am	Caernarvon shunt	229
5.15 am	'F' shunt	225
5.25 am	Amlwch	40
11.40 am	Amlwch	130
3.55 pm	Amlwch	133
5.30 am	Pwllheli	107
11.50 am	Afonwen	112

Time	Destination	Turn No.
6.00 am	Caernarvon	101
11.30 am	Pwllheli	110
6.45 am	Amlwch	50
12.40 pm	Amlwch	131
6.45 am	Llan. Jctn.	80
12.20 pm	Afonwen	113
5.48 am	Llan. Jctn.	77
6.58 am	Holyhead	69
7.10 am	Amlwch	231
7.30 am	Nantlle	209
7.35 am	'P' shunt	141
7.45 am	Llan. Jctn.	79
8.40 am	Amlwch	224
9.00 am	Caernarvon	230
11.25 am	'F' shunt	115
12.55 pm	Menai Bridge	249
12.55 pm	Llanfair	242
6.20 pm	Llan. Jctn.	86
2.40 pm	Llan. Jctn.	87
3.50 pm	Chester	97
4.38 pm	Llan. Jctn. goods	83

The centrepiece of shed working was the engine arrangements board shown here with Norman Kneale and Barry Wynne contemplating their special allocation efforts on 13th May 1964. The shed was nearing the end of its working life when many of the regular workings were local trips. *E. N. Kneale*

LOCOMOTIVE ALLOCATIONS

Records of LMS allocations are poor, and the former shed-master at Bangor, J. M. Dunn, compiled a study of the shed from information available to him in his official capacity. The first list of locomotives in detail (apart from a reference for 1908 which listed 2—4—0ST engines 1000 and 1001 being stationed at Bangor for working the Red Wharf Bay and Bethesda branches), is dated 1929 (no month but believed to be the summer period) when the allocation was as follows:-

PASSENGER LOCOMOTIVES

5152 'Renown' class	6578 4' 6" Motor
5157	6579
5371 'George V' class	6633 5' 6" ST
5372	6635
5373	6636
	6637
6026 'Claughton' class	6748
6027	
6028	6963 5' 6" Superh. ST
	6964
5545 'Experiment' class	6965
5546	

FREIGHT LOCOMOTIVES

4146 Standard 0—6—0	8354 18" Goods
4147	8355
4148	8370
	8537
7557 STC (Motor)	8538
7654	8539
7679	8540
7680	8541
	8542
7795 STC	
7796	8779 19" Goods
7797	8780
7799	8781
7801	
7802	9644 ex ROD
7803	9645
7805	9646
	9647
8158 Small coal	9649
8159	

MARCH 1933

4305 Standard 0—6—0	7606 Class '2F'
4359	7613
4369	7654
4370	7669
4487	7679
4507	7680
4509	7729
	7764
5309 Class '3P'	7772
5343	7780
5371	7797
5372	7829
5373	
	8158 Class '2F'
5545 Class '3P'	8159
	8356
6026 Class '5P'	8538
6027	8539
	8540
6146 Class '6P'	8541
	8542
6633 Class '1P'	
6669	8779 Class '4F'
6681	8781
6683	8830
6703	
6963 Class '4P'	
6964	
6965	

DECEMBER 1937

10 Class '3P' 2—6—2T	6956 Class '4P' 4—6—2T
52	6980
101 Class '3P'	7728 Class '2F' 0—6—2T
121	7729
	7764
4075 Class '4F' 0—6—0	7812
4081	27572
4121	27596
4340	27654
4375	27678
5317 Class '5MT' 4—6—0	8158 Class '2F' 0—6—0
5318	
5346	8392 Class '2F' 0—6—0
	8404
2351 Class '4T' 2—6—4T	8485
2390	8618
6681 Class '1P. 2—4—2T	12214 Class '2F' 0—6—0
6683	12605
6703	
6710	

JULY 1938

2 Class '3P' 2—6—2T	6681 Class '1P' 2—4—2T
12	6683
48	6703
51	6710
52	
55	7728 Class '2F' 0—6—2T
70	7729
	7764
101 Class '3P' 2—6—2T	7812
207	
	8158 Class '2F' 0—6—0
2539 Class '4P' 2—6—4T	8455
2581	8618
2593	
	25277 Class '3P' 4—4—0
4075 Class '4F' 0—6—0	
4121	25374 Class '2P' 4—4—0
4305	
4340	27572 Class '2F' 0—6—2T
4375	27596
	27604
5070 Class '5MT' 4—6—0	27654
5317	27678
5318	
5346	12214 Class '2F' 0—6—0
	12605
6106 Class '6P' 4—6—0	
6113	

MARCH 1949

72 Class '3P' 2—6—2T	2948 Class '5' 2—6—0
73	2951
87	2984
124	
134	4305 Class '4F' 0—6—0
143	4445
1200 Class '2P' 2—6—2T	6687 Class '1P' 2—4—2T
1221	
1222	6899 Class '1P' 0—6—2T
1223	6906
1224	
	7711 Class '1F' 0—6—2T
524 Class '2P' 4—4—0	
	12118 Class '2F' 0—6—0
2258 Class '4P' 2—6—4T	12176
2259	12239
2260	12407
2261	
	28543 Class '2F' 0—6—0
2460 Class '4T' 2—6—4T	
2628	

A fine view of Bangor shed, taken from Bangor mountain looking towards Belmont tunnel and Menai Bridge. The restricted space for the station and shed can be appreciated from this location. The position of the turntable, literally perched over Caernarvon road, ensured that anyone approaching it did not become too casual about speed. To the left of the turntable road next to the goods shed can be seen three carriage sidings. Bangor possessed no mechanical coaling facilities and engines were loaded by hand from the old LNWR 'coal hole'.

G. H. Platt

SEPTEMBER 1954

40122 Class '3P' 2—6—2T

41200 Class '2P' 2—6—2T
41223
41230
41239
41321
41323
41324

42156 Class '4P' 2—6—4T
42157
42178

42415 Class '4P' 2—6—4T
42416
42417
42418

42444 Class '4P' 2—6—4T
42455
42460
42588
42617
42662

44305 Class '4F' 0—6—0
44445

44913 Class '5MT' 4—6—0
45144
45417

52119 Class '2F' 0—6—0
52230
52269

58394 Class '2F' 0—6—0

16th MAY 1955

41200 Class '2P' 2—6—2T
41230
41239
41321
41322
41323
41324

42156 Class '4P' 2—6—4T
42157
42178

42415 Class '4P' 2—6—4T
42416
42417
42418

42444 Class '4P' 2—6—4T
42455
42460
42588
42617

44305 Class '4F' 0—6—0

44913 Class '5MT' 4—6—0
45144
45417

52119 Class '2F' 0—6—0
52230
52269

58394 Class '2F' 0—6—0

JUNE 1957

40003 Class '3P' 2—6—2T
40132 Class '3P' 2—6—2T

41200 Class '2P' 2—6—2T
41230
41233
41234
41239

42415 Class '4P' 2—6—4T

80087 Class '4P' 2—6—4T
80088
80089
80090
80091
80092
80094
80095

44445 Class '4F' 0—6—0

44913 Class '5MT' 4—6—0

75010 Class '4MT' 4—6—0
75012

52119 Class '2F' 0—6—0
52230
52269

12th JUNE 1965

Final allocation on day Bangor shed closed

41200 Class '2P' 2—6—2T
41204
41233
41234
41241

44821 Class '5MT' 4—6—0
45145
45223
45298
45345

78003 Class '2MT' 2—6—0
78032
78058
78059

80131 Class '4MT' 2—6—4T
(Condemned)

From 1948 until the shed closed, much of the local traffic was worked by 2—6—4T locomotives. Four of the Fairburn tanks were delivered new to Bangor, including No. 42258 seen here resting between turns outside the shed. Despite the tricky injectors they were popular with the crews and comfortable to work, even on bunker first trips back off the Afonwen line. Eventually these locos were transferred to Gourock in exchange for Fowler parallel boiler versions, which were equally popular, if a trifle hot in the summer months. They were considered slightly more powerful than their younger cousins.

Author

Extract from

LNWR SERVICE TIMETABLE – JULY, AUGUST & SEPTEMBER 1904

BANGOR, CARNARVON PEN-Y-GROES, & AFONWEN. (Single Line Carnarvon to Afonwen.)

Train Staff Stations: Carnarvon, Dinas, Groeslon, Pen-y-Groes, Brynkir, Chwilog, and Afonwen.

Passenger Trains can cross each other only at Dinas, Pen-y-Groes, and Brynkir.

WEEK DAYS. (Nos. 1–30); Suns. (Nos. 31–32)

Miles.	STATIONS.	1	2	3	4	5	6	7	8	9	10	11	12	13	14	15	16
	DOWN.	Gd	Pas	Gd	Fast Gd	Empty Coach SO	Fast Coal	Pas	Pas	Goods and Empty Coach SO	Gd	Gd	Season Excursion	Season Excursion	Pas	Gd	Empty Ca'ges SO
		1	2	3				5	6		1	7				4	
•		a m	a m	a m	a m	a m	a m	a m	a m	a m	a m	a m	a m	a m	a m	a m	p m
...	BANGOR...dep	..	4 46		...	...	7 25	8 15	8 52	...	...	8 20	9 28	9 34	10 55	...	...
1¼	Menai Bridge arr	...	...	...	...	...	7 30	8 19	8 56	...	...	8 25	9 32	9 38	10 59	...	...
	Menai Bridge dep	5 35	4 49	...	...	...	8 30	8 20	9 1	...	...	9 10	9 33	9 40	11 0		.
1⅝	Davies Siding	...	...	...	SO	...	...	...	...	...	S	...	...	...	...	For Nantlle.	...
2¼	Treborth	...	...	...	...	...	M	8 24	...	...	...	...	See note	C	11 4		
2½	Treborth Siding	...	...	...	...	...		...	...	...	...	...			...		...
3¾	Port Siding ...	...	...	...	...	...	...	...	...	...	...	...	...	...	..		..
4½	P. DINORWIC	...	4 57	...	...		..	8 29	9 8	...	...	X	...	...	11 10	...	...
6⅜	Griffith's Cr'sing		..	...	..	...	..	8 34	...	...	...	...	...	...	11 15	...	...
8½	CARNARVON arr	6 0	5 4	...	...	...	8 55	8 38	9 15	...	...	9 35	9 45	9 52	11 19	...	..
	CARNARVON dep	6 45	5 6	6 0	6 20	8 30	1.40 a.m. from Bamfurlong.	8 45	9 20	9 45	9 45	10 12	10 25	...	...	11 16	12 5
9	Quay Siding ...	7 10	See	6 10	6 30	...		...	See	...	..	...	..			...	...
11¾	DINAS Junction arr	7 20	5 16	6 20	6 40	8 40		8 55	9 30	9 55	9 56	10 23	10 35	...	...	11 26	12 10
	DINAS Junction dep	7 30	5 17	6 35	7 10	8 40		8 57	9 30	10 0	9§56	10 55	..	...	...	11 55	12§15
12⅜	Llanwnda	7 35	note	...	7 25	...		9 0	note	X	...	...	When No. 13 runs No. 12 will be accelerated, and will not call at Menai Bridge.		...	X	...
13½	Groeslon	Saturdays excepted Carnarvon to Llanwnda	5 21	7 10	7 38	8 45		9 4	9§34	10 7	10 §5	11 2			...	12 10	12§22
14	Tudor Siding...		...	X		...		...	...	X	...	X			...	X	...
15⅜	PENY-GROES arr		5 26	7 17	7 45	8 50		9 9	9 38	10 20	10 12	11 10			...	12 20	12 30
	PENY-GROES dep		5 27	For Nantlle.	8 0	...	...	9 12	9 40	...	10 32	11 30			...	Works Traffic to and from Tudor Siding when required.	For Nantlle.
19¼	Pant Glas Crs'g		...		...	...	...	9 21	...	...	...	X			...		
21	BRYNKIR arr		5 41		8 25	...	...	9 26	9§49	...	10 55	11 48			...		
	BRYNKIR dep		5 41		8 40	...	...	9 27	9§49	..	11 7	12 0			...		
23	Ynys Crossing		...		...	...	...	9 32	...	.	...	X			...		
24¾	Llangybi .,		...		..	...	...	9 36			...	X			...		
26	Chwilog (for Nevin) arr		5 51	...	8 55	...	...	9 39	9§58	...	11 25	12 20			...		...
	Chwilog (for Nevin) dep		5 53	...	9 0	...	...	9 42	9§58	...	11 30	12 25			...		...
27¼	AFONWEN ...	...	5 56	..	9 5		...	9 45	10 0		11 35	12 40			...		...

Miles.	STATIONS.	17	18	19	20	21	22	23	24	25	26	27	28	29	30	31 (Suns.)	32 (Suns.)
	DOWN.	Pas	Pas	Empty Wagns	Pas	Gd	Pas	Pas	Pas	Gd	Pas	Pas	Pas	Gd	Pas	Pas	Pas
				3		8		SO		C				C			
•		noon	p m	p m	p m	p m	p m	p m	p m	p m	p m	p m	p m	p m	p m	a m	a m
...	BANGOR...dep	12 5	1 20	C	2 28	...	3 25	...	5 25	...	7 22	8 0	9 5	...	11 0	4 46	9 5
1¼	Menai Bridge arr	12 9	1 24		2 32	...	3 29	.	5 29	...	7 26	...	9 9	...	11 4	...	9 9
	Menai Bridge dep	12 10	1 25	2 0	2 33	2 40	3 30	...	5 31	7 0	7 27	...	9 10	9 30	11 5	4 49	9 10
1⅝	Davies Siding	...	...	...	...	X	...	...	...	...	...	...	...	...	...	...	...
2¼	Treborth	...	1 29	...	2 37	.		...	5 35	...	7 31	...	...	...		...	...
2½	Treborth Siding	...	...	...	...	X	...	...	...	...	...	...	...			.	...
3¾	Port Siding ...	...	...	2 10	...	...	...	...	...	..	...	...	...	...	...	...	...
4½	P. DINORWIC	12 16	1 34		2 42	X	3 37	...	5 41	...	7 36	8 10	9 18	...	11 12	4 57	9 18
6⅜	Griffith's Cr'sing	...	1 39	...	2 47	X	.	...	5 46	...	7 41	...	...	...	...	...	...
8½	CARNARVON arr	12 23	1 43	...	2 51	3 10	3 44	...	5 50	7 30	7 45	8 18	9 26	9 55	11 20	5 4	9 26
	CARNARVON dep	12 32	...	To be worked by Engine and Men of 8.15 a.m. from Mold Jc.	3 2	...	3 48	5 20	6 5	...		8 25	...		...	7 55	..
9	Quay Siding ...	...	...		...	...	See	...	...		..	...		..	...	...	...
11¾	DINAS Junction arr	12 42	...		3 12	...	3 58	5 30	6 13	...	...	8 35	..	...	...	8 5	...
	DINAS Junction dep	12 44	...		3 12	...	3 58	5 31	6 15	...	..	8 36	..	...	...	8 §5	...
12⅜	Llanwnda	12 47	...		3 15	..	note	5 35	6 18	..	...	8 39	...		..	8 8	...
13½	Groeslon	12 51	...		3 19	..	4§2	5 39	6 22	...	...	8 43	..	...	...	8 12	...
14	Tudor Siding...	...	...		...	...	...	...	...	...	..	...	...		...	.	
15⅜	PENY-GROES arr	12 56	...		3 24	...	4§6	5 44	6 27	...	...	8 48	...	...	...	8 17	...
	PENY-GROES dep	12 58	...		3 25	...	4 6	...	6 28	...	...	8 49	...	...	...	8 18	...
19¼	Pant Glas Crs'g	1 8	...		3 34	...	...	...	6 37	...	...	8 58	...	...	...	...	...
21	BRYNKIR arr	1 14	...		3 39	...	4 16	...	6 42	...	...	9 3	...	...	...	8 31	...
	BRYNKIR dep	1 15	...		3 40	...	4§17	...	6 43	...		9 4	..	...	...	8 32	...
23	Ynys Crossing	1 20	...		3 45	...	See	...	6 48	...	...	9 9	...	...	...	...	...
24¾	Llangybi .,	1 24	...		3 49	...	note	..	6 52	...	..	9 14		..	...	...	.
26	Chwilog (for Nevin) arr	1 27	...		3 52	...	4 26	..	6 55	...	..	9 17	...	...	...	8 41	...
	Chwilog (for Nevin) dep	1 29	...	...	3 55	...	4 29	...	6 57	-		9 20	...	...	...	8 44	..
27¼	AFONWEN ...	1 32			3 58		4 32		7 0	...	...	9 23	...	..		8 47	...

A Conditional Empty Wagon Train leaves Menai Bridge at 8.0 a.m. for Port Siding.

No. 2—Is advertised to call at Dinas Junction when required to set down, on notice being given by the passenger to the guard.

No 3.—This Train not to convey Traffic for Pen-y-Groes, except from Quay Siding, unless short of a load. Arrives Groeslon 6.40.

Nos. 1. 4, and 15 shunt coal siding and warehouse at Dinas.

No. 5—Runs on Carnarvon Fair Days also,

No. 8—Calls at Dinas Junction to set down Passengers for the North Wales Narrow Guage Railway. Tickets to be collected at Pen-y-Groes.

No. 11—Works Tranship Van, stops at Pant Glas, Ynys, and Llangybi when required Not to be kept at Brynkir to do Shunting. To leave Dinas at 11.5 a.m. on Saturdays after arrival of 10.40 a.m. (Saturdays only Train) from Nantlle

A Mineral Train leaves Carnarvon at 1.0 p.m. for Quay Siding.

No 15—To do what shunting is required at Dinas. Calls at Llanwnda on Saturdays to pick up and detach important Traffic.

No 22—Calls at Chwilog to set down from beyond Rhyl when required. Dinas and Afonwen tickets to be collected at Carnarvon.

Afonwen Tickets of all Down Trains, except No. 8, to be collected at Chwilog.

A Coal Train leaves Bangor at 6.0 a.m. and arrives Carnarvon at 6.30 on Sundays.

AFONWEN, PEN-Y-GROES, CARNARVON, & BANGOR. (Single Line Afonwen to Carnarvon.)

TRAIN STAFF STATIONS: Afonwen, Chwilog, Brynkir, Pen-y-Groes, Groeslon, Dinas, Carnarvon.

Passenger Trains can cross each other only at Brynkir, Pen-y-groes, and Dinas.

WEEK DAYS. (Nos. 35–65); Sundays (Nos. 66–67)

Miles.	STATIONS.	35	36	37	38	39	40	41	42	43	44	45	46	47	48	49	50
	UP.	Fast Min. Empties.	Pas	Pas	Pas	Pas	Pas SO	Pas	Gd		Pas SO	Pas	Pas	Pas	Gd	Relief Pas	Gd See Note
				6	2			5	1			6		1	3		7
		a m	a m	a m	a m	a m	a m	a m	a m		a m	a m	p m	p m	p m	p m	p m
...	AFONWEN dp	...	...	...	7 25	...	...	10 10	Saturdays excepted, Llanwnda to Carnarvon	...	...	10 45	..	12 50	...	...	1 35
1¼	Chwilog (for N.)	MO	...	...	7 30	...	...	10X12		...	...	10 50	...	12 55	...	..	1 40
2½	Llangybi Cross.		...	...	X	...	...	See		...	...	10 55	...	12 59	C	SO	X
4¼	Ynys Crossing	...	...	...	X	...	...	Note		...	...	11 0	...	1 3			X
6¼	BRYNKIR arr	...	...	...	7 40	...	...	10§21		...	...	11 5	..	1 8	...	1.50 p.m. from Nantlle.	2 0
	BRYNKIR dep	...	...	...	7 41	...	...	10§21		...	..	11 6	...	1 15	...		2 40
8	Pant Glas Cross.		...	...	7 46	..	...	...		...	...	11 11	...	1 21	...		X
11⅞	PEN-Y-GROES arr		...		7 56	...	...	10§31		...	...	11 20	...	1 31	...		3 5
	PEN-Y-GROES dep	For Birmingham.	...	...	7 57	..	9 17	10§31		...	10 50	11 22		1 32	...	2 5	3 30
13¼	Tudor Siding...		...	...	...	...	...			...	...	...	...	...	...		...
13¾	Groeslon		...	...	8 2	...	9 22	10§35	...	...	10 55	11 27		1 37	...	2 10	3 35
14⅞	Llanwnda		...	.	8 6	...	9 26	...	7 50	...	10 59	11 31	...	1 41	...	2 14	X
15½	DINAS Junction arr		...	...	8 9	...	9 29	10 39	7 58	...	11 3	11 34	...	1 44	...	2 18	3 42
	DINAS Junction dep		...	...	8 11	...	9 31	10 46	8 25	...	11 4	11 35	...	1 45	...	2 18	4 0
18¼	Quay Siding	...	...	...	...	...	...	Note	8 35	...	...	...	...	..	...	...	...
18¾	CARNARVON arr	...	...	...	8 21	...	9 41	10 50	8 40	...	11 15	11 45	...	1 55	...	2 28	4 10
	CARNARVON dep	5 0	7 10	7 25	8 25	9 20		10 55	10 20	...		12 10	12 40	2 10	...	...	...
20⅞	Griffith's Cross.	...	...	X	8 30	9 27	...	...	10 40	...	See	12 15	12 45	2 15	...	...	...
22¾	P. DINORWIC	...	7 18	7 33	8 36	9 33	...	11 3	11 15	...	Note	12 21	12 51	2 21	...	...	...
23½	Port Siding arr	...	...	...	...	...	...	...	11 20	...	...	...		...	...	...	...
	Port Siding dep	...	...	...	...	...		...	1 20	...	...	...	...	...	2 55	...	...
25	Treborth	...	...	...	X	9 40	...	..	...	...	...	...	12 58	2 28	...	...	...
26	Menai Bridge arr	5 25	7 24	7 39	8 43	9 44	...	11 10	1 32	...	...	12 30	1 2	2 32	3 7	...	...
	Menai Bridge dep	5 55	7 28	7 42	8 45	9 48	...	11 16	8	...	...	12 36	1 6	2 36		...	...
27¼	BANGOR	6 0	7 31	7 46	8 49	9 51	...	11 20	...	...	...	12 40	1 10	2 40		..	...

Miles.	STATIONS.	51	52	53	54	55	56	57	58	59	60	61	62	63	64	65	66 (Sundays)	67 (Sundays)
	UP.	Pas	Gd	Fast Gd	Pas	Cattle SO	Pas	Gd	Pas		Empty Carrs. SO	Pas	Gd	Gd C	Fast Coal Empties	Pas	Pas	Pas
			3	7										4			1	2
		p m	p m	p m	p m	p m	p m	p m	p m		p m	p m	p m	p m	p m	p m	a m	p m
...	AFONWEN dp	2†0		...	...	2 45	4 40	...	...	...	...	7 15	7 25	6.30 p.m. from Nantlle.	S	9 35	...	7 0
1¼	Chwilog (for N.)	2 5	..	...	...	3 0	4 45	...	...	...	...	7 20	7 45			9 40	...	7 5
2½	Llangybi Cross.	†See	...	...	...	...	4 49	C	...	...	..	7 25	X		...	...	...	...
4¼	Ynys Crossing	Note	...	...	...	...	4 53		...	...	..	7 30	X		...	...	...	...
6¼	BRYNKIR arr	2§15	...	...	...	3 15	4 58		...	..	..	7 35	8 5			9 50	...	7 15
	BRYNKIR dep	2§15	...	...	...	3 40	4 59	...	...	...	...	7 36	8 10			9 51	...	7 16
8	Pant Glas Cross.	...	...	...	...	...	5 4	...	...	...	..	7 41	X		For Bamfurlong.	X	...	...
11⅞	PEN-Y-GROES arr	2§25	..	...	...	3 55	5 13	...	...	..	...	7 50	8 30	...		10 4	...	7 29
	PEN-Y-GROES dep	2X26	2 45	...	...	4 25	5 16	...	...	...	6§55	7 51	8 55	9 10		10 5	...	7 30
13¼	Tudor Siding...	...	...	...	...	...	...	...	...	...	...	...	...	...		...	...	...
13¾	Groeslon	2§30	2 51	...	...	4§30	5 21	...	...	..	7§0	7 56	...	9 17	...	10 10	...	7 35
14⅞	Llanwnda		...	...	...	...	5 24	...	...	...	...	7 59	...	...	...	10 14	...	7 39
15½	DINAS Junction arr	2§39	3 0	...	...	...	5 27	...	...	...	...	8 2	9 5	9 22	...	10§17	...	7§42
	DINAS Junction dep	2§45	3 15	...	...	4§37	5 30	...	...	.	7§5	8 3	9 10	9 30	..	10§17	...	7§42
18¼	Quay Siding	...	3 25	...	...	...	...	...	...	...	...	...	...	...	...	...	...	...
18¾	CARNARVON arr	2 55	3 30	...	...	4 45	5 40		...	...	7 15	8 13	9 20	9 41	...	10 27	...	7 52
	CARNARVON dep	3 0		4 20	4 40	4 52	5 43	5 45	6 35	...	...	8 20	10 10		9 45	...	6 30	8 20
20⅞	Griffith's Cross.	...	...	For Crewe	4 45	...	5 48	...	6 40	...	...	...	...	...	...	...	...	...
22¾	P. DINORWIC	3 8	...		4 51	...	5 54	...	6 46	...	...	8 28	X	...	...	...	6 38	8 28
23½	Port Siding arr	...	...		...	...	...	...	...	...	...	...	...	...	...	...	...	...
	Port Siding dep	...	...		...	...	...	...	..	...	...	...	...	...	...	...	...	...
25	Treborth	...	...		4 58	...	6 1	...	6 53	...	...	...	...	...	...	...	...	...
26	Menai Bridge arr	3 15	...	4 50	5 2	5 12	6 5	6 15	6 57	...	...	8 35	10 30	...	10 5	...	6 46	8 35
	Menai Bridge dep	3 16	...	6 35	5 4		6 6		6 58	...	...	8 38	10 40	...	10 55	...	6 48	8 38
27¼	BANGOR	3 20	...	6 40	5 8	...	6 10	...	7 1	...	..	8 42	10 45	...	11 0	...	6 52	8 42

A Light Engine (C M) leaves Port Siding 8.25 a.m., and arrives Menai Bridge 8.32 a.m.

No. 37—Calls at Griffith's Crossing when required to pick up passengers on notice being given at the station, or to set down on notice being given by the passenger to the guard.

No. 38—Calls at Llangybi at 7.33, Ynys at 7.37, and Treborth at 8.40, to set down on notice being given by the Passenger to the Guard, & to pick up Passengers on notice being given at the Station. The Engine of this Train to do the necessary Shunting at Bangor until 12.0 noon.

No. 40—Runs on Carnarvon Fair Days also.

No. 41—Calls at Chwilog when required to pick up Passengers for Crewe and beyond on notice being given to the Station Master.

No. 42—Engine of 10 20 a.m. from Carnarvon to come out at 8 0 a.m. to shunt at Carnarvon.

No. 44—Calls at Dinas for Staff purposes only, unless the 10.45 a.m. from Afonwen is running late, in which case No. 41 may be held back at Dinas for N. W., N. G. connection.

A Mineral Train leaves Quay Siding at 1.35 p.m., and arrives Carnarvon at 1.40 p.m.

No 48—If the Engine of the 8.15 a.m. Goods, Mold Junc. to Menai Bridge, is not required to work the 2.55 p.m. "C" Train, Port Siding to Menai Bridge, the Engine to be uilised at Menai Bridge for shunting purposes and marshalling traffic for other trains to pick up, also to Shunt the Local Goods Sidings and then work a train at 4.30 p.m. to Bangor.

No 50—Stops at Chwilog for Live Stock, Foreign Empties, and Tranships only, and at Groeslon and Llanwnda when required to pick up or put off Cattle Traffic, and to pick up Tranships.

A Conditional Goods (MS) leaves Carnarvon at 4.52 p.m. (when required) for Menai Bridge.

No. 51—Calls at Pen-y-groes if required to set down passengers from the Cambrian Line on notice being given by the passenger to the guard, or to pick up passengers for Chester and beyond on notice being given at the Station.

No. 55—Conveys pig traffic for Birmingham. To be extended to Mold Junction, if required.

No. 65 Calls at Pantglas at 9 55 p.m. if required to pick up passengers on notice being given at the station, or to set down on notice being given by the passenger to the guard

Extract from

LNWR SERVICE TIMETABLE – 2nd OCTOBER 1922 until further notice

BANGOR, CARNARVON, PEN-Y-GROES, & AFONWEN. (Single Line, Carnarvon to Afonwen.)

Train Staff Stations: Carnarvon, Dinas, Groeslon, Pen-y-Groes, Brynkir, Llangybi, Chwilog, & Afonwen.

Passenger Trains can cross each other only at Dinas, Groeslon, Pen-y-groes, Brynkir, and Llangybi.

WEEK DAYS ONLY.

Miles	Down.	1	2	3	4	5	6	7	8	9	10	11
		B Goods	PAS	G Goods	D Goods	G Goods	PAS	G Goods	PAS		G Goods	G Goods
		M										
		a.m.	a m	a m	a m	a m	a.m.	a.m.	a m		a.m.	a m
...	BANGOR dep.	3 45	4 46	...	...	...	...	...	8 55	...	...	...
1¼	Menai Bridge arr	...	...	...	...	...	...	...	8 59	...	...	...
	Menai Bridge dep	3 50	4 48	...	5 30	...	...	7 20	9 0	...	9 50	10 45
1¾	Davies' Siding	...	...	...	...	...	...	...	...	...	...	X
2¼	Treborth	...	See	...	...	...	...	...	9 4	...	X	See
2½	Treborth Sdg.	...	note	...	...	...	...	...	...	...	See	note.
3¼	Port Siding	...	...	...	...	...	...	...	...	...	note.	10 55
4¼	Port Dinorwic	...	4†55	...	...	...	...	...	9 9	...	10x15	...
6¼	Griffith's Cr'sing	...	...	...	...	...	...	...	9 14	...	X	...
8¼	CARNARVON arr	4 10	5 4	...	5 50	...	...	7 40	9 20	...	10 25	...
	CARNARVON dep		5 11	5 30		6 10	8 48	9 55	9 25	...	10 55	...
9	Quay Siding	...	...	...	...	...	...	...	...	...	...	...
11¼	Dinas Junction arr	...	...	...	...	...	...	...	9 37	...	...	...
	Dinas Junction dep	...	5†22	5§45	...	6§25	8§59	10§10	9 38	...	11§10	...
12¼	Llanwnda	...	5†25	...	...	...	...	...	9 41	...	11 30	...
13	Groeslon arr	...	...	...	...	...	...	...	...	...	11 35	...
	Groeslon dep	...	5 30	5§53	...	6§33	9§ 4	10§17	9 46	...	11 52	...
14	Tudor Siding	...	...	...	...	6 45	...	...	...	...	X	...
15¼	Penygroes arr	11.50 p.m. (S) from Mold Jct.	5 36	...	...	6 50	9 10	10 25	9 52	...	12 0	...
	Penygroes dep		5 38	6 §1	...	7 5	9 13	10§30	9 54	...	12 30	...
19¼	Pant Glas		...	...	...	...	...	...	10 4	...	X	...
21	Brynkir arr		5 52	...	...	For Nantlle.	...	...	10 8	...	12 50	...
	Brynkir dep		5 53	6§21	...		...	10§50	10 15	...	1 35	...
23	Ynys		...	...	...			...	10 20	...	...	...
24¼	Llangybi arr		...	...	...	...	For Nantlle.	11 0	...	...	1 45	...
	Llangybi dep		6 §0	6§31	...	...		11§15	10 25	...	2§25	...
26	Chwilog arr		6 4	...	...	...		11 20	10 28	...	2 35	...
	Chwilog dep		6 5	6§38	...	...	...	11 30	10 30	...	2 45	...
27¼	AFONWEN arr	...	6 8	6 43	...	...	...	11 35	10 33	...	2 50	...

Miles	Down.	12	13	14	15	16	17	18	19	20	21	22
		PAS	G Goods	PAS	PAS		PAS	PAS		Engine and Van.	PAS	PAS
							SO			C		
		a m	a.m.	noon	p.m.		p.m.	p.m.		p.m.	p m	p.m.
...	BANGOR dep.	11 10	...	12 0	1 10	...	2 15	2 43	..	...	3 25	4 45
1¼	Menai Bridge arr	11 14	...	12 4	1 14	...	2 19	...	...	...	3 29	...
	Menai Bridge dep	11 16	C on S	12 5	1 16	...	2 20	2 46	...	3 10	3 31	4 48
1¾	Davies' Siding	...		...	...	...	...	...	...	...	...	...
2¼	Treborth	11 20		...	1 20	...	...	...	...	...	3 35	...
2½	Treborth Sdg.	7.30am from M'cher		...	..	...	...	...	...	...	...	...
3¼	Port Siding			...	...	...	...	...	...	3 20	...	...
4¼	Port Dinorwic	11 25	...	12 13	1 25	...	2 28	...	...		3 41	...
6¼	Griffith's Cr'sing	11 31	...	...	1 31	...	...	...	...	...	3 46	...
8¼	CARNARVON arr	11 37	...	12 21	1 37	...	2 36	2 56	...	...	3 52	4 58
	CARNARVON dep	...	11 25	12 26		...	2 40	2 59	...	...	4 7	5 2
9	Quay Siding	...	11 40	...	...	...	...	...	...	...	...	...
11¼	Dinas Junction arr	...	11 50	12 37	...	...	...	...	...	...	4 18	...
	Dinas Junction dep	...		12 38	...	...	2§51	3§10	...	...	4 19	5 13
12¼	Llanwnda	...	...	12 41	...	...	2 54	...	...	...	4 23	5 16
13	Groeslon arr	...	...	...	...	...	...	...	...	...	—	5 20
	Groeslon dep	...	...	12 46	...	...	2 59	3§14	...	...	4 28	5 21
14	Tudor Siding	...	Arrives Quay Siding 11.30.	...	...	...	...	...	...	...	...	...
15¼	Penygroes arr	...		12 52	...	...	3 5	...	...	...	4 34	5 27
	Penygroes dep	...		12 54	...	...	...	3§20	...	...	4 39	5 28
19¼	Pant Glas	...		1 4	...	...	...	...	...	...	4 49	...
21	Brynkir arr	...		1 8	...	...	...	...	...	...	4 53	5 39
	Brynkir dep	...		1 10	...	...	...	3§31	...	...	4 55	5 40
23	Ynys	...	...	1 15	...	...	...	...	...	...	5 0	...
24¼	Llangybi arr	...	...	1 20	...	...	...	...	...	...	...	...
	Llangybi dep	...	...	1 23	...	...	...	3§36	...	...	5 5	5§45
26	Chwilog arr	...	...	1 26	...	...	...	...	...	...	5 8	5 48
	Chwilog dep	...	...	1 30	...	...	...	3§39	...	...	5 10	5 49
27¼	AFONWEN arr	...	...	1 33	...	...	..	3 42	...	...	5 13	5 52

Miles	Down.	23	24	25	26	27	28	29	30	31	32
			PAS	PAS		PAS	PAS	PAS	PAS	E Min'rl	PAS
			HC	HC		HC FS	HC FO	HC SO	SO	SO	Th SO
			p.m.	p m		p m	p.m.	p.m.	p m	p.m.	p.m.
...	BANGOR dep.	...	5 45	6 55	...	8 50	8 50	9 10	...	9 50	10 40
1¼	Menai Bridge arr	...	5 49	6 59	...	8 54	8 54	9 14	...	...	10 44
	Menai Bridge dep	...	5 51	7 1	...	8 56	9 0	9 16	Not Advertised.	9 56	10 45
1¾	Davies' Siding	...	...	4.15 p.m. from Liverpool.	...	...	...	...		...	...
2¼	Treborth	...	5 55		...	...	...	...		...	...
2½	Treborth Sdg.	...	...		...	...	...	...		...	...
3¼	Port Siding	...	...		...	...	...	...		..	...
4¼	Port Dinorwic	...	6 0	7 10	...	9 4	9 8	9 24		...	10 53
6¼	Griffith's Cr'sing	...	6 6	...	...	...	...	...	...	..	...
8¼	CARNARVON arr	...	6 12	7 19	...	9 15	9 19	9 35	...	10 20	11 1
	CARNARVON dep	...	...	7 24	...				9 55		
9	Quay Siding	...	...	...	...	...	...	...	...	...	...
11¼	Dinas Junction arr	...	...	7 35	...	...	...	...	...	...	...
	Dinas Junction dep	...	...	7 36	...	...	...	...	10 §6	...	...
12¼	Llanwnda	...	...	7 39	...	...	...	...	10 9	5.50 p.m. from Mold Junction	...
13	Groeslon arr	...	...	7 43	...	...	...	...	10 13		...
	Groeslon dep	...	...	7 47	...	...	...	...	10 14		...
14	Tudor Siding	...	...	...	...	...	...	...	...		...
15¼	Penygroes arr	...	...	7 53	...	...	...	...	10 20		...
	Penygroes dep	...	..	7 54	...	...	...	...	10 23		...
19¼	Pant Glas	...	...	8 5	...	...	...	...	For Nantlle.	...	...
21	Brynkir arr	...	...	8 10	...	...	...	...		...	...
	Brynkir dep	...	...	8 11	...	...	...	...		...	...
23	Ynys	...	...	8 16	...	...	...	...		...	...
24¼	Llangybi arr	...	...	...	...	...	...	...	...	...	...
	Llangybi dep	...	...	8 21	...	...	...	...	...	...	...
26	Chwilog arr	...	...	8 24	...	...	...	...	...	...	...
	Chwilog dep	...	...	8 28	...	...	...	...	...	...	...
27¼	AFONWEN arr	...	...	8 31	...	...	...	...	...	...	...

No. 2—† Calls at Port Dinorwic and Llanwnda for Postal purposes only.

No. 10—Arrives Port Dinorwic 10.5. Calls at Port Dinorwic on Wednesdays to detach, and on other days for tranships only.

No. 11—Calls at Davies' Siding to detach.

AFONWEN, PEN-Y-GROES, CARNARVON, & BANGOR. (Single Line, Afonwen to Carnarvon.)

TRAIN STAFF STATIONS: Afonwen, Chwilog, Llangybi, Brynkir, Pen-y-Groes, Groeslon, Dinas, Carnarvon.

Passenger Trains can cross each other only at Llangybi, Brynkir, Pen-y-groes, Groeslon and Dinas.

WEEK DAYS ONLY.

Up.	1	2	3	4	5	6	7	8	9	10	11
	Pas	Pas	PAS	Pas	G Mineral.		Pas	PAS		Pas	Pas
	S	SO			M						HC
	a.m.	a.m.	a m	a.m.	a.m.		a.m.	a.m.		a.m.	a.m.
AFONWEN dp	...	...	7 0	...	...	...	...	9 55	...	...	11 0
Chwilog arr.	...	...	7 4	...	...	...	...	9 59	...	...	11 4
Chwilog dep.	...	...	7 5		C	...	...	10 0	...	...	11 6
Llangybi arr	...	...	...	From Nantlle.		...	...	...	...	...	...
Llangybi dep	...	...	7 10		...	...	...	10 5	...	...	11 11
Ynys	...	...	7 14		...	...	...	...	...	...	11 16
Brynkir arr.	...	...	7 19		...	...	...	10 13	...	...	11 21
Brynkir dep.	...	...	7 20		...	...	...	10 14	...	...	11 23
Pant Glas	...	...	7 25	...	...	...	...	10 19	...	...	11 28
Penygroes arr	...	...	7 35	8 15	...	...	...	10 28	...	...	11 37
Penygroes dep.	...	...	7 36	8 21	...	...	...	10 29	...	...	11 40
Tudor Siding	...	...	...	...	...	...	...	...	...	...	...
Groeslon arr.	...	...	...	...	...	...	...	...	...	—	...
Groeslon dep.	...	...	7 41	8 26	...	...	...	10 35	...	...	11 46
Llanwnda	...	...	7 44	8 29	...	...	...	10 38	...	...	11 49
Dinas Junction arr.	...	...	7 47	8 32	...	...	...	10 41	...	...	11 52
Dinas Junction dep	...	...	7 48	8 33	...	...	...	10 42	...	...	11 53
Quay Siding	...	...	...	...	...	...	...	...	...	...	...
CARNARVON arr.	...	...	7 57	8 42	...	...	..	10 51	...	...	12 2
CARNARVON dep.	6 42	7 5	8 2		...	...	10 30	10 55	...	11 45	12 6
Griffith's Cross.	6 47	7 10	8 7	...	...	...	10 35	...	...	11 50	12 11
Port Dinorwic	6 53	7 16	8 13	...	...	...	10 41	...	...	11 56	12 17
Port Siding arr.	...	...	...	...	...	...	...	...	...	...	...
Port Siding dep.	...	...	...	...	8 50	...	...	...	...	...	...
Treborth	...	...	8 19	...	..	...	10 47	...	...	12 2	12 23
Menai Bridge arr	7 0	7 23	8 21	...	9 5	...	10 49	11 8	...	12 4	12 25
Menai Bridge dep	7 1	7 24	8 22	...			10 51	11 11	...	12 7	12 26
BANGOR arr	7 5	7 28	8 25	—	...	...	10 55	11 15	...	12 11	12 30

Up.	12	13	14	15	16	17	18	19	20	21	22
	G Goods.	G Mineral.	G Mineral	Pas	G Mineral.	PAS	PAS	E Mineral.	Pas	G Mineral.	G Goods
		SO		SO					HC		
	p.m.	p m	p.m.	p m	p m	p.m.	p.m.	p.m.	p.m.	p. m.	p.m
AFONWEN dp	...	...	S	...	...	1 10	...	...	...	...	2 0
Chwilog arr.	...	...		...	...	1 14	...	...	...	...	2 5
Chwilog dep.	...	C	Quay Siding arrive 1.33.	...	...	1 16	...	...	...	...	2 20
Llangybi arr	...	...		...	...	1 21	...	...	...	C	...
Llangybi dep	Arrives Griffiths Crossing 12.50, Port Dinorwic 1.15.	...		...	...	1 24	...	...	...	...	2§25
Ynys		Quay Siding arrive 1.8.		...	...	1 29	...	...	...	...	...
Brynkir arr.				...	...	1 34	...	...	...	...	2 40
Brynkir dep.				...	...	1 35	...	...	...	...	2 55
Pant Glas				...	...	1 40	...	...	...	...	...
Penygroes arr			...	...	...	1 49	...	...	...	...	3 15
Penygroes dep.			...	1 15	...	1 50	...	...	...	...	3 35
Tudor Siding			...	...	...	...	...	For Mold Jct.	...	...	...
Groeslon arr.		...	...	1 20	...	1 55	For Chester.		...	...	...
Groeslon dep.		...	...	1 21	...	1 56			...	...	3§42
Llanwnda		...	...	1 24	...	1 59			...	...	...
Dinas Junction arr.		...	...	1 27	...	2 2			...	...	..
Dinas Junction dep	...	1 0	1 25	1 28	...	2 3	..		...	...	3§50
Quay Siding	...	1 17	1 42	...	...	...	...		...	...	...
CARNARVON arr.	...	1 20	1 45	1 37	...	2 12	...	...	...	...	4 2
CARNARVON dep.	12 40		...	1 45	...	2 17	3 35	3 50	4 20	...	4 40
Griffith's Cross.	1 10	...	...	...	...	2 22	3 40	...	4 25	...	...
Port Dinorwic	1 35	...	...	1 55	...	2 28	3 46	...	4 31	...	...
Port Siding arr.	...	...	...	...	...	...	...	...	...	.	...
Port Siding dep.	...	...	...	...	2 5	...	...	...	...	4 10	...
Treborth	...	...	...	...	...	2 34	3 52	...	4 37	...	...
Menai Bridge arr	1 50	...	...	...	2 20	2 36	3 54	4 10	4 39	4 25	5 0
Menai Bridge dep		...	...	2 2		2 38	3 56	4 25	4 42		
BANGOR arr	...	...	...	2 5	...	2 42	4 0	4 30	4 46	...	...

Up.	23	24	25	26	27	28	29	30	31	32	33
	Pas	Pas	G Mineral.	G Goods.	PAS	D Goods	MIXED HC			D Goods.	Light Engine.
					HC	SO				S	SO
	p m	p.m.	p m	p m	p m	p.m.	p m			p.m.	p m
AFONWEN dp	4 0	5 33	From Nantlle. Arrive Penygroes 3.40 p.m. on Saturdays.	6 30	7 0	..	9 0	...	...	...	...
Chwilog arr.	4 4	5 37		...	7 4	...	9 5	...	...	...	...
Chwilog dep.	4 5	5 38		6x§35	7 5	...	9 6	...	...	...	
Llangybi arr	4 10	5 43		...	...	...	9 11	...	...	...	From Nantlle
Llangybi dep	4 11	5 46		6 40	7 10	...	9 12	...	...	...	
Ynys	4 15	5 51		...	7 15	...	9 18	...	...	...	
Brynkir arr.	4 20	5 56		...	7 20	...	9 25	...	...	...	
Brynkir dep.	4 21	5 57		6x§55	7 21	...	9 26	...	...	...	...
Pant Glas	4 27	6 3			7 27	...	9 33	...	...	...	...
Penygroes arr	4 36	6 12	2:20		7 36	...	9 46	...	...	...	...
Penygroes dep.	4 37	6 14	6 40	7§x15	7 40	...	9 47	...	...	...	10§40
Tudor Siding	...	...	...	See	...	...	...	...	...	...	...
Groeslon arr.	...	...	...	note.	7 46		9 55	...	...	...	...
Groeslon dep.	4 43	6 20	6§x50	7§23	7 49	For Mold Jct.	9 56	...	...	...	10§46
Llanwnda	4 46	6 23	6x55	...	7 52		See	...	...	...	...
Dinas Junction arr.	4 49	6 26	7 0	7 31	7 55		note	...	...	For Mold Jct.	...
Dinas Junction dep	4 50	6 27	7 5	7 41	7 56		10 §3	...	...		10§52
Quay Siding	...	...	...	...	...	...	...	...	...		...
CARNARVON arr.	4 59	6 35	7 20	7 53	8 5	...	10 16	...	...		11 2
CARNARVON dep.	5 4	6 40	Calls at Groeslon & Llanwnda for tranship purposes.	...	8 12	9 40	...	...	...	10 50	...
Griffith's Cross.	5 9	6 45		...	...	...	...	...	...	...	...
Port Dinorwic	5 15	6 51		...	8 22	...	...	...	...	...	...
Port Siding arr.	See	...		...	...	...	...	...	...	...	...
Port Siding dep.	note	...		..	...	...	—	...	...	...	...
Treborth	5 21	...		...	...	...	...	...	...	...	...
Menai Bridge arr	5 23	6 58		...	8 29	10 5	...	...	...	11 15	...
Menai Bridge dep	5 25	7 0		...	8 31	10 45	...	...	...	11 50	...
BANGOR arr	5 29	7 4		.	8 35	10 50	...	...	...	11 55	...

No. 23—When the 5.0 p.m. "C" from Holyhead runs, will dep. Menai Bridge 5.33, and arr. Bangor 5.37 p.m.

No. 29—On Saturdays departs Dinas 10§7, and arrives Carnarvon 10.20.

No. 26 calls at Chwilog to attach live stock traffic.

Extract from

LMS SERVICE TIMETABLE FOR FREIGHT —MAY to SEPTEMBER 1939

WEEKDAYS. 330

Miles.	For continuation of trains from junctions, see page	Station	1	2	3	4	5	6	7	8	9	10	11	12	13	17	19	20	21	22	23	24	25	26	27	28	29
			Freight.	Freight.	Freight.	Freight.	Freight.	Freight	Light Engine.		Mineral.	Mineral.	Freight.	Freight.	Freight.		Freight.	Freight.	Freight	Freight.	Light Engine to Bangor.	Freight.	Freight.	Freight.	Freight.	Freight.	Freight.
				SX			SO		M SX					SO	SX		SO	SX	SX	SO	SX		SO	SX		SX	SX
			a.m.	a.m.	a.m.	a.m.	a.m.	a.m.	p.m.		p.m.	p.m.	p.m.	p.m.	p.m.		p.m.	p.m.	p.m.	p.m.	p.m.	p.m.	p.m.	p.m.	p.m.	p.m.	p.m.
0		AFONWEN ⊕ dep.															2 25	2 25		2 50		6 30	6 35				
1¼		Chwilog ⊕ arr.															2 32	2 32		2 57		X	X				
		Chwilog dep.															2 48	2 48		3 7		6*37	6*42				
2¼		Llangybi ⊕ arr.																									
		Llangybi dep.											Commencing July 8 will be SX.	Commences July 8.			2*53	2*53		3*12		6*42	6*47				
4¼		Ynys																				V	V				
6¼		Brynkir ⊕ arr.															3 6	3 6		3 24							
		Brynkir dep.															3 26	3 26		3 50	After shunting.	6*57	7* 2				
8		Pant Glas															V	V				V	V				
	0	Nantlle dep.						10 15																			
11¼	1¼	Penygroes ⊕ arr.						10 25										3 46				X	X				
		Penygroes dep.	SUSPENDED		Commencing May 29 will be SO.	SUSPENDED							12 20	12 45	Commences June 19.		3*45	3 58	Runs May 29 to June 16 inclusive.	4*10		7*18	7*20	Runs July 3 to September 8 inclusive.		SUSPENDED commencing July 3.	Commences July 3.
13¾		Groeslon ⊕ arr.											12 27										7*28				
		Groeslon dep.											12 38	12*52			3*50	4* 5		4*17		7*26	7*34				
15		Llanwnda arr.											V														
		Llanwnda dep.																									
15½		Dinas ⊕ arr.											12 45							4*24		7*34					
		Dinas dep.											1 28	12*59			3*55	4*11		4*14		7*37	7*40				
18½		Quay Siding arr.											1 38														
		Quay Siding dep.	6 57				SUSPENDED	Freight.	To work 1.25 p.m. to Caernarvon.				1 48														
	0	LLANBERIS ⊕ dep.			9 55	10 15									2 15				3 20								
	¾	Glynrhonwy Siding dep.			V	V							X—Calls when required to attach.		V												
	2¼	Cwm-y-Glo arr.			V	V									V												
		Cwm-y-Glo dep.																		SUSPENDED		X—Stops to attach live stock traffic and for tranship purposes.	X—Stops to attach live stock traffic and for tranship purposes.				
	3½	Pontrhythallt ⊕ arr.			10 23	10 43		SO							2 35				3 40								
		Pontrhythallt dep.			10 33	10 53		p.m.			SUSPENDED	Departs Port Siding 2.21 p.m. (SO). Menai Bridge arr. 2.31.			3 7				4 5								
	7¼	Peblig Siding			V	V									V				V								
	7½	Seiont Mill Siding			V	V									V				V					8 0			
18½	9	CAERNARVON ⊕ ⊕ arr.	7 2		11 14	11 34							1 53	1 11	4 0		4 4	4 23	4 50	4 55		7 47	7 50	8 10			
		CAERNARVON dep.		11 0			11 45	12 25	12 30				2 18	2 18			4 30	5 7		5 37	7 5				8 25	9 53	10 50
20¼		Griffith's Crossing arr.		V			V	V																			
		Griffith's Crossing dep.																									
22¼		Port Dinorwic arr.		11 15			12 0	12 40																			
		Port Dinorwic dep.		11 25			12 8	12 48														Commencing July 8 will be SX.	Commences July 8.				
[illegible]		Port Siding arr.											X														
		Port Siding dep.									1 45	1 57															
		arr.															4 30	[illegible]		[illegible]					8 45	10 13	11 10

WEEKDAYS.

Miles.	For continuation of trains from junctions, see page	Station	[illegible]	[illegible]	[illegible]	[illegible]	[illegible]	[illegible]	40	41	42	43	44	45	47	48	50	51	52	53	55	56	58	59	60
				12.1 a.m. Express Freight from Mold Jn.	12.1 a.m. Express Freight from Mold Jn.	Through Freight.		Through Freight.	Freight.	Freight.	Freight.	Freight.	Freight.	Freight.		Freight.	Freight	Freight.	Freight.	Freight.	Light Engine.	Light Engine.			Freight.
				MX	SO								SO	SO		SX	SO	SX	SO	M SX	SX	Q M SX			SX
				a.m.	a.m.	a.m.		a.m.	a.m.	a.m.	a.m.	a.m.	a.m.	a.m.		a.m.	a.m.	a.m.	a.m.	p.m.	p.m.	p.m.			p.m.
0		MENAI BRIDGE dep.		3 45	4 5	5† 5		5 40	6 10			7 15		7 15		9 25	9 25	10 20	10 40	1 25		2 45			
½		Davies' Siding								SUSPENDED			SUSPENDED					X	X		Runs May 29 to June 16 inclusive.				Runs July 3 to September 8 inclusive.
		Treborth																X	X						
		Treborth Siding																							
2½		Port Siding																10 43	11 5						
3		Port Dinorwic arr.										7 30		7 30											
		Port Dinorwic dep.										7 40		7 40											
5		Griffith's Crossing										V		V											
7	0	CAERNARVON ⊕ ⊕ arr.		4 5	4 25	5†25		6 0	6 33			7 55		7 55		9 45	9 45			1 45		3 0			
		CAERNARVON dep.				5 30		6 30		6 47	7 45	8 0	8 5	8 20		10 11	10 11				2 25				7 40
	1¼	Glan Morfa Siding		Commencing July 8 will be MSX.	Commences July 8.						V		V									To shunt.			
	1½	Seiont Mill Siding				†—Mondays only.																			7 45
	5¼	Pontrhythallt ⊕ arr.									8 5		8 25												
		Pontrhythallt dep.									8 25		8 45								2*45				
	6¾	Cwm-y-Glo arr.						Arrives Tudor Siding 7.5.			8X30		8X50	SUSPENDED											
		Cwm-y-Glo dep.									8X55		9X15						X—Stops when required to detach.						
	8¼	Glynrhonwy Siding																							
	8½	Hickman's Siding																X—Stops when required to detach.							
	9	LLANBERIS ⊕ arr.									9 5		9 25								2 52				
7½	—	Quay Siding arr.								6 52						10 16	10 16								
		Quay Siding dep.									X—Stops to detach only.	V		V		10 26	10 26								
10¼		Dinas ⊕ arr.										8 25	X—Stops to detach only.	8 45		10 39	10 39								
		Dinas dep.				5*45		6*45				8 35		8 55		10 45	11 32								
10¾		Llanwnda arr.										8 40		9 0		10 50	11 37								
		Llanwnda dep.										8 50		9 10		11 0	11 47								
11½		Groeslon ⊕ arr.						6 50				8 55		9 15		11 5	11 52				To work 3.20 p.m. to Caernarvon.				
		Groeslon dep.				5*53		7 0				9 5		9 25		11 20	12 5								
12½		Tudor Siding						7 15																	
14		Penygroes ⊕ arr.						7 22				9 12		9 32		11 32	12 12								
	0	Penygroes dep.				6* 1		7 35				10 6		10 34		12 10	1 5								
	1½	Nantlle arr.						7 45																	
17¾		Pant Glas																							
19½		Brynkir ⊕ arr.										10 26		10 54		12 30	1 25								
		Brynkir dep.				6*21						10 36		11 5		1 0	1 35								
21¼		Ynys														V	V								
23¼		Llangybi ⊕ arr.										10 46		11 15			1*45								
		Llangybi dep.				6*31						11 17		11 35		1*10	1*50								
24½		Chwilog ⊕ arr.										11 22		11 40		1 15	1 55								
		Chwilog dep.				6*38						11 32		11 50		1 25	2 5								
25½		AFONWEN ⊕ arr.				6 43						11 37		11 55		1 30	2 10								

331

7

Extract from
LMS SERVICE TIMETABLE – JULY to SEPTEMBER 1939

AFONWEN, LLANBERIS, CAERNARVON AND BANGOR.

WEEKDAYS.

Reporting Nos.: 38, 54, 488, 496, 216, 494, 256, 256, 84, 86, 86

Miles	Station																	
1¼	AFONWEN dep.			7 3	7 50		9 20	9 20				10+ 8	10 40	10 54	11 5			
2¼	Chwilog			7 7	7 54		9 24	9 24				10 12	10 44	10 58	11 9			
4¼	Llangybi arr./dep.			7 13	7 59		9 29	9 29				10*17	10*49	11 3	11 14			
6¼	Ynys			7 17	8 6		9 34	9 34					11 8	11 19			
8	Brynkir arr./dep.			7 21	8 11		9 36	9 38				10 23	10 55	11 12	11 23			
11¼	Pant Glas			7 26	8 15			9 43				10 24	10 56	11 13	11 31			
	PEN-Y-GROES arr./dep.			7 34 / 7 37	8 23 / 8 24		9 46 / 9 49	9 51 / 9 52				10 33 / 10 35	11 6	11 27	11 43			
13½	Groeslon arr./dep.			7 41 / 7 42	8 28 / 8 29		9 53 / 9 54	9 56 / 9 57				10 39 / 10 40	11 11	11 32	11 48 / 11 49			
15	Llanwnda			7 45	8 32		9 57	10 0				10 43	11 35	11 52			
15½	Dinas arr./dep.											10 45	11 37	11 54			
	(Caernarvon) dep.			7 47	8 34		9 59	10 2				10 46	11 37	11 54			
0	LLANBERIS dep.					9 35			9 40	10 25							
2½	Padarn Halt					9+37			9+42	10 27							
	Cwm-y-Glo					9+42			9+47	10 32							
	Pontrhythallt					9+51			9+51	10 36							
18½	CAERNARVON arr.	6 38	7 40	7 55	8 42	9 58	10 7		10 10		10 3	10 48	10 54	11 24	11 45	12 2		
22½	Port Dinorwic	6 47		8 5	8 54		10 12		10 14	10 25	10 40	11A		12 14			
25	Treborth			9 0	9 2				10 33	10 48			12 11			
25¼	Menai Bridge arr./dep.	6 54		8 12	9 2				10 39	10 54		11 31	12 13			
27½	BANGOR arr.	6 59	7 53	8 17	9 7		10 26		10 27	10 46	11 1	11 16	11 41	12 22			

WEEKDAYS—continued.

Reporting Nos.: 264, 114, 170, 40, 40, 128, 240, 162

(continued columns 18–36)

Passenger trains cannot cross at Chwilog and Pontrhythallt.

AFONWEN, LLANBERIS, CAERNARVON AND BANGOR—*CONT.*

WEEKDAYS—continued.

Reporting Nos.: 162, 168, 178, 26, 296, 250, 190

(columns 37–56)

WEEKDAYS—continued.

Reporting Nos.: 190, 188, 188

(columns 57–75)

Passenger trains cannot cross at Chwilog and Pontrhythallt.

Extract from

LMS SERVICE TIMETABLE – JULY to SEPTEMBER 1939

BANGOR, CAERNARVON, LLANBERIS AND AFONWEN.

WEEKDAYS.

Miles	Miles		1	2	3	4	5	6	7	8	9	10	11	12	13	14	15	16	17	18
			PARCELS.	PASSENGER.	PASSENGER.	PASSENGER.		PASSENGER.	PASSENGER.	PASSENGER.	PASSENGER.	Light Engine.	PASSENGER 9.15 a.m. from Rhyl.	PASSENGER 9.45 a.m. from Llandudno Jn.	PASSENGER † 9.30 a.m. from Rhyl.	PASSENGER. 10.20 (SX) from Llandudno, 9.45 a.m. (SO) from Rhyl.	Light Engine.	MOTOR TRAIN.	PASSENGER.	
		Reporting Nos. ..											71	83	65	17				
								SX	SO	SX	SO	SX	SX	SO	SX		SO	SO	SX	
			a.m.	a.m.	a.m.	a.m.		a.m.	a.m.	a.m.	a.m.	a.m.	a.m.	a.m.	a.m.	a.m.	a.m.	noon	p.m.	
		BANGOR ....dep.	4 25	4 46	6 50	7 55				9† 0	9 0	9 35	10 25	10 30	10 40	11A15	11 50	12 0	12 5	
1½		Menai Bridge arr.			6 54	7 59				9 4	9 4			10 34	10 44	11 19		12 4	12 9	
		Menai Bridge dep.	4 28	4 49	6 55	8 2				9 5	9 5	9 40	10 28	10 35	10 45	11 20	11 55	12 5	12 10	
2¼		Treborth								9 8	9 8							12 8		
4½		Port Dinorwic		4†55	7 0	8 8				9 13	9 13			10 41	10 51	11 26		12 13		
8½	0	CAERNARVON ⊕ ⊕ arr.	4 38	5 3	7 9	8 16				9 21	9 21	9 55	10 38	10 49	10 59	11A34	12 10	12 21	12 21	
		CAERNARVON ⊕ ⊕ dep.	4 55	5 14	7 14			8 45	8 45	9 25	9 25		10 50	10 53	11 3	11 40		12 32	12 35	
	5¼	Pontrhythallt ⊕						9† 1	9† 1				11* 5			11*55		12*48	12†50	
	6¾	Cwm-y-Glo......							9† 5										12†54	
	8¾	Padarn Halt							9†10										12†59	
	9	LLANBERIS ⊕ .. arr.						9 7	9 12				11 11			12 1		12 54	1 1	
11¾		Dinas ⊕ (Caernarvon) arr.			7 23					9 33	9 34			11 2	11 11					
		Dinas (Caernarvon) dep.	5* 4	5*23	7 24					9 34	9 35			11 3	11 12					
12¾		Llanwnda			7 27					9 37	9 38			11 6	11 15					
13¾		Groeslon ..⊕ arr.	5 9	5 29	7 30					9 40	9 41			11 9	11 18					
		Groeslon dep.	5 10	5 31	7 31					9 41	9 42			11 12	11 19					
15¼		PENY-GROES ⊕ arr.	5 15	5 36	7 36					9†46	9 47			11 17	11 24					
		PENY-GROES dep.	5 17	5 40	7 41					9 52	9 48			11 18	11 28					
19¼		Pant Glas ..dep.			7 49					10 0	9 56			11 26	11 36					
21		Brynkir ..⊕ arr.	5 27	5 50	7 52					10 3	9 59			11 29	11 39					
		Brynkir dep.	5 31	5 53	7 53					10 4	10 0			11 30	11 40					
23		Ynys..............			7 57					10 8	10 4			11 34	11 44					
24½		Llangybi ..⊕ arr.			8 0					10 11	10 7			11 37	11 47					
		Llangybi dep.	5*37	5*59	8 1					10 18	10 12			11 38	11 48					
26		Chwilog ..⊕.. ..	5 40	6 2	8 4					10 21	10 15			11 41	11 51					
27½		AFONWEN⊕..arr.	5 43	6 5	8 7					10 24	10 18			11 44	11 54					
		Notes	To run Saturdays only after September 9th.	†—Calls for postal purposes only.				†—Not advertised. Not to run after September 8th.	†—Not advertised.	†—On Thursdays, also on Tuesdays, August 8th and 15th, and on Wednesdays August 9th to 30th, to run 3 minutes later, Bangor to Caernarvon.		To work 10.44 a.m. Caernarvon to Llanberis.	Will not run after September 8th.		Starts from Bangor commencing September 11th.	A—Commencing Sept. 11th to run 2 mins. later, Bangor to Caernarvon (SX).	Not to run after September 9th. To work 1.0 p.m., Caernarvon to Manchester.	Not to run after September 9th.	†—Not advertised.	

WEEKDAYS—continued.

	19	20	21	22	23	24	25	26	27	28	29	30	31	32	33	34	35	36
		PASSENGER.	PASSENGER 11.40 a.m from Llandudno Jn.	Light Engine.		PASSENGER 12.41 p.m. from Llandudno Jn.	PASSENGER 12.41 p.m. from Llandudno Jn.	PASSENGER 11.15 a.m. from Manchester (Ex.).	MOTOR TRAIN.	PASSENGER † 1.20 p.m. from Llandudno Jn		PASSENGER.		PASSENGER † 11.15 a.m. from Manchester (Ex.).	PASSENGER 12.43 p.m. from Chester.		PASSENGER 12.25 p.m. from Liverpool (L. St.).	
Reporting Nos.........						69	69	463		103				463	465		413	
		SO	SX	SO		SO	SO	SO	SO	SO		SX		SX	SO		SO	
		p.m.	p.m.	p.m.		p.m.	p.m.	p.m.	p.m.	p.m.		p.m.		p.m.	p.m.		p.m.	
BANGOR ....dep.		12†15	12 20	12 40		1†12	1†12	1†26		2 5		2 10		2 28	2†30		2 55	
Menai Bridge .... arr.		12 19	12 24	12 44						2 9		2 14		2 32	2 34			
Menai Bridge dep.		12 20	12 25			1 15	1 15	1†29		2 10		2 15		2 33	2 35		2 58	
Treborth																		
Port Dinorwic												2 21		2 39				
CAERNARVON .. ⊕ ⊕ arr.		12 31	12 34	1 0		1 25	1 25	1†39		2 21		2 29		2 47	2 46		3 8	
CAERNARVON dep.		12 35	12 40			1 30		1 57	2 0	2 35		2 35		2 51	2 51		3 12	
Pontrhythallt ⊕......									2†16			2†51						
Cwm-y-Glo									2†20			2†55						
Padarn Halt.........									2†25			3† 0						
LLANBERIS ⊕ .. arr.									2 27			3 2						
Dinas ⊕ (Caernarvon) arr.		12 43	12 49			1 39				2 44				3 0	3 0		3 21	
Dinas (Caernarvon) dep.		12 45	12 50			1 48		2* 6		2 47				3 1	3 3		3 22	
Llanwnda		12 48	12 53			1 53				2 50				3 4	3 6		3 25	
Groeslon ....⊕ .. arr.		12 51	12 56			1 56				2 53				3 7	3 9		3 28	
Groeslon dep.		12 52	12 57			1 57		2*11		2 54				3 8	3 10		3 29	
PENY-GROES ⊕ .. arr.		12 57	1 2			2 2		2 16		2 59				3 13	3 15		3 34	
PENY-GROES dep.		1 6	1 9			2 3		2 18						3 14	3 16		3 36	
Pant Glas .. .. dep.		1 14	1 17			2 11								3 22	3 24			
Brynkir ....⊕ .. arr.		1 17	1 20			2 14		2 28						3 25	3 27		3 46	
Brynkir dep.		1 21	1 21			2 15		2 34						3 26	3 28		3 48	
Ynys		1 25	1 25			2 19								3 30	3 32			
Llangybi ..⊕ .. arr.		1 28	1 28			2 22								3 33	3 35		3 53	
Llangybi dep.		1 29	1 29			2 26		2*39						3 34	3 36		3 54	
Chwilog .. ⊕		1 32	1 32			2 29		2 42						3 37	3 39		3 57	
AFONWEN ⊕ ....arr.		1 35	1 35			2 32		2 45						3 40	3 42		4 0	
Notes		†—Public Bills 12.10 p.m.		To work 1.45 p.m. Caernarvon to Manchester.		Not after Sept. 9th. †—Public Bills 1.10 p.m.	To run September 16th and 23rd only. †—Public Bills 1.10 p.m.	Will not run after August 26th. †—1 minute later on August 5th and 12th.	†—Not advertised.	† On August 5th & 12th is the 1.25 p.m. from Llandudno Jn.		Not to run after September 8th. †—Stop not advertised.		†—Starts from Chester at 12.33 p.m. commencing September 11th.	Commences September 2nd. †—Public Bills 2 28 p.m. On September 2nd and 9th is the 11.40 a.m. from Liverpool (L. St.).		Will not run after Aug. 26th.	

Passenger trains cannot cross at Chwilog and Pontrhythallt.

BANGOR, CAERNARVON, LLANBERIS AND AFONWEN—*CONT.*

WEEKDAYS—continued.

	37	38	39	40	41	42	43	44	45	46	47	48	49	50	51	52	53	54	55
	MOTOR TRAIN.	PASSENGER † 2.15 p.m. from Rhyl.	PASSENGER.	PASSENGER.	Light Engine.	EXPRESS 11.5 a.m. from Euston.	Light Engine.	PASSENGER 11.15 a.m. from Euston.	PASSENGER 11.5 a.m. from Euston.	Light Engine.	PASSENGER.	PASSENGER. (1.45 p.m. from Manchester (FO). Rep. No. 471).	PASSENGER.	MOTOR TRAIN.	PASSENGER.	PASSENGER.	PASSENGER.	PASSENGER 5.45 p.m. from Llandudno Jn.	MOTOR TRAIN.
Reporting Nos. ..		95				67		67	67									37	
	SO	SX	SO	SX	SX	SO	SX	SX	SO	SX	SO	SX	SO	SO	SO	SX	SX	SO	SO
	p.m.	p.m.	p.m.	p.m.	p.m.	p.m.	p.m.	p.m.	p.m.	p.m.	p.m.	p.m.	p.m.	p.m.	p.m.	p.m.	p.m.	p.m.	p.m.
BANGOR ....dep.		3 25	3 30			3 57		4 13	4 13		4 30	5 0	5 0		5 20	5 57		6 20	
Menai Bridge arr.		3 29	3 34					4 17	4 17		4 34	5 4	5 4		5 24	6 1		6 24	
Menai Bridge dep.		3 30	3 35			4 0		4 18	4 18		4 35	5 5	5 5		5 25	6 2		6 25	
Treborth																6 5		6 28	
Port Dinorwic		3 36	3 41													6 10		6 33	
CAERNARVON ⊕ ⊕ arr.		3 44	3 49			4 10		4 29	4 29		4 46	5 16	5 16		5 36	6 18		6 41	
CAERNARVON dep.	3 35			3 57	3 57	4 14	4 15	4 33	4 33	4 40	4 50	5 21	5 24	5 30	5 40		6 30		7 0
Pontrhythallt ⊕	3†51			4†13	4*13		4*30			5A 7				5†46			6†46		7†16
Cwm-y-Glo......	3†55			4†17										5†50			6†50		7†20
Padarn Halt	4† 0			4†22										5†55			6†55		7†25
LLANBERIS ⊕ ..arr.	4 2			4 24	4*21		4 38			5 15				5 57			6 57		7 27
Dinas ⊕ (Caernarvon) arr.						4*22		4 42	4 42		4 59	5 30	5 32		5 49				
Dinas (Caernarvon) dep.						4*24		4 45	4 45		5 0	5 31	5 33		5 50				
Llanwnda								4 48	4 48		5 3	5 34	5 36		5 53				
Groeslon ..⊕ arr.								4 51	4 51		5 6	5 37	5 39		5 56				
Groeslon dep.						4*30		4 53	4 53		5 8	5 38	5 40		5 57				
PENY-GROES ⊕ arr.						4 35		4 58	4 58		5 13	5 43	5 45		6 2				
PENY-GROES dep.						4 36		4 59	4 59		5 15	5 44	5 46		6 4				
Pant Glas ..dep.								5 7	5 7		5 23	5 52	5 54		6 12				
Brynkir ..⊕ arr.						4 46		5 10	5 10		5 26	5 55	5 57		6 15				
Brynkir dep.						4 48		5 11	5 11		5 27	5†58	5†58		6 18				
Ynys..............								5 15	5 15		5 31	6 2	6 2		6 23				
Llangybi ..⊕ arr.						4 53		5 18	5 18		5 34	6 6	6 6		6 26				
Llangybi dep.						4 54		5 19	5 19		5 35	6 7	6 7		6 27				
Chwilog ..⊕.. ..						4 57		5 22	5 22		5 38	6 10	6 10		6 30				
AFONWEN⊕..arr.						5† 0		5 25	5 25		5 41	6 13	6 13		6 33				
Notes	†—Not advertised.	Starts from Llandudno Jn. at 2.45 p.m. commencing Sept. 11th. Rep. No. 97.		Not to run after Sept. 8th. †—Not advertised.	To commence Sept. 11th. To work 5.0 p.m. to Llandudno.	†—Public Bills 5.23 p.m. Will not run after September 9th.	Not to run after Sept. 8th. To work 5.25 p.m. to Rhyl.		Commences September 16th.	A—Arrives 4*57 p.m. Not to run after September 8th.	Not to run after Sept. 9th.	†—Public Bills depart 5.56 p.m.	†—Public Bills 5.56 p.m. To commence September 16th.	†—Not advertised.	Not to run after Sept. 9th.		†—Not advertised. Not to run after September 8th.		†—Not advertised.

WEEKDAYS—continued.

	56	57	58	59	60	61	62	63	64	65	66	67	68	69	70	71	72	73	74	75
	PASS. 6.35 p.m. (SX) from Llandudno Jn., 3.38 p.m. (SO) f'm Manchester (Ex.).	Empty Stock.		MOTOR TRAIN.		PASSENGER 7.45 p.m. from Llandudno Jn.	PASSENGER 7.25 p.m. from Rhyl.	PASSENGER.		PASSENGER †8.15 p.m. from Rhyl.			PASSENGER 9.25 p.m from Llandudno Junction.	PASSENGER 9.25 p.m. from Llandudno Junction.	PASSENGER.	PASSENGER.	PASSENGER.	PASSENGER.	PASSENGER 11.28 p.m. from Llandudno Jn.	
Reporting Nos. ..	225					213	143			147			205	205					219	
		SX		SO		SO	SX	SO		SX			Th SX	ThO	SO	SO	SO	SX	SO	
	p.m.	p.m.		p.m.		p.m.	p.m.	p.m.		p.m.			p.m.	p.m.	p.m.	p.m.	p.m.	p.m.	night	
BANGOR ....dep.	7 6					8 28	8 45	9 10		9 30			10 10	10 15	10 20		11 10	11 10	12 3	
Menai Bridge arr.	7 10					8 32	8 49	9 14		9 34			10 14	10 19	10 24		11 14	11 14	12 7	
Menai Bridge dep.	7 11					8 33	8 50	9 15		9 35			10 15	10 20	10 25		11 15	11 15	12 8	
Treborth																				
Port Dinorwic						8 39	8 56	9 21		9 41			10 21	10 26	10 31		11 21	11 21		
CAERNARVON ⊕ ⊕ arr.	7 22					8 47	9 4	9 29		9 49			10 29	10 34	10 39		11 29	11 29	12 19	
CAERNARVON dep.	7 26	7 30		8 20		8 51	9 10	9 35		9 55					10 43	10 45	11 40			
Pontrhythallt ⊕		7*47		8†36			9†26	9†51								11† 1	11†56			
Cwm-y-Glo......				8†40			9†30	9†55								11† 5	12† 0			
Padarn Halt				8†45			9†35	10† 0								11†10	12† 5			
LLANBERIS ⊕ .. arr.		7 55		8 47			9 37	10 2								11 12	12 7			
Dinas ⊕ (Caernarvon) arr.	7 35					9 0				10 4					10 52					
Dinas (Caernarvon) dep.	7 36					9 1				10 5					10 53					
Llanwnda	7 39					9 4				10 8					10 56					
Groeslon ..⊕ arr.	7 42					9 7				10 11					10 59					
Groeslon dep.	7 46					9 8				10 12					11 0					
PENY-GROES ⊕ arr.	7 51					9 13				10 17					11 5					
PENY-GROES dep.	7 52					9 18									11 6					
Pant Glas ..dep.	8 0					9 26									11 14					
Brynkir ..⊕ arr.	8 3					9 29									11 17					
Brynkir dep.	8 4					9 30									11 18					
Ynys..............	8 8					9 34									11 22					
Llangybi ..⊕ arr.	8 12					9 38									11 25					
Llangybi dep.	8 13					9 39									11 26					
Chwilog ..⊕.. ..	8 16					9 42									11 29					
AFONWEN⊕..arr.	8 19					9 45									11 32					
Notes	On Sats. Rep. No. 479.	Not to run after September 8th. To work 8.30 p.m. to Llandudno.		†—Not advertised.			†—Not advertised.	†—Stop not advertised.		†—Starts from Llandudno Jn. at 8.50 p.m. commencing Sept. 11th.						†—Not advertised.	†—Stop not advertised.			

Passenger trains cannot cross at Chwilog and Pontrhythallt.

AFONWEN, LLANBERIS, CAERNARVON AND BANGOR.

SUNDAYS.

	1	2	3	4	5	6	7	8	9	10	11	12	13	14	15	16	17	18	19	20
		PASSENGER to Llandudno Junction.	PASSENGER.		PASSENGER 12.15 p.m. from Pwllheli.		PASSENGER to Llandudno Junction.		Empty Stock.				PASSENGER to Rhyl.	PASSENGER 5.0 p.m. from Pwllheli.	PASSENGER to Llandudno.		PASSENGER.	PASSENGER.	Empty Stock.	Light Engine.
Reporting Nos. ..		84					102						40		114					
		a.m.	p.m.		p.m.		p.m.		p.m.				p.m.	p.m.	p.m.		p.m.	p.m.	p.m.	p.m.
AFONWEN⊕ dep.					12 35									5 25						
Chwilog ..⊕......					12 40									5 30						
Llangybi ⊕ arr.					12 45									5 35						
Llangybi dep.					12 46									5 36						
Ynys..																				
Brynkir ..⊕ arr.					12 52									5 42						
Brynkir dep.					12 54									5 43						
Pant Glas																				
PENY-GROES ⊕ arr.					1 3									5 52						
PENY-GROES dep.					1 5									5 53						
Groeslon ..⊕ arr.					1 9									5 57						
Groeslon dep.					1 11									5 58						
Llanwnda																				
Dinas ⊕ (Caernarvon) arr.					1 15									6 1						
Dinas (Caernarvon) dep.					1 16									6 2						
LLANBERIS⊕..dep.															6 10					
Padarn Halt.. ..																				
Cwm-y-Glo																				
Pontrhythallt ⊕															6†16					
CAERNARVON ⊕⊕ arr.					1 24									6 10	6 28					
CAERNARVON dep.		10 0	12 10		1 28		2 25		2 50				4†45	6 18	6 35		7 15	8 5	11 15	11 55
Port Dinorwic																				
Treborth																				
Menai Bridge arr.		10 11	12 21				2 36										7 26			
Menai Bridge dep.		10 15	12 22		1 40		2 37		3 5				4†58	6 29	6 45		7 27	8 16	11 29	12 11
BANGOR ....arr.		10 20	12 27		1 44		2 42		3 10				5 1	6 33	6 48		7 32	8 20	11 33	12 15
Notes		Not to run after September 10th.			To run July 30th to September 10th inclusive.				To run July 9th, 16th and 23rd.				†—3 minutes recovery time.	Runs July 30th to September 10th inclusive.	Not to run after September 10th. †—Not advertised.				Not to run after September 10th.	

Passenger trains cannot cross at Chwilog and Pontrhythallt.

BANGOR, CAERNARVON, LLANBERIS AND AFONWEN.

SUNDAYS.

	1	2	3	4	5	6	7	8	9	10	11	12	13	14	15	16	17	18	19	20
		Light Engine	PASSENGER to Pwllheli.	PASSENGER.				PASSENGER.	PASSENGER.	PASSENGER to Pwllheli.	EXPRESS 2.30 p.m. from Llandudno.		Light Engine.	PASSENGER.	PASSENGER	PASSENGER	PASSENGER 9.30 p.m. from Rhyl.	PASSENGER 10.25 p.m. from Rhyl.		
Reporting Nos. ..											25						137	143		
		a.m.	a.m.	a.m.				p.m.	p.m.	p.m.	p.m.		p.m.	p.m.	p.m.	p.m.	p.m.	p.m.		
BANGOR ....dep.		9 15	10 20	11 20				1 25	2 0	2 0	3 25		3 38	3 50	5 30	7 10	10 40	11 23		
Menai Bridge arr.			10 24					1 29	2 4	2 4	3 29			3 54	5 34	7 14	10 45	11 27		
Menai Bridge dep.		9 20	10 25	11 23				1 30	2 5	2 5	3 30		3 43	3 55	5 35	7 15	10 46	11 28		
Treborth																				
Port Dinorwic																				
CAERNARVON ⊕ ⊕ arr.		9 35	10 36	11 33				1 41	2 16	2 16	3 41		3 58	4 6	5 46	7 26	10 57	11 39		
CAERNARVON dep.			10 40							2 20	3 50									
Pontrhythallt ⊕..											4* 5									
Cwm-y-Glo																				
Padarn Halt																				
LLANBERIS⊕ .. arr.											4 11									
Dinas ⊕ (Caernarvon) arr.			10 49							2 29										
Dinas (Caernarvon) dep.			10 50							2 30										
Llanwnda																				
Groeslon ..⊕ arr.			10 54							2 34										
Groeslon dep.			10 55							2 35										
PENY-GROES ⊕ arr.			11 0							2 40										
PENY-GROES dep.			11 1							2 41										
Pant Glas ..dep.																				
Brynkir ..⊕ arr.			11 12							2 52										
Brynkir dep.			11 13							2 53										
Ynys..............																				
Llangybi ..⊕ arr.			11 21							3 1										
Llangybi dep.			11 22							3 2										
Chwilog ..⊕.. ..			11 25							3 5										
AFONWEN⊕ arr.			11 28							3 8										
Notes		To work 10.0 a.m. to Llandudno Jn. Not to run after September 10th.	To run July 30th to September 10th inclusive.						To run on July 9th, 16th and 23rd only.	To run July 30th to September 10th inclusive.	Will not run after September 10th.		Not to run after September 10th. To work 4.45 p.m. Caernarvon to Rhyl.	To run on September 17th and 24th only.			Not to run after September 10th.			

Passenger trains cannot cross at Chwilog and Pontrhythallt.

Extracts from
PASSENGER TRAIN MARSHALLING INSTRUCTIONS — SUMMER 1934

Marshalling.	Circuit No.
7.50 a.m., AFONWEN TO LIVERPOOL (Lime Street).	
Inter-Corridor Set ⎱ Afonwen (3 vehicles) ⎰ Liverpool (L.St.)	101
Attach rear Bangor:—	
Third —Bangor Liverpool	763
cbBrake Van (Milk) —Amlwch Manchester	
Attach rear Llandudno Junction :—	
CacLavatory Set ⎱	1214
(3 (NC) vehicles) ⎰ Llandudno	
CacComposite ⎰ Manchester (Ex.)	587
a Received off 9.40 a.m. from Llandudno.	
b Received off 7.50 a.m. from Amlwch.	
c Transferred Chester to 11.37 a.m. to Manchester (Ex.).	
C Except on May 26th and Saturdays commencing June 30th, when vehicles run independently.	
Tonnage— 85 Afonwen.	
139 Bangor.	
247 Llandudno Junction (C).	
113 Chester.	

Marshalling.	Circuit No.
10.48 a.m. (SO), AFONWEN TO EUSTON.	
(10.25 a.m. from Pwllheli.)	
(10.10 a.m. from Portmadoc.)	
(Class " A " Stock.)	
Compo. Brake (60 ft.) ⎱ Pwllheli Euston	373
Third (42) ⎰	655
Compo. Brake (60 ft.) ⎱ Portmadoc Euston	295
Third (42) ⎰	
Attach rear Llandudno Junction :—	
bCompo. Brake (60 ft.) —Bangor Euston	368
Attach rear Rhyl :—	
aThird Brake	
aThird Vestibule	
(60 ft.)	
aKitchen Car ⎱ Llandudno Euston	
aFirst Vestibule	
(60 ft.)	
aComposite (18/24)	
aThird Brake ⎰	
a Received off 11.50 a.m. from Llandudno.	
b Received off 11.40 a.m. from Bangor.	
Tonnage—120 Afonwen.	
150 Llandudno Junction.	
324 Rhyl.	

Marshalling.	Circuit No.
10.48 a.m. (S), AFONWEN TO BANGOR.	
(10.25 a.m. from Pwllheli.)	
Two Coach Set (NC) —Bangor	1304
AaCompo. Brake (60 ft.)—Pwllheli Euston	373
a Transferred Bangor to 10.50 a.m. Holyhead to Euston.	
Tonnage—85.	

Marshalling.	Circuit No.
12.30 p.m. (SO), AFONWEN TO MANCHESTER (Exchange).	
(12.10 p.m. from Pwllheli.)	
Lavatory Set ⎱ Afonwen	1248
(3 (NC) vehicles) ⎰ Manchester (Ex.)	
Compo. Brake ⎱ Pwllheli	454a
Third ⎰ Manchester (Ex.)	768
Attach front Bangor:—	
BTwo Thirds ⎱	787
BComposite ⎰ Manchester (Ex.)	594c
CLavatory Set ⎱	1223
(3 (NC) vehicles) ⎰	
B Until June 2nd.	
C Commences June 9th.	
Tonnage—141 Afonwen.	
225 Bangor.	

Marshalling.	Circuit No.
1.45 p.m., AFONWEN TO LLANDUDNO JUNCTION.	
(Runs to Liverpool (Lime Street) (SO) commencing June 30th.)	
(1.5 p.m. from Portmadoc.)	
(1.20 p.m. from Pwllheli.)	
BTwo Thirds (SO) ⎱ Afonwen	767a
BComposite (SO) ⎰ Liverpool	594
aThird ⎰ (L.St.)	767
aCompo. Brake ⎰ Portmadoc	451
aCompo. Brake ⎱ Liverpool (L.St.)	450
DaThird ⎰ Pwllheli	768a
⎰ Manchester (Ex.)	
Attach front Bangor :—	
BBrake Van (SO) ⎱ Liverpool (L.St.)	—
BTwo Thirds (SO) ⎰	764a
a Transferred Llandudno Junction to 3.25 p.m., Llandudno to Manchester (applies to Manchester vehicle only on Saturdays, commencing June 30th).	
B Commencing June 30th.	
C Except Saturdays, commencing June 30th.	
D Commencing June 16th.	
Tonnage— 86 Afonwen (C).	
170 (SO) Afonwen ⎱	
252 (SO) Bangor ⎰ (B).	
223 (SO) Llandudno Junc.	
28 tons extra Afonwen to Llandudno Junc., commencing June 16th.	

Marshalling.	Circuit No.
11.15 a.m. (SO), EUSTON TO AFONWEN.	
(Class " A " Stock.)	
Compo. Brake (60 ft.) ⎱ Pwllheli	335
Third (42) ⎰	622
Third (42) ⎱ Portmadoc	294
Compo. Brake (60 ft.) ⎰	
bCompo. Brake —Llanfairfechan (B)	340b
aThird Brake	
aComposite (18/24)	
aFirst Vestibule (60 ft.) ⎱ Llandudno	20
aKitchen Car	
aThird Vestibule (60 ft.)	
aThird Brake ⎰	
a Transferred Rhyl to 3.25 p.m. to Llandudno.	
b Transferred Llandudno Junction to 3.47 p.m. to Bangor.	
B Llandudno Junction to relabel to Bangor.	
Tonnage—333 Euston.	
149 Rhyl.	
120 Llandudno Junction.	

BANGOR CARRIAGE WORKING — *shown overleaf*

All stock movements on the LMS and LMR were planned, and allocated circuit numbers. Whilst inter-district stock working was generally listed and published in the Passenger Train Marshalling Instructions booklet (issued at the commencement of each time-table change) and as such could readily be identified, local stock circuit numbers were not widely known. Little or no information about circuit numbers came to light until recently when the carriage workings for Bangor station for the period 31st May to 26th September 1948 for down trains on Saturdays and Sundays only were made available by Eric Lynn who fortunately had held on to them. This enabled a comprehensive picture to be ascertained and many of the up workings can be deduced, not only for a Saturday, but also for the weekday period. It will be noted that the information only deals with stock that actually stopped at Bangor, hence the 'Irish Mail' is not shown. This information can be obtained from the marshalling book for the period. The number shown in the left-hand column relates to the train reporting number that signalmen would have to note, and in some cases, report to control as part of their normal working duties. The second column indicates the time the train started from its commencing point. In some cases the working is conditional and this is prefixed by a 'Q' whilst empty stock working is indicated by 'E.C.S.' In some timings the letter 'L' is shown between the hours and the minutes; this indicates that the locomotive or locomotives are changed at Bangor and the working is allowed time to effect the change.

BANGOR COACH DIAGRAMS

SATURDAYS ONLY		UP TRAINS					CARRIAGE WORKINGS	31st MAY to 26th SEPTEMBER 1948
Number	Time	FROM	TO	Arrive	Depart	Circuit	Details	Return Bangor arr
38		Bangor	Llandudno		6.45am			arr Llandudno 7.25am
42	6.45am	Caernarvon	Llandudno	7.06am	7.13am		Lav set. arr Llandudno 7.52am	
Mtr		Bangor	Bethesda		7.25am	1700	arr Bethesda 7.40am	8.01am
52	7.15am	Caernarvon	Llandudno	7.36am	7.40am	230	3 coach set	arr Llandudno 8.33am
	6.50am	Amlwch	Bangor	7.48am		1311	3 coach set	works 11.25am Caernarvon
114	6.40am	Afonwen	Bangor	7.55am		1235 743	Lav set works forward 8.20am Bangor- Manchester Rep no 58 CF ; works forward 8.20am Bangor-Manchester Rep no 58	
148	7.15am	Holyhead	Bangor	8.10am			C H ; CBB; CBC;2-QF; C H : CBC. works forward 8.20am Bangor - Manchester returns 10/20pm Manchester - Holyhead	
58		Bangor	Manchester		8.20am	1235 743	Lav set ex 6.40am Afonwen returns 1/40pm Manchester - Llandudno CF; ex 6.40am Afonwen as above C H : CBB;CBC;2-QF;C H ;CBC. returns 10/20pm Manchester-Holyhead	
ECS- Mtr	8.18am	Menai Bridge	Bangor	8.22am		1700		
Mtr		Bangor	Bethesda		8.24am	1700	arr Bethesda 8.39am	8.58am
238	8.35am	Holyhead	Liverpool	9.20am	9.28am		IDZ Lav set	) 6 coaches)
488	8.10am	Afonwen	Llan. Jctn.	9.33am	9.40am	1232 2020	Lav set 2 - F	arr Llan. Jctn. 10.16am works forward 10.42am Manchester
164	8.50am	Penychain	Llan. Jctn.	10.24am	10.29am		L - changes locomotives and crews	arr Llan. Jctn. 10.48am
	10.30am	Caernarvon	Llan. Jctn.	10.50am	10.55am	1230	Lav. set	arr Llan. Jctn. 11.25am
138	9.40am	Penychain	Manchester	11.14am	11.17am		L - changes engines and crews	
498	10.00am	Holyhead	Manchester	11.09am	11.24am	748	C H ; 2-QF; CBC;CBB, ex 2.10am Crewe. works 4/30pm Manchester -Chester QF; CBC ; CH ex 7.30am Bangor works 4/30pm Manchester - Chester	
Mtr		Bangor	Bethesda		11.30am	1700	arr Bethesda 11.45am	
270		Bangor	Euston		11.45am		L- Change loco & crew at Sorting Sidings South, Crewe.	
	10.55am	Amlwch	Bangor	11.59am		1310	3 coach set	ex 6.35am Bangor-Amlwch
272	11.00am	Holyhead	Bangor	12/13pm				
454	10.45am	Afonwen	Manchester	12/05pm	12/22pm	2677 1235	6-B RSD 237 Lav set	
Q - 142	10.50am	Penychain	Llan. Jctn.	12/19pm	12/27pm			arr Llan. Jctn. 12/47pm
90	11.15am	Afonwen	Manchester	12/30pm	12/45pm		GWR stock	
Mtr		Bangor	Bethesda		12/50pm	1700	arr Bethesda 1/05pm	
Q - 318	11.25am	Penychain	Llan. Jctn.	12/58pm	1/11pm			arr Llan. Jctn. 1/32pm
	12/55pm	Caernarvon	Bangor	1/19pm		1311	3 coach set	
216	12/30pm	Holyhead	Manchester	1/27pm	1/35pm			
	12/50pm	Amlwch	Bangor	1/50pm		1316	3 coach set	
Mtr	2/10pm	Caernarvon	Bangor	2/31pm				works 3/00pm Bethesda
252		Bangor	Liverpool		2/45pm	229a	3 coach set ex 8.35am Manchester - Bangor arr 11.35am	
Mtr		Bangor	Bethesda		3/00pm	1700	arr Bethesda 3/15pm	
82	1/55pm	Holyhead	Ordsall Lane	2/36pm	3/23pm			
	2/20pm	Amlwch	Bangor	3/15pm		1232 2020	Lav set F	
278	2/35pm	Holyhead	Birmingham	3/35pm	3/45pm		10 vehicles ex Crewe IDZ; CBC; 2-CF ex Bangor.	
Mtr		Bangor	Bethesda		4/25pm	1700	arr Bethesda 4/40pm	
156		Bangor	Llan. Jctn.	4/50pm		127	5 coach set. ex 1/50pm Llan. Jctn.	
	3/58pm	Afonwen	Bangor	5/25pm		1220 1982	Lav set 2 - F	
172	4/15pm	Holyhead	Manchester	5/07pm	5/11pm		CH ; 2 - QF; CBC ; CBB ; CBR ; QF; CBC ; CH.	
Mtr	5/30pm	Menai Bridge	Bethesda	5/34pm	5/35pm	1700	arr Bethesda 5/50pm ECS from Menai Bridge - Bangor	
162		Bangor	Llan. Jctn.		5/40pm			
382	5/10pm	Holyhead	Bangor	6/09pm		5304	CBD included	
	5/10pm	Amlwch	Bangor	6/16pm		1311	3 coach set	
	5/10pm	Afonwen	Bangor	6/45pm		1230 2007	Lav set 2 - F	
182		Bangor	Manchester		7/00pm	1973	F . ex 10.25am Manchester - Bangor included	
Mtr		Bangor	Bethesda		7/30pm	1700	arr Bethesda 7/45pm	
160	6/30pm	Holyhead	Bangor	7/44pm			works forward dep Bangor 9/15pm	
332	7/15pm	Amlwch	Llan. Jctn.	8/20pm	8/30pm	235	3 coach set	
	7/05pm	Afonwen	Bangor	8/27pm		1232 2020	Lav set 2 - F	
196	7/35pm	Holyhead	Crewe	8/38pm	8/51pm		CBR ; PQR ;CBR ;CBB ;CBC ; 2-QF ; CH ;	
Mtr		Bangor	Bethesda		9/00pm	1700	arr Bethesda 9/15pm	
186	7/40pm	Chwilog	Bangor	8/56			works forward to Broad Green Rep no 160	
160		Bangor	Crewe		9/15pm		includes milk to Broad Green	
Q	7/35pm	Penychain	Llan. Jctn.	9/10pm	9/35pm		arr Llan. Jctn. 9/58pm	
	9/00pm	Amlwch	Bangor	9/59pm		1230	Lav set	
	8/35pm	Afonwen	Bangor	10/04pm		1316	3 coach set	
		Bangor	Llan. Jctn.		10/10pm		arr Llan. Jctn. 10/41pm	
	9/45pm	Afonwen	Bangor	11/07pm		1220 1982	Lav set 2 - F	
200	10/25pm	Holyhead	Bangor	11/22pm				

SATURDAYS ONLY   DOWN TRAINS   CARRIAGE WORKINGS   31st MAY to 26th SEPTEMBER 1948

Number	Time	FROM	TO	Arrive	Depart	Circuit	Details	Return Bangor arr.
47	1.45	Chester	Bangor	4.15am			Parcels	
1	2.10	Crewe	Holyhead	4.34am	4.36am			
		Bangor	Afonwen		4.51am	1235	Lav. set due 11/7pm ex Afonwen. 743 CF due 1/19pm fr. ex Cvon	7.53am
		Bangor	Amlwch		5.05am	1311	3 coach set due 6/16pm ex Amlwch	8.09am
		Bangor	Afonwen		5.45am	1232	Lav. set due 9/51pm ex Llan. Jctn & 2020 2F due 11/7 fr. Afonwen	9.30am
		Bangor	Amlwch		6.35am	1310	3 coach set due 10/4pm ex Afonwen	9.25am
ECS		Bangor	Caernarvon	6.40am		230	3 coach set due 11/38 fr. Llan. Jctn (191) 7.15.to Llandudno	7.36am
5	4.15	Chester	Bangor	7.10am				
7		Bangor	Holyhead		7.30am	237	3 coach set due 11/18 fr. Holyhead . 742 C.F.	
Q- ECS	7.25	Llan. Jctn.	Penychain	7 L 45am	7 L 50am		works 10.50am Penychain to Llan. Jctn. Changes loco & crews	
Mtr.	7.45	Bethesda	Menai Bridge	8.01am	8.10am	1700	works 8.24am Bethesda	8.22am
Q-ECS	7.55	Llan. Jctn	Penychain	8 L 11	8 L 15		works 11.25am Penychain to Llan. Jctn. Changes loco & crews	
15	5.45	Chester	Bangor	8.41am		235	3 coach set for 5/25pm Amlwch. Cir.397CF & CBC for 1/30pm Holyhead	
3	6.10	Chester	Holyhead	8.54am	9.23am			
Mtr.	8.42	Bethesda	Bangor	8.58am		1700	for 11 30am Bethesda	
		Bangor	Afonwen		9.00am	2677	6 B RSD 237 stock circuit 1235	12/10pm
309	3.50	Manchester	Bangor	9.06am			Parcels	
			Bangor	9.43am		1316	3 coach set for 11.30am Amlwch, June 5th & 12th ;Sept. 18th & 25th for 11.00am ECS to Gaerwen June 19th to Sept. 11th inc.	
	9.10	Llan. Jctn	Bangor	9.43am				
ECS		Bangor	Caernarvon	9.45am		1230	Lav set . 3/7 to 18/9 due 6/23 fr. 10.30 to Llan. Jctn.	10.50am
107	8.10	Chester	Bangor	11.00am			Parcels	
ECS		Bangor	Amlwch		11.00	1316	3 coach set due 9/43am June 19th to Sept. 11th inc.	1/50pm
61	7.40	Liverpool	Bangor	11.16am		1220 1982 2576	Lav set for 12/20pm Afonwen 2 -F for 12/20pm Afonwen 4 bogies RSD	
		Bangor	Caernarvon		11.25am	1311	3 coach set due 7.48am fr. Amlwch. return with 12/55pm fr. C/von	1/19pm
315	9.05	Crewe	Holyhead	11.23am	11.30am		June 19th to Sept. 11th inc.	
		Bangor	Amlwch		11.30am	1316	June 5th,12th; Sept. 18th,25th only 3 coach set due 9.43am Llan. Jctn	1/51pm
453	8.35	Manchester	Bangor	11.35am		229a 2711 3102	3 coach set for 2/45pm Liverpool (Comm. 26/6) 8B RSD 259 comm 26/6 11BRSD June 5th, 12th 19th only	
55	9.20	Crewe	Holyhead	11.50am	12.00pm			
Mtr.		Bethesda	Bangor	12/06pm	12/15pm	1700	ECS to Menai Bridge. to work 12/50pm Bethesda.	
	11.35	Llan. Jctn	Bangor	12/10pm		1232	Lav set for 12/39pm Amlwch. LSV front	
		Bangor	Afonwen		12/20pm	1220	Lav set 1982 2F due 11.16am	5/25pm
		Bangor	Amlwch		12/39pm	1232	Lav set 2020 F due 12/10pm ex Llan. Jctn.	3/16pm
427	12/20	Llan. Junction	Penychain	12/41pm	12/45pm		L - changes Locomotives and crews	
Mtr.	1/12	Bethesda	Bangor	1/28pm		1700	for 1/40pm Caernarvon	
107		Bangor	Holyhead		1/30pm	397 5304	CF & CBC due 8.41am fr. Chester(15) CBD due 6/09pm Holyhead (392)	
Mtr.		Bangor	Caernarvon		1/40pm	1700	due 1/28pm dep C/von 2/10pm. Works 3/00pm Bethesda	
373	1/09	Llan. Jctn.	Bangor	1/44pm		1230 2007	Lav set for 3/10pm Afonwen 2F for 3/10pm	
467	1/30	Llan. Jctn.	Penychain	1/50pm	1/55pm		L - changes Locomotives and crews return ECS	
	1/50	Llan. Jctn.	Bangor	2/25pm		127	5 coach set for 4/50pm Llan. Jctn	
457	10.25	Manchester	Bangor	2/42pm		503 879 1199 1973 1984 2718	CBC for 3/23 H. & C. (Chester) CH spare Lav set for 7.30am Manchester F. for 7/00pm Manchester 2 - F. for 5/30pm Manchester 4 B RSD 253	
473	2/30	Llan. Jctn.	Penychain	2/51pm	2/55pm		L - changes Locomotives and crews . Q - runs as required, returns ECS dep A/w.7/50pm	9/10pm
		Bangor	Afonwen		3/10pm	1230 2007	Lav set due 1/44pm ex Llan. Jctn. 2 - F. due 1/44pm ex Llan. Jctn.	6/46pm
459	11.25	Manchester	Holyhead	3/13pm	3/20pm		Ty Croes next stop	
143	2/56	Llan. Jctn.	Holyhead	3/29pm	3/36pm			
Mtr.	3/25	Bethesda	Bangor	3/41pm		1700	for 4/25pm Bethesda	
		Bangor	Amlwch		3/55pm	1311	3 coach set ex 11.25am Afonwen 5/10pm fr. Amlwch	6/16pm
		Bangor	Afonwen		4/35pm	1232	Lav set 2020 2 -F due 3/15pm ex Amlwch	8/27pm
415	1/30	Liverpool	Bangor	4/53pm		151 490 784 786A	5 coach set for 7.35am Su. CBC for Llandudno CF for 7.35am Su. 2 - CF spare for 4.51am Mon. Afonwen	
Mtr.	4/45	Bethesda	Bangor	5/01pm		1700	for 5/35pm Bethesda	
89	11.15	Euston	Holyhead	5/05pm	5/12pm			
		Bangor	Amlwch		5/25pm	235	3 coach set due 8.41am ex Chester 7/15pm fr. Amlwch	8/30pm
147	5/00	Llan. Jctn.	Holyhead	5/35pm	5/45pm			
		Bangor	Afonwen		5/35pm	1316	3 coach set due 1/50pm ex Amlwch	
Mtr.	5/55	Bethesda	Bangor	6/11pm		1700	to work 7/30pm Bethesda	
433	6/43	Llan. Jctn.	Holyhead	7/20pm	7/30pm			
		Bangor	Amlwch		7/45pm	1230	Lav set due 6/46pm ex Afonwen	
127	7/20	Llan. Jctn.	Bangor	7/36pm		1220 1982	Lav set for 8/05pm Afonwen 2 - F for 8/05pm Afonwen	
		Bangor	Afonwen		8/05pm	1220 1982	Lav set ex 7/20pm Llan. Jctn 2 - F ex 7/20pm Llan. Jctn.	11/07pm
Mtr.	8/10	Bethesda	Bangor	8/26pm		1700	for 9/00pm Bethesda	
419	5/05	Liverpool	Holyhead	8/35pm	8/40pm			
		Bangor	Caernarvon		8/52pm	1232 2020	Lav set due 8/27pm. Stock stored C/von. Work milk. to Afonwen arr 10/09pm 1 - F Milk A/wen to Chwilog. L.E. dep 10/35pm to Bangor	11/35pm
Mtr.	9/20	Bethesda	Bangor	9/36pm		1700	for 7.35am Monday	
	9/18	Llan. Jctn.	Bangor	9/51pm		126	5 coach set for 9.40am Monday Crewe.	
187	9/50	Llan. Jctn.	Holyhead	10/24pm	10/30pm			
145	5/05	Euston	Holyhead	11/15pm	11/23			
191	11/05	Llan. Jctn.	Bangor	11/38pm		144	5 coach set for 7.35am Su. to Birmingham	
491	10/20	Manchester	Holyhead	1.41am	1.49am		SUNDAY MORNING	
29	3.15	Crewe	Bangor	6.41am		109	5 coach set for 2/35pm Su. + other stock - no details	
5	5.00	Chester	Bangor	7.40am			Parcels	
403	9.30	Liverpool	Bangor	1/16pm		763 119	2 - C F for 6/35pm no details	
53	1/50	Llan. Jctn.	Holyhead	2/11pm	2/14pm			
59	5/30	Llan. Jctn.	Bangor	6/01pm		218	3 coach set for 6.45am Monday to Llan. Jctn.	
119	5/45	Crewe	Holyhead	8/27pm	8/35pm			
137	9/35	Llan. Jctn.	Bangor	10/06pm	10/30pm	1207	Lav set for 5.45am no further details	
195	8/25	Crewe	Holyhead	11/24pm	11/30pm			
491	10/20	Manchester	Holyhead	1.41am	1.49am		MONDAY MORNING	

Beyond Treborth towards Caernarvon were the twin bores of Vaynol tunnel. The gradient fell away after the station and was 1 in 79 through the tunnel, which caused draughting problems with 'down' trains. Here Bangor's No. 42157 emerges from the dark and stifling heat and heads for Port Siding and Caernarvon with 11.25 a.m. Bangor to Pwllheli working on 4th October 1952.   *Author*

Working the line

Whilst branch line work possessed little of the prestige and appeal of working on the main line, each branch had its own character and requirements and preparation for each trip needed to be just as thorough and methodical. After the First World War the Afonwen line was usually worked by tank engines which were used increasingly after the turntable had been taken out of use. After the 0−6−2Ts had been tried on various turns, singly and in pairs, Bangor was allocated 4−6−2Ts which proved better suited to the work. Even so, Stanier had new designs under construction, and his 2−6−4Ts enabled the earlier Fowler version to be released to less profitable districts. Two were based at Bangor in 1937 and were the answer to most of the problems encountered on the Afonwen line. They were strong and carried sufficient coal and water to enable a trip to be made without anxiety.

About the same time, variations of the 2−6−2Ts appeared on the North Wales coast, but the general complaint about these engines was that they were unable to cope with the loads being worked to Afonwen. Time was booked against the engine repeatedly and this was reflected in the shed master's report to his superiors. Of the two types allocated to Bangor, staff preferred the earlier Fowler version to the Stanier taper boiler model.

The former had marginally more power and was less prone to rolling at speed. Nevertheless it was when the Stanier and Fairburn locomotives arrived in numbers after the war that good timekeeping was maintained on the Afonwen line.

In the mid 1950s there were the four versions of 2−6−4Ts on shed. The Fowler version, with enclosed cab, despite being hot in the summer months, was by agreement amongst most of the staff, the most powerful of the four models. The Fairburn engines were well received, but the injector was inclined to be temperamental and would 'knock off' when the regulator was closed. The Stanier version suffered a similar complaint, whilst the British Railways Standard type had none of the injector complaints but an unpopular design of reverse screw. On odd occasions there were complaints about the regulator sticking open, but apart from that they were well liked.

Once attached to the train, it was necessary to have sufficient water space available in the boiler to allow the use of the injectors to keep the engine quiet, whilst standing at the platform. When the 'right away' was received, the dampers were opened and the firebox doors shut. Usual loading to Afonwen was a three or four coach set, although some trips had extra vehicles included. The first train of the day, known as the 'Afonwen Mail' had six vehicles including two mail coaches which were despatched at Afonwen to Portmadoc and Pwllheli.

Once clear of Belmont tunnel, firing recommenced and it was necessary to have plenty of steam for the climb out of

Menai Bridge. There was a restriction over the junction onto the Caernarvon line of 10 mph, but the swing as one entered the points made it uncomfortable to take it at any greater speed. Of course, most trains stopped at Menai Bridge anyway, so speed was reduced for this stop. The climb out of the station was severe, and in wet weather could be tricky, so care was needed to avoid slipping. Judicious use of the sander on stopping and restarting was the norm, and the bank was forged with a cut-off of about 40% and the regulator on second valve. Provided the fire was bright by Menai Bridge station, things were straightforward and lumps added on leaving the station would be burnt through by Treborth, where the gradient changed direction.

At the levelling out it was essential that the boiler was full to the top nut, and the injector was watched closely as Treborth station was cleared. The 'stick' was wound back, and some drivers coasted a short way down the bank, but approaching the Vaynol tunnel it was injector full on, blower hard on, firehole doors closed and into the corner of the cab. The sensation of hitting a wall of air in tunnels of restricted clearance has been described elsewhere, but it is always an experience to live through. The regulator was always kept open and the train was driven through, speed climbing rapidly up to 60 mph before clearing the single bore. As the smoke cleared, drivers shut off, set the reverser to coast at 45%, while firemen looked over the side to the overflow pipe, usually re-setting the injector which had knocked off the moment the regulator was closed.

For the next mile one coasted, speed being kept in check by judicious use of the brake. By Port Siding it was necessary to pick up the shovel and give the box another good round, shut off the injector, and put the blower on again. The driver would be slowing down for Port Dinorwic and it was necessary to have some space in the boiler to keep the engine quiet whilst standing. On getting the 'right away', the fire doors were opened, injector shut off, blower off and another couple of rounds in the box.

The Fairburn engines were my personal favourites despite the injector, and 42259 in particular was a good performer. The climb up to Felin Heli crossing was straightforward, and the fire was given another round before the line levelled out. When the driver whistled up for Griffiths' Crossing, the dampers were closed to one notch and the doors opened. Speed built up and after whistling up for Pandy Lane crossing, the fire was given a pull through with the dart, before filling up the back corners of the box. Approaching Waterloo Port crossing, steam was shut off, and we coasted into Caernarvon. As the 'up' and 'down' platform approached, the injector was put on again, the blower was opened out slightly and the damper opened another notch. Some drivers made a point of drawing level with the column and topping up the tanks, especially if one had time to spare at Afonwen.

The signalman from No. 2 box brought the staff to the loco and, on getting the 'right away', drivers opened up briefly, sufficient to get the train moving, by which time we had negotiated the scissors crossover and taken the right

Taken from the footbridge at Caernarvon, looking towards Menai Bridge in 1964 before the track was singled, this view shows a 2—6—4T approaching with a Saturdays only special to Butlin's camp at Penychain. The access from the goods yards to the 'up' main line is on the left hand side of the picture. *Author*

hand track for Afonwen. The gradient fell away severely as we burrowed under Castle Square, and the flanges squealed as they rode round the twists and turns. As speed rose, and Caernarvon tunnel approached, the dampers were opened fully, and firing recommenced.

On leaving the tunnel, the injector was switched off, or reduced, another round of firing and then the doors were shut until Seiont bridge was in sight. Here the Llanberis line fell away to the left, but the Afonwen line continued to climb. By milepost 8 another round of firing, and the injector was increased. The climb was severe, and controlled firing of half a dozen shovels full, close the door, watch the chimney until the smoke had cleared, then repeat the process, was for me the most acceptable method of firing.

The driver had his own method of tackling his side of the job and he had to be vigilant. The line was not one for speed merchants, and it was necessary to keep the regulator well open and cut off in the 40% region. There was little time to look around until the gradient eased off just before Dinas Junction. When it showed signs of easing, the blower went on, the injector was checked and then the staff was taken off the water gauge cock, or wherever the driver required it. Some wanted instant sight of it, whilst others left it to the fireman to look after. As he checked speed entering the loop, the staff was taken in the left hand and held between finger and thumb at arms length out of the opening by the cab door, if one had a clear road. The

At Dinas Junction, Huw Williams is standing ready to exchange the token from Dinas Junction to Groeslon for the staff for the Caernarvon No. 2 to Dinas Junction section, with the fireman of a Bangor to Afonwen train.   *Author*

signalman would hold up the token carrier with his left hand. The fireman's right hand was extended forward, allowing the loop of the token carrier to ride up the sleeve, at the same time releasing the staff to the signalman. It was a skilled operation and to have dropped the token would have caused delay which would have to be explained. Speed for exchanging staffs was supposed to be at ten miles per hour, but if one was behind time, it was much higher. I recall exchanging staffs at at least 25 miles an hour one snowy morning on the Afonwen Mail at Dinas with Bob

'Joy' Williams, and the smack as the loop rode up my arm and the leather pouch hit the back of my head, created a sensation I can still recall to this day. All this for one minute regained time.

The moment the token was on board, it was back to the shovel and another round, watch the chimney, then another. The injector was left on, and if it was necessary to stop at Llanwnda, the blower was put on and the injector checked as speed dropped for the halt.

Llanwnda was a difficult station to see what was happening, particularly on the 'Mail' as the curve of the track meant that the platform was out of sight. Depending on who the guard was, it was necessary to get down from the cab and climb the bank to get the 'right away', which was usually relayed by the station staff. The 'Mail' in fact did not stop at Llanwnda for passengers, but if any train had four coaches, then the engine was off the platform. Once on the move, it was back to the shovel, and the injector was left on until the distant for Groeslon was sighted. Another firing round, then the token hoop was taken off the handbrake column. As we ran over the level crossing it was held in the left hand by the pouch and the right hand was extended to grasp the staff from the porter signalman at the leading end of the platform.

Whilst standing at Groeslon, the fire was given another going over with the dart, or the rocker grate (if fitted) was shaken, before filling in the back corners of the box. At this time, I usually sorted out a few large lumps for the grate and kept them to one side. Once clear of Groeslon, the injector was shut down slightly and on the easing of the gradient once clear of Tudor siding, the opportunity was taken for a sit down for a minute, before closing the damper a notch, putting the blower on and the cab tidied up. As the distant for Penygroes was sighted, the lumps were thrown into the box and a double round put in. The injector was put on as the platform face came alongside, and the doors were left open to cut down smoke emission.

Penygroes had a signal box, and so the token exchange was conducted at a civilised rate. The staff was exchanged for a token, the fastidious driver checking that the contents were correct. The dampers were opened, and, as the valves began to lift, if timing was right, the green flag was waved. The climb now was on in earnest and, apart from minor changes of grade up and down for the first few yards, the climb continued at 1 in 49 for over a mile. This was full regulator and 45-50% cut-off or even more. Some drivers could pull the unburnt coal off the shovel as it was approaching the firehole ring and many a fireman has had his carefully prepared fire torn to pieces before the climb was half way through, although I fortunately never experienced that. Nevertheless, the effect was devastating for an inexperienced fireman. Even double-headed ten coach trains were at risk, and most mates would ensure that the fire was in the best state possible before leaving Penygroes.

One advantage of working on a single line branch like the Afonwen line was that everyone knew one another, and tolerance was part of the way of life. Trains did not leave

Penygroes until they were in a fit condition to do so, and drivers have been known to make up time from Groeslon and overstay by a couple of minutes until they were satisfied that things were ready for making the top. If possible, the injectors were left on all the way up, and approaching the summit the dampers were closed down.

On the descent, as Pant Glâs drew near, it was not necessary to build the fire up, merely sufficient to see that it was in reasonable shape. This was the time to sit down and have a drink of tea. I used the time to tidy up the footplate, hose down the coal and generally straighten things up. After Pant Glâs all that was necessary was to keep an eye on the boiler water level, and peep into the firebox, perhaps putting a shovel or two into the back corners to keep things hot. Approaching Brynkir the hoop would be retrieved and as the train stopped, handed over to the porter signalman, who gave up a large staff again. A couple of puffs from the cylinders and the train coasted down, stopping at Ynys.

I recall one trip, when approaching Ynys, I was fascinated to see three quarters of a van plus assorted debris and groceries scattered along the track on the driver's side, just as we ran into the station. The van had stalled on the crossing and the driver had been unable to re-start it in time. A photograph was taken at the time. As far as I know, they are still talking about it in Ynys. It was the only

exciting thing to happen since they opened the line, apart from when they closed it again.

A slight climb out of the station meant that the fire was given another round or two, before settling down to relax, only moving to check the injectors, and the business of exchanging token for staff at Llangybi.

This was the pattern as one coasted down the grade to Chwilog. The platform was on the fireman's side, and the token was exchanged when stationary. As the train drew away, it was my practice to open the dampers, give the fire a rocking and put in one or two large lumps into the corners. I also allowed the water level to go down and, unless there was a long layover at Afonwen, I prepared the fire for the return journey. As we ran in to the LMS platform, the token was given up to the GWR staff at the platform ramp, and the injector was put on to fill up the boiler. There was rarely less than twenty minutes before departure, and after 'hooking off', the loco would run forward onto the main line, unless there was a through train to Portmadoc due. If there was, depending on the time of day, it was then the practice to run into the sidings before setting back through the goods avoiding line that ran alongside the LMS platform face line. There was a point on this line where clinker could be dumped, and it was my practice to have any such debris ready and dump it at the prescribed

The van shown at a small ungated occupation crossing north of Ynys station was given a glancing blow by the 'down' train. The outcome was very lucky for all concerned.   *Author's collection*

spot, before pulling on to the main down line and setting on to the stock. Usually a halt was made short of the stock by the column to fill up the tanks before coupling up. The fire would then be built up, using large coal if it could be found, and the boiler was filled to the top nut. By this time it was possible that the bunker doors could be opened, and the opportunity was taken to hose down the coal with the slaking pipe. This was particularly important as the return journey was made bunker first and coal dust blowing in the face was not in anyone's interest. After checking that all was in order and that the correct lamps were in position, the opportunity was taken for a quick inspection around the loco, ensuring that nothing had fallen off, or was working hot or loose.

As time drew near for departure, and the usual pleasantries or insults exchanged with the guard or the station staff, and checking that the train was in proper order, the dampers would be opened and the blower increased. If the valves lifted, the injector was put on, and when the staff arrived, the handbrake was unscrewed and a lookout was kept for the green flag.

The climb out of Afonwen was as severe in its own way as was the climb out of Penygroes in the 'down' direction. It

was necessary to keep the fire healthy and, although the gradient was not quite so severe, it was certainly longer, nearly eleven miles of uphill slog before one could relax. Consequently, very great care was taken to ensure that pressure did not drop more than a few pounds, and that every halt at a station was used to the best advantage. Running times to each station were only minutes apart, but that was sufficient to lose pressure, and time. Chwilog was reached after three minutes, and after changing the staff and checking the injector, because it was necessary to steam right up to the level crossing as the platform ramp was approached, together with the need to change the staff on the move, one had plenty to do. I used to put the blower on as the distant signal was passed and shut off the injector, because if it blew back as the driver shut off, the distraction of an injector misfeed could cause a lapse of concentration as the tokens were being exchanged.

As the staff was brought into the cab, the injector was reset, and it was then necessary for the fireman to get to his window and watch for the green flag. Most drivers would cross over and see for themselves but one or two were reluctant to leave their controls, particularly the brake, with the train on the slope, and delegated their mate to watch out.

No. 42444 departing from No. 3 platform at Afonwen with the 3.50 p.m. to Bangor in 1952. The 'down' line three arm signal was replaced by a two arm signal some time between 1955 and 1960. The locomotive siding under the tanks is clear of stock.   *Author*

On 29th June 1935 severe flooding at Brynkir washed away a small bridge over a stream north of the station. For a while trains terminated at Penygroes and Brynkir and Crosville provided a shuttle service of buses between the two points. The district engineers erected a temporary bridge with severe weight restrictions, but sufficient to enable train services to resume. The restricted axle weight loadings continued until the rebuilding was completed. Here an Afonwen train is working past the bridge. *Author's collection*

One could understand their caution in these conditions. The moment the signal was received, the fire would be topped up, and after shutting off the blower the injectors would be set to maintain a decent level. The blast kept the fire bright, and it was necessary to fire continuously without overdoing things.

The procedure at Llangybi was the same as at Chwilog. The staff was changed as one entered the platform; the platform face was on the fireman's side, and there was still a gradient — and so it went on. At Ynys there was a levelling off of the climb somewhat, and the opportunity was taken to build up the fire if the driver was heavy handed. The boiler was kept fully topped up, and once Brynkir had been cleared, it was back to the shovel.

The platform at Pant Glâs was on the driver's side so he had the job of looking for his own green flag, and the fire was tended carefully, ensuring that the back of the grate was packed up. As Grianog crossing was cleared, the damper was closed, and the going was now easier. The drop down to Penygroes was very carefully controlled, and the continuous braking meant that the injectors were popping off and on all the way down.

As the station approached and the gradient levelled out, the dampers were opened and the fire built up as we ran past the goods yard. The tokens were exchanged again as we entered the platform, and as we drew up the valves usually lifted. The injector was checked, and on receiving the 'right away', the fire was rocked and then topped up.

Progress was relatively easy to Groeslon, and all that was needed was a watchful eye on the controls. The damper was shut to one notch on leaving the station and one could roll down to Llanwnda, then on to Dinas Junction. It was the practice at Dinas to keep the distant and the home on until the train was nearly stopped, before dropping the arm which enabled the signalman to get down the steps and exchange tokens outside his front door. The 'up' line entrance to the loop was very severe, and everyone treated the access to the platform face with the greatest respect. Once clear of the platform, the gradient fell away again, and it was coasting all the way down to Seiont bridge. There I opened the dampers again and built up the fire, ensuring that by the time the foot of the gradient had been reached, there was a full head of steam for the climb under Castle Square and up to Caernarvon station.

On emerging from Caernarvon tunnel, the line dropped momentarily under Turf Square, and the signals for Caernarvon could be sighted. The climb in the confined space ensured a noisy entrance up the 1 in 40, and as No. 2 box came into view, the signalman could be seen waiting in the 'six foot' for the staff. This meant opening the cab door, getting low down and stretching out. I always hated this change more than any other because of this difficult position. Mind you, the signalmen were not happy either, as they had to reach up.

As the track levelled, the run into the 'up' platform was slow and steady, and usually the loco was drawn up to the water tank at the end of the platform. If the duty meant that the loco was working forward beyond Bangor, the practice was to top up the tanks here.

The driver took the opportunity to check over the engine here whilst the fireman was on the tank top, and when duties were over, the time was taken to build up the fire, particularly if the train or loco was working forward. I used to rock the grate again, just to keep the bars clear, and then it was away again, with the same pattern of work. Six or seven shovelsful of coal, close the doors, watch the chimney until the smoke was clear, then repeat. The injector was kept on, and progress to Port Dinorwic was brisk. As the gradient fell away, drivers would shut off steam, and the train would roll down, being brought to a halt at the platform. The fireman had to watch for the flag, and when it was received, fire again, building up the fire for the climb through to Treborth. It was also necessary to ensure that one was not firing going into Vaynol tunnel, although the danger of a blow back was less than on the 'down' journey. Nevertheless, the bore was tight and, despite the fact that the chimney was behind you, it got very stuffy. Once clear of the tunnel, the damper was closed a notch and the injector feed rate increased. The descent to Menai Bridge was severe and the distant was usually left on. Speed was brought to about 25 miles an hour before the descent proper began, and speed was reduced all the way.

The platform was approached at walking pace. As the train stopped, I opened the damper again if we were being relieved on the platform at Bangor and, on getting the 'right away', built up the fire and topped up the boiler. Just before Belmont tunnel I would soak the coal and the floor with the slaking pipe, and put the blower on as the tunnel mouth was entered. The signals controlling entrance to Bangor platforms were in the tunnel mouth and speed was progressively reduced. Most local trains were brought to a dead stop before entering the platform, particularly for the down passenger loop, and as one negotiated the points and ran in, the cab was checked over for the last time. The injectors were checked to see that all was well; if the train was standing for some time, the dampers were closed down and the blower was put on just sufficient to ensure there was no blow back. The doors were opened slightly. As the train stopped, the handbrake was screwed on, while the driver set the loco in mid gear and opened the drain cocks. A remanned job meant that the relieving crew were on the platform waiting for you, and they boarded the footplate before you left. Any comments were made between drivers and firemen and, after a last look over to ensure that nothing had been left behind, one made one's way across the tracks to the shed, to sign off and make for home.

Some turns, of course, worked more than one trip. For instance, the crew that worked the Afonwen mail worked a second trip to Afonwen at 9.00 a.m. from Bangor, with the same locomotive. The stock was left in the down passenger

loop to be dealt with by the passenger shunt, and after detaching, the engine would draw forward into Bangor tunnel before setting back and running through the station into Belmont tunnel, in order to pull on to the shed road. After topping up the tanks, pulling coal forward and checking the motion, we would go into the mess room for a 'cup and a bite', before repeating the process.

Some duties worked through from Afonwen to Llandudno Junction and back to Bangor. Others worked to Llandudno Junction, then through to Afonwen and back to Bangor. On a Saturday, a crew with a class '2' 2—6—2T would work a trip to Amlwch and back to Bangor, then work a trip to Afonwen and back to Bangor as part of their turn of duty. On Saturdays, in the summer months, with ten coach trains, heavily loaded, pairs of locomotives would work the Butlin's specials from Penychain to Bangor, the pilot locomotive coming off at Bangor, and the permutations and combinations of locomotives were numerous and varied. Class '3' and class '2' 2—6—2Ts were common. Class '4' 2—6—4Ts were also common. A class '4' 2—6—4T with a class '5MT' 4—6—0 was not unknown, and on one occasion two class '5MTs' were worked. It was attempted to work the double-headed trains bunker to bunker so that the pilot engine was facing in the normal direction of travel. However, it did not always work out, and some very weird arrangements were seen. It was the practice for a traffic inspector to be on duty at Afonwen to sort out the tangles.

Now Afonwen was not overblessed with spare track capacity and it was necessary to park empty stock, locos, etc. wherever possible. The peak times of crisis were between 10.00 a.m. and 12.00 noon, and again from 2.00 p.m. to 4.30 p.m. On one occasion, it is said, two class '5s' worked tender to tender back to Bangor. The train engine which was working forward after the pilot had been detached at Bangor was scheduled to work through to Manchester Exchange — tender first. I believe that the language of the relieving crew from Chester could be heard all along the coast, and that one traffic inspector was discreetly kept away from Afonwen after that.

On another occasion, due to a slip-up on someone's part, a class '2' 2—6—2T was supposed to work a ten coach train to Bangor on its own. I cannot vouch for the accuracy of these two instances, but can well believe the possibility of it happening. It was the practice in the late 1950s on a Saturday morning to work engines to Afonwen for return working in groups of twos and threes. For certain, on at least one occasion, one of the engines going off shed in a threesome had no pressure on the clock, and a very weak fire. By the time it got to Afonwen, things were picking up, and at departure time, after a stint of hard work and bad language, pressure was within sight of the red line, and by means of some hard work and an unofficial arrangement of a banker being provided to Chwilog, it managed to get the Penychain to Sheffield trip away and out of sight on time.

No. 41221 working bunker first with the 12.40 p.m. Bangor to Amlwch train at Menai Bridge main line 'down' platform on 10th May 1949.

E. S. Russell

Menai Bridge

Menai Bridge, on the main Chester to Holyhead line, was the commencing point for the Caernarvon and Afonwen line. It was opened to traffic in 1858 as a junction for the Bangor & Caernarvon Railway which, by Act of 20th May 1851, was worked by the Chester & Holyhead Railway. Details of the wrangles and construction difficulties can be found in Peter Baughan's book which covers the historical background to all the lines featured here.

Initially there was no 'down' connection with the Chester & Holyhead line, trains from Bangor to Caernarvon having first to set back into the branch platform. However, following an accident in 1865, the track layout was altered to provide a direct double junction and an additional platform. The line to Caernarvon was doubled in 1872 and remained so until 1966 when it reverted to a single line, worked by miniature train staff. For the Investiture of the Prince of Wales in 1969, the section was split at Felin Heli crossing, but reverted to a single section immediately afterwards.

Apart from the building on the main 'up' platform, which was an imposing stone structure, the island platform and the Afonwen line 'down' platform were very humble affairs connected by a subway. The island platform, which handled the main line 'down' traffic and the 'up' traffic

Distance from Menai Bridge No. 1 box to Bangor No. 2 box:	1 mile 275 yds up direction
Distance from Menai Bridge No. 1 box to Treborth:	1700 yards down direction
Distance from Menai Bridge to Port Siding signal box:	2 miles 819 yds down direction
Running time:	
up direction	
passenger trains	3 minutes to Bangor
freight trains	5 minutes to Bangor
down direction	
passenger trains	3 minutes to Treborth
freight trains	5 minutes to Treborth
Intermediate siding:	
down direction – Davies' siding. 680 yards from signal box	

from Afonwen, was of timber construction and devoid of enclosed shelter. The Afonwen line 'down' platform at least had an open shed to offer some measure of protection, but certainly no comfort.

For many years there were two signal boxes controlling the site, No. 1, at the east end of the station at the Bangor end, controlling the junction and the small goods yard, and number 2 box the goods sidings with access to the Caernarvon line. No. 2 box was dismantled some time in the 1930s, its function being replaced by two ground frames

Two 2—6—4Ts work a 4 coach train back to Bangor from Afonwen. Such abundance of power was not necessary, but coupling a light engine to a scheduled train prevented congestion on the single line sections between Caernarvon and Afonwen. Oswald Jones, the linesman, occasionally had to travel over the line to transfer single line tokens and train staffs between signal boxes and stations to avoid 'running out' of tokens in peak traffic periods.
E. N. Kneale

controlled by No. 1 box. The track plan shows the two boxes and the location of Davies' siding on the 'down' Afonwen line 840 feet from the quarter-mile post.

The Afonwen line commenced from the station with a climb of 1 in 128 from the platform which almost immediately stiffened to 1 in 79. As the track was lined with trees on the 'down' side, screening it from the Vaynol estate, the going could be quite tricky in wet weather and particularly in autumn. Drivers calling at Davies' siding were particularly at risk, but fortunately the siding was little used and was dismantled before nationalization. The gradient stiffened still further to 1 in 60 after the bridge.

Many of the goods trains for the Caernarvon line started from Menai Bridge yard or terminated there. Light engine working to and from the motive power depot at Bangor was frequent and such was the density of traffic to the sidings that a shunter was on duty for much of the day, although some trains worked through without calling at the yard, particularly the through freights from Holyhead to Crewe, Liverpool or Manchester and their return workings. Some worked through to Caernarvon, usually from Mold Junction, and involved a change of locomotive and crew. This was

effected on the goods avoiding line at Bangor. Details of the locomotive workings starting or terminating at Menai Bridge yard for the Afonwen and Amlwch lines can be found in the section dealing with locomotive workings on page 3.

Passenger traffic to and from the station on the Caernarvon line was usually healthy. Some trains were particularly well patronized, especially the early morning and evening workings which catered for folk going to work in upper Bangor or Menai Bridge, but few changed at Menai Bridge, most going through to Bangor and changing there.

By contrast, the small goods yard off the 'up' main line serving Menai Bridge saw little traffic. The afternoon goods from Llangefni usually dealt with any requirements but there were normally only one or two wagons a week.

The line from Menai Bridge to Caernarvon was split into block sections as follows: Menai Bridge to Port Siding; Port Siding to Port Dinorwic; and Port Dinorwic to Caernarvon No. 1 box. Port Siding box was opened from 6.00 a.m. to 6.00 p.m. but that at Port Dinorwic saw only occasional use. Outside these hours the intermediate boxes were switched out and one through section sufficed.

Right: At Menai Bridge the main station building was beside the 'up' main line. The station was always kept clean and tidy by the platform staff as this view shows. *British Railways*

The island platform as seen from the Holyhead end of the 'up' main line on 12th August 1953.

H. C. Casserley

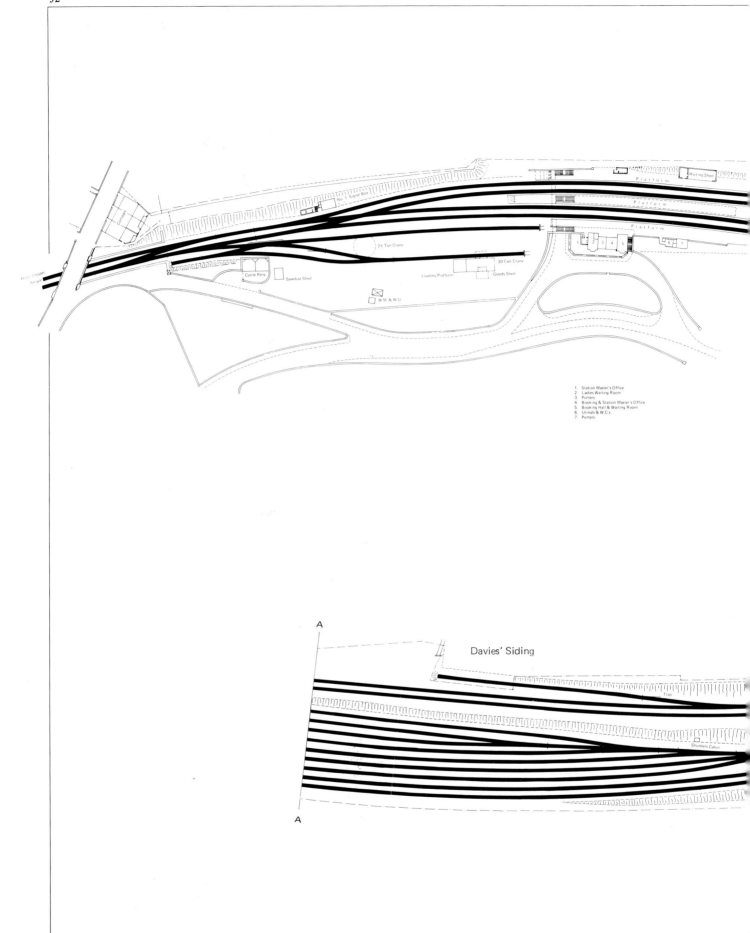

1. Station Master's Office
2. Ladies Waiting Room
3. Porters
4. Booking & Station Master's Office
5. Booking Hall & Waiting Room
6. Urinals & W.C.s
7. Porters

Davies' Siding

MENAI BRIDGE

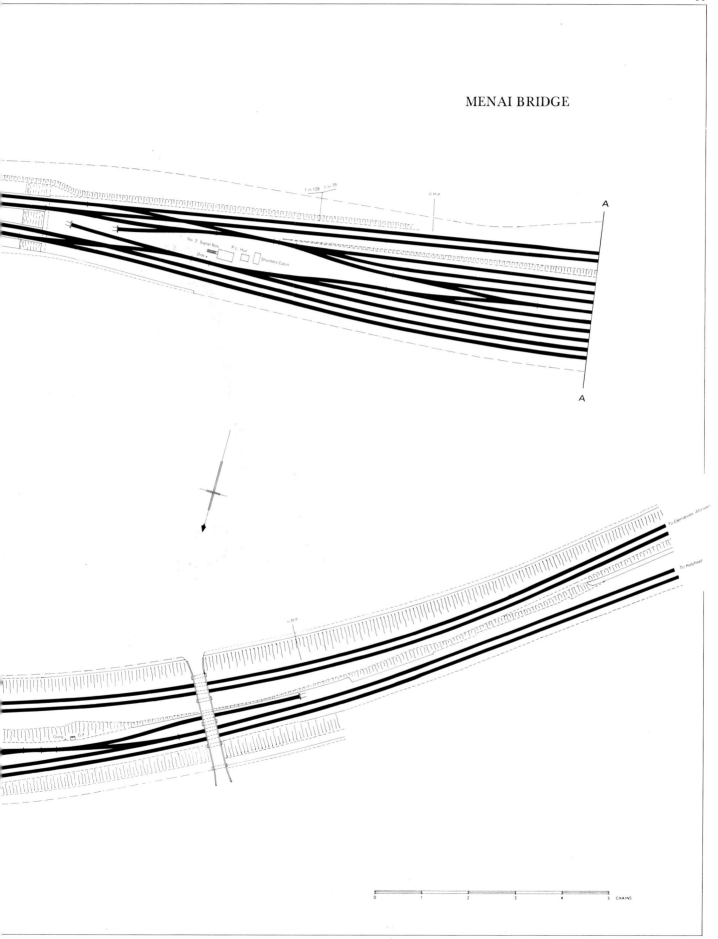

A

A

1 in 128 1 in 79

R M P

No. 2 Signal Box   P L Hut

Disc   Shunters Cabin

To Caernarvon, Afonwen

To Holyhead

R M P

Gong   G F

0   1   2   3   4   5 CHAINS

A departing Afonwen train climbing the grade towards Treborth. The spartan cover afforded on the island platform can be seen on the left.

E. N. Kneale

The sidings at Menai Bridge situated between the main Chester & Holyhead line on the left and the Afonwen line, to the right of the photograph. This view is looking towards Menai Bridge station in 1952. Davies' siding, removed shortly after the last world war, connected off the Caernarvon 'down' line at the extreme right hand side of the picture, in line with the hut in the lower goods yard.

Author

British Railways standard class '4' No. 75039, coasting down the bank from Treborth with an Afonwen to Bangor local working. The use of tender locomotives, whilst not unknown, was comparatively rare, and for such a locomotive to work in this direction was even more so. The lower level tracks are the main line to Holyhead.

E. N. Kneale

Treborth station was at the summit of the climb out of Menai Bridge. It is seen here looking towards Caernarvon, the change in gradient being clearly visible.
J. M. Dunn

Treborth

Treborth opened initially in 1855, closed in 1858 and reopened again the following year. It had a very quiet existence, being one of those oddities where an agreement over its construction led to a clause which stipulated the number of trains that had to call each day.

The main building was on the 'down' side, and incorporated a house, booking & waiting hall and booking office. On the 'up' side a small wooden shelter was provided, access to the platform being by means of a walkway across the tracks. The occupation crossing at the Bangor end was interlocked with the signals, and the up distant for Menai Bridge was located at the Caernarvon end of the 'up' platform.

The goods siding, brought into use in 1902, was rarely used in later years, apart from a short period in 1952 when the CEGB delivered some materials there for a sub-station built immediately behind the station site. For a while, a camping coach was located here but even this was not very successful, and after a couple of seasons was withdrawn.

Distance from Treborth to Menai Bridge:	1700 yards up direction
Distance from Treborth to Port Dinorwic station	2 miles 548 yds down direction
Distance from Treborth to Port Siding Box	1 mile 879 yds down direction
Running time:	
up direction	
passenger trains	3 minutes to Menai Bridge
freight trains	4 minutes to Menai Bridge
down direction	
passenger trains	5 minutes to Port Dinorwic
freight trains	5 minutes to Port Siding signal box
Gradient leaving station: *up direction* 1:132 falling	
down direction 1:132 rising	

According to J. M. Dunn, the sparseness of passenger traffic was such that the small change float in the till had gone mouldy, or green, when the station finally closed on 2nd March 1959.

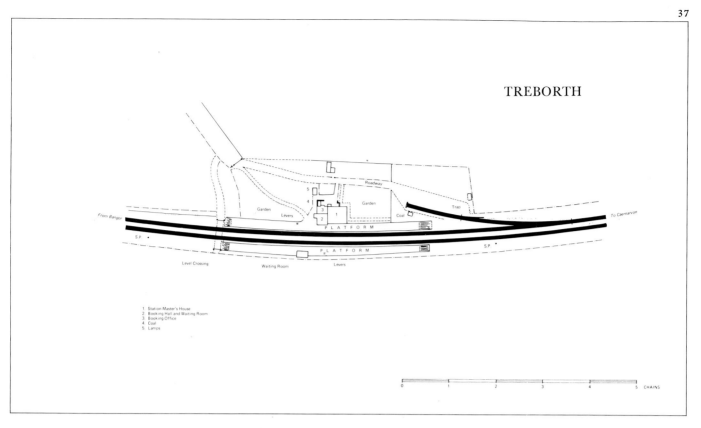

TREBORTH

1. Station Master's House
2. Booking Hall and Waiting Room
3. Booking Office
4. Coal
5. Lamps

Treborth station 'down' platform looking towards Caernarvon. Traffic was always sparse and freight traffic non-existent. A camping coach, located here for a couple of seasons, can be seen partially concealed behind the house.

W. A. Camwell

38

A 2—6—4T climbing the gradient from Port Siding to Treborth before plunging into Vaynol tunnel with an Afonwen to Bangor train. When the line was singled following closure of the section from Caernarvon to Afonwen, the 'up' line tunnel remained in use until final closure.

E. N. Kneale

A 2—6—4T working back to Menai Bridge yard from Caernarvon in 1953, stops to pick up wagons which have been brought up from the quayside by the 'Port Siding shunt' locomotive, 0—6—0 No. 52407, before resuming their separate duties. The Port Siding signal box of Saxby and Farmer origin was taller than usual to give the signalman an uninterrupted view over the road overbridge from which the photograph was taken.

Author

Port Siding

The Port Siding branch was promoted by the Bangor & Carnarvon Railway, with the Chester & Holyhead Railway's support, to facilitate the transport of the slate products inland from the Dinorwic Quarry via the quayside at Port Dinorwic. The Bangor & Carnarvon Railway opened the line to Port Dinorwic on 10th March 1852, the first station being replaced by another to the west in 1875. Narrow gauge wagons from Penscoins were offloaded from their 4 ft gauge transporters and lowered down to the quayside on an incline, which passed over the standard gauge on a skew bridge, and under the main Caernarvon to Bangor road. However, considerable difficulties were experienced in effecting the transhipment of slates to the standard gauge and consequently a branch from the Bangor to Caernarvon line was proposed early in 1856 to run down to the quayside at Port Dinorwic. The work was completed and the line brought into use in the summer of that year, the route down to the quayside following the course of the final stretch of the first Dinorwic tramroad. Details of the tramroad can be found in 'The Padarn & Penrhyn Railways' by Susan Turner, and in a series of articles entitled 'Slates to Felin Heli' in the Journal of the Stephenson Locomotive Society.

The interior of Port Siding signal box taken shortly after it had been taken out of commission. The points had been disconnected and the signal arms removed, but the block instruments were still in position .

Author

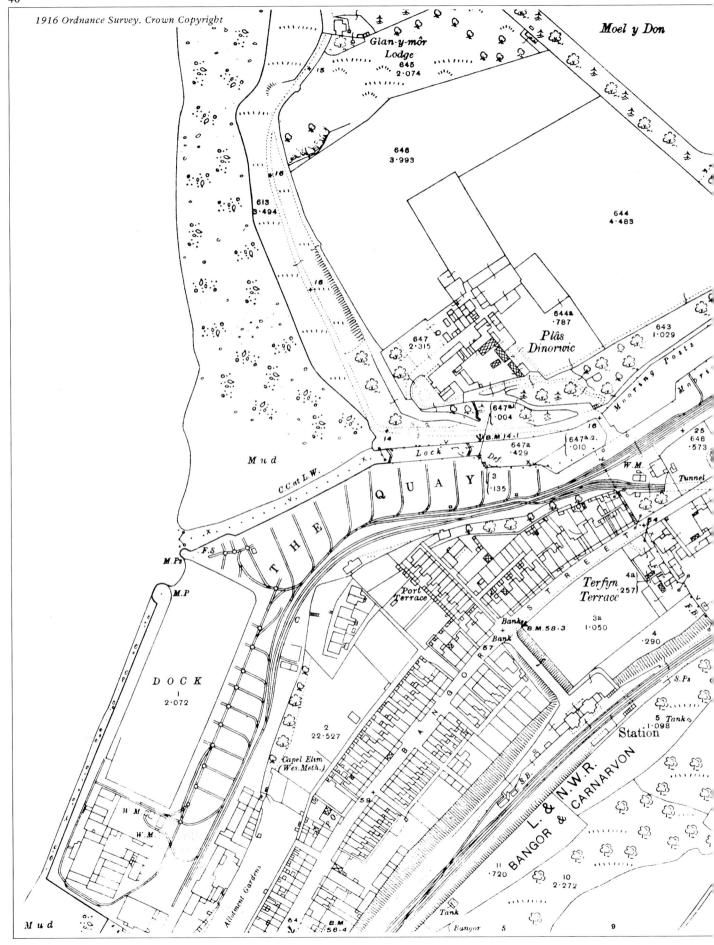

Moel y Don

Glan-y-môr
Lodge
645
2·074

646
3·993

644
4·483

613
3·494

644a
·787

643
1·029

*Plâs
Dinorwic*

647
2·315

647
·004

B.M 14·1

647a
·429

647a.2.
·010

648
·573

647a
·010

Mud

C.C. at L.W.

Lock

Def.

W.M.

Tunnel

3
·135

W.M.

THE QUAY

M.Ps

F.S.

M.P

Port
Terrace

*Terfyn
Terrace*
257

4a

3a
1·050

Bank
B.M.58·3

Bank

57

4
·290

S.Ps

DOCK
1
2·072

2
22·527

S.P.s

5 Tank
1·098

Station

W.M.

W.M.

Capel Elim
(Wes. Meth.)

Allotment Gardens

L. & N.W.R.
BANGOR & CARNARVON

S.B.

11
·720

10
2·272

Tank

Mud

B.M
56·4

Bangor

5

9

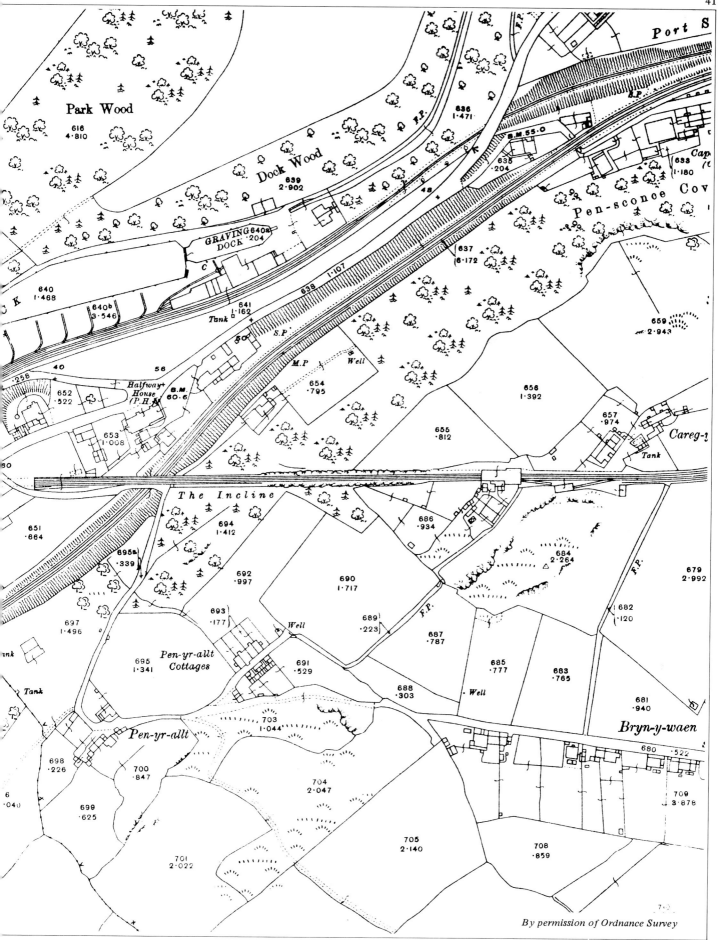

Park Wood

616
4·810

Dock Wood

636
1·471

B.M.55·0

Port S

635
·204

633
1·180

Cap

Pen-sconce Cov

639
2·902

GRAVING 640a
DOCK ·204

637
6·172

659
2·943

640
1·468

640b
3·546

641
1·162

Tank

638
1·107

S.P.

·258

652
·522

Halfway
House
(P.H.)

B.M.
60·6

M.P

Well

654
·795

656
1·392

657
·974

Careg-

Tank

653
1·008

655
·812

The Incline

651
·664

694
1·412

690
1·717

686
·934

684
2·264

679
2·992

695a
·339

692
·997

682
·120

697
1·496

693
·177

Well

689
·223

687
·787

685
·777

683
·765

681
·940

Pen-yr-allt
Cottages

695
1·341

691
·529

688
·303

Well

Bryn-y-waen

Tank

Pen-yr-allt

703
1·044

680
·522

698
·226

700
·847

704
2·047

709
3·878

699
·625

701
2·022

705
2·140

708
·859

By permission of Ordnance Survey

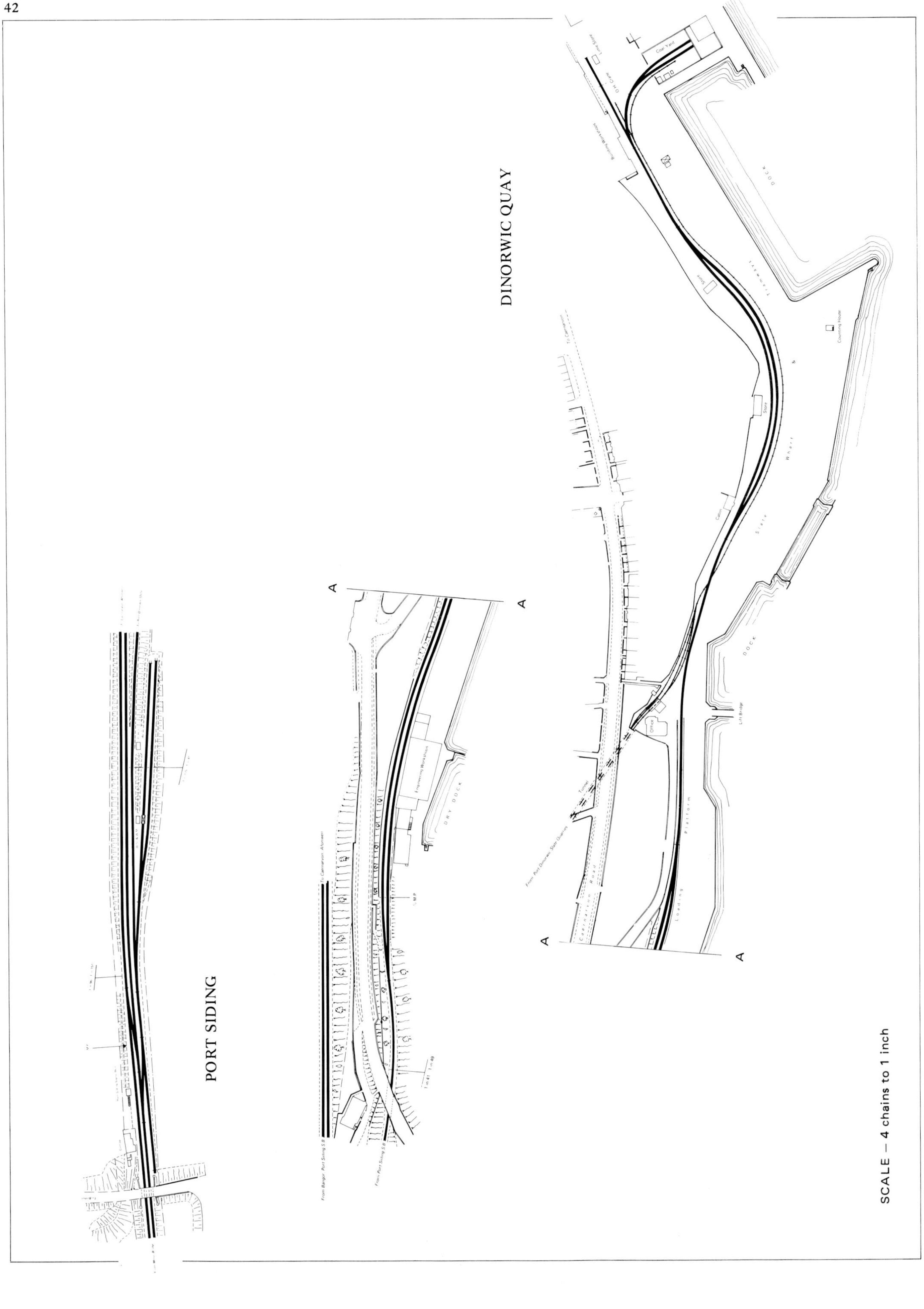
DINORWIC QUAY
PORT SIDING
SCALE — 4 chains to 1 inch
A
A
A
A
DOCK
Slate Wharf
Counting House
Store
Cabin
Coal Yard
DOCK
Lift Bridge
Office
Loading Platform
Carnarvon Road
Tunnel
Engineering Workshops
DRY DOCK

The general bustle and stacks of slates unloaded from the narrow gauge wagons at Port Dinorwic are indicative of a period of activity long gone. Standard gauge wagons stand alongside narrow gauge trucks along the extent of the harbour. *National Library of Wales*

The branch commenced at Port Siding signal box, about a mile from Port Dinorwic, on the 'up' side of the Bangor to Caernarvon line. The signal box itself, measuring some 14 ft x 12 ft, was of brick construction, and at 18 ft 6 ins above ground level, gave the signalmen visibility over the bridge from Deiniolen to the Caernarvon to Bangor road. While the siding was in use, the box was opened from 6.00 a.m. to 6.00 p.m. and was switched out outside working hours. The branch junction trailed from the 'up' line and a short shunting neck facilitated access to two storage sidings. An adjacent crossover between the running lines allowed access to and from the 'down' line. On the 'Port Siding trip' (turn 125 in 1955) it was the practice to work empty wagons from Menai Bridge yard to Port Siding in the morning, arriving about 10.30 a.m. After reversing over the trailing crossover and onto the up running line, the train entered the sidings loco first. With no loop in the top sidings the necessary run-round was sometimes effected by gravity, although more usually the Afonwen goods, which passed around this time, stopped here while its locomotive was used to draw off the wagons from the 'Port Siding trip' and release the engine.

The guard's brake van was then left in one of the sidings and shunting began. The gradient of 1 in 41 meant that there was a limit to the numbers of wagons allowed either way between the siding and the quay. The locomotive generally worked smokebox first to the Port, propelling the empties down from the main line.

The branch fell away down the gradient and the Caernarvon to Bangor road passed over by means of seven

0–6–0 No. 52230 shunting the harbour, alongside narrow gauge loco and wagons at Port Dinorwic quayside on 25th August 1954. This scene was typical of the daily work at the harbour, until the closure of the feeder service from Dinorwic quarry. *H. C. Casserley*

stone skew arches, known as Cross Bridge. The line then passed through a small valley alongside a stream, which fed the dock at the port, before levelling out at the quayside, where the track doubled, forming a transhipment siding and loop, at the end of which the narrow gauge lines emerging from the tunnel and off the incline, in front of the weigh-bridge office, crossed the standard gauge tracks. Throughout its existence the layout of standard gauge tracks appears to have remained unchanged.

At the port there were similarities between working methods and practices on the Padarn and Penrhyn Railways, each port having its own narrow gauge locomotive to shunt

The cottage at Port Siding, taken from the signal box and looking towards Bangor. *Author*

the quarry stock. It must be remembered that in both cases the ports were established first for the shipment of slate, each quarry owning its own vessels. The standard gauge lines were additional features which offered increased trade. After the First World War, and the immediate boom which resulted as a consequence of war damage, slate demand slumped and so did the degree of standard gauge traffic. However, there was sufficient traffic to justify one train daily to each port until the increased use of lorries within the quarries brought about a withdrawal of the narrow gauge railway workings and the total withdrawal of traffic from both Port Dinorwic and Port Penrhyn. The last working to Port Siding was on 30th October 1961, the track being lifted shortly afterwards. Port Siding box was stripped of its fittings, although the shell of the building remained for some time afterwards. The trackbed was reclaimed by nature although its course can still be followed.

Until the late 1950s the Port Siding crew brought up the loaded wagons from the quay about eight at a time and stored them in the top sidings opposite the signal box. A rake of empty wagons was then propelled down the gradient with brakes pinned down and the shunter or guard walking in front, until the line doubled and levelled out. Empties were worked beyond the point where the narrow gauge lines crossed the standard gauge tracks and spaced out alongside the various stacks of slates which were graded by size. Loaded wagons would be drawn onto the 'up' side of the loop before being taken up to Port Siding box. The standard gauge track extended for some way beyond the loading bays, ending in a coal yard, where the narrow gauge locomotives based at the quay were stored. Coal and other supplies were propelled to these points as and when necessary, the distance from the Port Siding signal box to the harbour coal yard being 1 mile 4 chains.

The locomotives used latterly on the Port Siding turn were the ex-Lancashire & Yorkshire 0—6—0s based at Bangor. These also worked smokebox first to Port Siding, travelling back tender first after the day's work with empties, any loaded wagons being left at the top sidings.

The morning return freight workings from Nantlle or Llanberis would call at Port Siding to pick up wagons and deposit them in Menai Bridge yard, the brake van and other wagons being left on the 'up' line, suitably protected by the signalman while the locomotive ventured into the sidings for stock. Quite often the 0—6—0 on the shunt would be at the top level and would draw into the shunting neck, out of the way. The L & Y locomotives were preferred to the Fowler '4F' 0—6—0s as they were stronger engines and better suited to the conditions on the quayside. With either type it could be decidedly unpleasant working back tender first to Bangor with coal dust from the tender blowing back into our eyes and bitter winter weather blowing off the Irish Sea as one came over the summit at Treborth. However, it was deemed necessary to work this way back through the narrow confines of Vaynol tunnel as the combination of gradient, weather and load could prove somewhat difficult struggling back from the Port with empties, and, although slipping to a standstill inside the tunnel was rare, it was not unknown, and if the locomotive chimney had been leading, there could have been serious difficulties in breathing for the train crews.

It was rare to find tank engines working the turn as there were no facilities for taking water. On one occasion I recall working down to the Port with a 'Q' working and a 2—6—2T specially called out to clear a backlog of loaded wagons. On this occasion it was merely a question of an engine and brake van working out to the sidings and leaving the brake van there while one trip was made down to the harbour for eight wagons. These were brought up and, after being coupled to the brake van, were deposited on the 'up' line while a further five wagons were cleared from No. 2 siding. When they were all coupled up we took them back to Menai Bridge. The path for the working was included in the freight working timetable, but this was the only time I have personal knowledge of it being used, although no doubt there were others. For the record, the locomotive used was Ivatt 2—6—2T No. 41223.

The main building on the 'up' platform at Port Dinorwic was a grand structure built in a rather depressing yellow brick. It contrasted sharply with the somewhat primitive shelter built of the same materials, for the 'down' line passengers.

L & GRP, courtesy David & Charles

Port Dinorwic

Port Dinorwic opened to traffic on 10th March 1852 with the objective of collecting slate from the Padarn Railway. The original line terminated at the quayside and it was not until the extension from Port Siding to Caernarvon that the line took on its final form. A new station, south of the original, was built in 1874 and the station building still survives under private ownership. It was built to a very optimistic design in view of the traffic that materialized, although optimism by the promotors was no bad thing. It was executed in a yellow brick, giving a somewhat depressing appearance but, in contrast to this grand structure, the 'down' side was provided with an open shed, similar to Menai Bridge. Access to the 'down' platform was by a subway passing under the tracks at the 'up' end. The small signal box was, most unusually for a Saxby & Farmer structure, built in the same yellow brick, producing a set of buildings which harmonized with each other,

There was one siding off the 'up' line and, until 1930, a connection from the 'down' line incorporating a single slip which provided a trailing crossover between the two lines. There was a cattle landing and dock adjoining the 'down' end of the 'up' platform ramp together with a fixed yard crane and at one time a mobile rail-mounted crane, although these were derelict or removed before 1956.

Distance from Port Dinorwic to Treborth station	2 miles 548 yds up direction
Distance from Port Dinorwic to Port Siding Box	1429 yards up direction
Distance from Port Dinorwic to Griffiths' Crossing	2 miles 1425 yds down direction
Running time:	
up direction	
passenger trains	5 minutes to Treborth
freight trains	10 minutes to Treborth
down line	
passenger trains	5 minutes to Griffiths' Crossing
freight trains	7 minutes to Griffiths' Crossing
Gradient leaving station: *up direction*	1:292 falling
down direction	1:292 rising
Up platform length — 300 feet	
Down platform length — 300 feet	

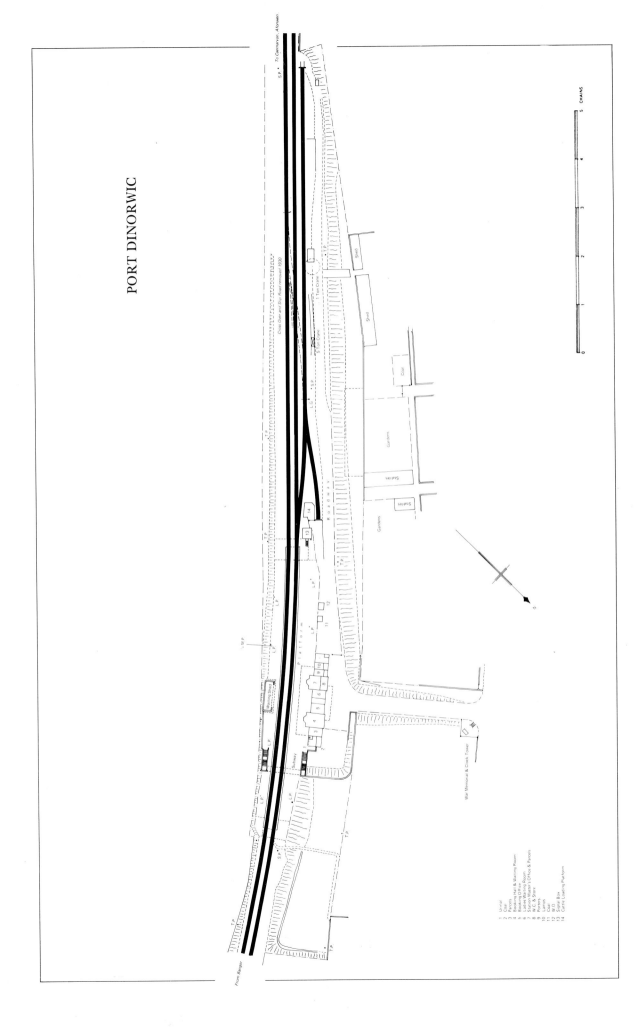

PORT DINORWIC

1 Urinal
2 Coal
3 Parcels
4 Booking Office
5 Booking Hall & Waiting Room
6 Ladies Waiting Room
7 Station Master's Office & Parcels
8 W.C. & Store
9 Porters
10 Lamps
11 Coal
12 W.O.
13 Signal Box
14 Cattle Loading Platform

CHAINS

0   1   2   3   4   5

The exterior of Port Dinorwic station seen from the end of the private road on 24th August 1954. For such a small amount of traffic the premises proved excessive.

R. M. Casserley

Left: The signal box, cattle dock, and general sweep of the station are shown here, looking towards Bangor. *Right:* The goods siding at Port Dinorwic supplied a builder's merchants' yard. Despite the quantity of materials shown, only the odd wagon load was delivered, most having been brought to the site by road. This was reflected in the timetable which listed freight trains to stop conditionally. The fixed yard crane remnants can be seen, but the rail-mounted crane shown in the diagram had long since disappeared.

Author

Taken from the signal protecting the level crossing on the 'down' side, this photograph shows the station, looking towards Caernarvon. The entrance to the siding is just visible beyond the 'down' platform whilst the entrance to the Parkia brick works siding is in front of the home signal on the 'up' line. After closure, the buildings and platforms were demolished. *Author's collection*

Griffiths' Crossing

Opened in 1854, Griffiths' Crossing had little traffic of note apart from one moment of glory when King George V and Queen Mary alighted there on the occasion of the investiture of the Prince of Wales at Caernarvon Castle on 13th July 1911. The station was closed to all traffic on 5th July 1937 and demolished almost immediately.

The platforms were 320 feet long, of stone construction and sub-standard height. The buildings were of local stone with slate roofs, the 'up' platform having a semi-open shelter, and the 'down' platform another of similar appearance but incorporating a booking office. A small lever frame stood on the 'down' platform to control the signals and these were interlocked with the crossing gates which were hand-operated. After demolition the lever frame was moved to the 'up' side and located in a small wooden hut.

The goods siding, opened in 1874, was equipped on the 'down' side with a loading platform and pens for cattle traffic, but these were removed on closure.

Just before running into the station in the 'up' direction, a private siding joined the main line with a trailing connection. Originally the property of the Parkia Brick Company, it fell out of use just before the last war, and the site became a fuel store for petroleum for a while, after which it became a pre-cast concrete works for Dow Mac. Amongst the products made were concrete sleepers.

Distance from Griffiths' Crossing to Port Dinorwic:	2 miles 1425 yds up direction
Distance from Griffiths' Crossing to Caernarvon No. 1 box:	1 mile 1638 yds down direction
Running time:	
up direction	
passenger trains	5 minutes to Port Dinorwic
freight trains	7 minutes to Port Dinorwic
down direction	
passenger trains	5 minutes to Caernarvon
freight trains	8 minutes to Caernarvon
Gradient leaving station:	*up direction* 1:74 rising
	down direction 1:74 falling

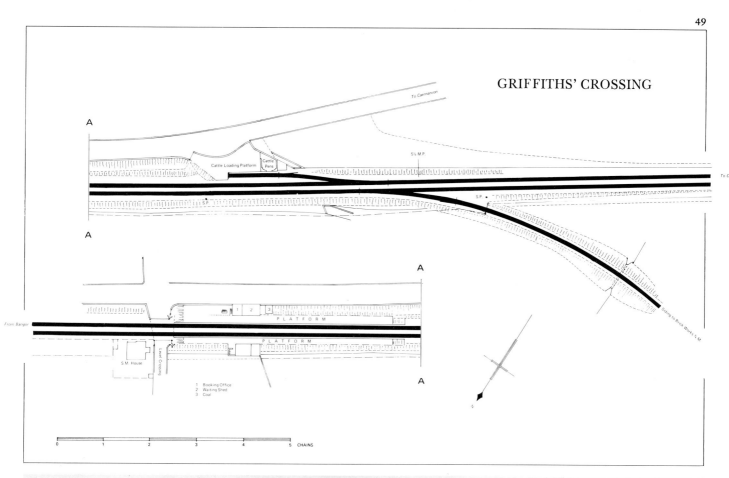

GRIFFITHS' CROSSING

To Caernarvon

To Caernarvon

5¼ M.P.

Cattle Loading Platform

Cattle Pens

S.P.

S.P.

Siding to Brick Works S.M.

From Bangor

PLATFORM

PLATFORM

A

A

A

A

S.M. House

Level Crossing

1 Booking Office
2 Waiting Shed
3 Coal

0   1   2   3   4   5   CHAINS

The former station master's house at Griffiths' Crossing, taken from the site of the 'down' platform and looking towards Bangor. A small crossing keeper's hut was erected to house the lever frame controlling the signals and the instruments.   *W. A. Camwell*

50

Caernarvon shed and station approach on Investiture day, 13th July 1911. Every platform face was occupied, including the excursion or No. 6 bay platform.

British Railways

Caernarvon station, taken from the 'up and down' platform, looking towards Afonwen and Llanberis, about 1924.   *C. L. Mowat*

Caernarvon

Caernarvon station was the largest of all the branch line stations in North Wales in terms of traffic density, and was only equalled in length by Afonwen and Denbigh. Llandudno station was somewhat larger, but regarded as a main line station. Technically, the railway itself never regarded Caernarvon as a main line station, although some main line traffic originated here.

The station opened to traffic from 1st July 1852 as a terminus with a single platform face. The Carnarvonshire Railway and the Carnarvon & Llanberis Railway extended their lines from their termini at the quayside station under Castle Square to the LNWR station, the development being known as the 'Carnarvon Town Line' which was brought into use on 5th July 1870, forming an end-on junction. The original LNWR station was enlarged at this time when bay platforms were provided, the goods shed moved to a new position, a scissors crossover installed in the centre of the platform lines, and a new locomotive shed with a 42ft turntable provided. Further developments took place in 1894 when an island platform was constructed, together with an 'up' loop and additional freight sidings. As part of the scheme, the scissors crossover junction at Caernarvon Quay (No. 3 cabin), between the Llanberis and Afonwen lines, was removed and the double line from there to the station made into two single lines. No. 3 cabin was abolished and a ground frame provided to work the connection onto the quay sidings. At the station a new scissors crossover between the two single lines to the south was provided while the crossovers at the centre of the main platform, no longer required with the provision of the addi-

tional through platforms, were removed. Two new signal cabins, No. 1 with 68 levers and No. 2 with 51 levers, were brought into use to work the station area. In 1911 two temporary platforms were constructed for the investiture, and an additional footbridge, connecting North Road with the 'up' and 'down' and island platforms was erected at the Bangor end of the station. At the same time a new booking hall was added onto the original building on the 'down' side.

A wagon repair shop was located west of the locomotive shed but no details of the building are forthcoming, and it is understood that it was closed and demolished before 1926.

Rebuilding and alterations between the wars included the removal of the footbridge from North Road to the island platform, closure of the locomotive shed in 1931, although the structure was not removed until the period 1938-9, removal of the engine release crossover in the Bangor bay platform and the siding off the Llanberis bay in 1939. The track for the wagon repair shop was lifted about the same time. In the period after the war, between 1956 and 1960, the island platform buildings were in need of extensive renovation and the decision was taken to remove them together with the platform canopy and cover for the footbridge connecting the two platforms. A brick shelter was provided which was warmer for the occupants but there was otherwise much less shelter from the elements. The 'up' and 'down' platform canopy was also cut back and the goods shed offices were replaced with a spacious brick building. Some signalling alterations were effected during this period. In 1952-3, two three-arm signals on the 'down' line by No. 1 signal box were replaced with one four-arm. The starting signal at the Afonwen end of the island platform controlling movements from the local platform was

52

An afternoon train from Afonwen to Bangor pulling out of Caernarvon with extra empty stock. The triple arm bracket signal in the distance beyond No. 1 signal box was replaced the following year with a four-arm upper quadrant signal. The lines to the lower goods yard branch off in the right foreground.

Author

replaced with a tubular post upper quadrant two arm signal, which contrasted with the wooden posted two arm version on the 'down' platform alongside.

With the closure of the Llanberis branch and the Afonwen line to all traffic, the station layout was altered significantly. No. 1 signal box was closed and control of the remaining point and signal work transferred to the spare levers of No. 2 box. No. 1 box was dismantled and the line to Menai Bridge singled. The 'up' platform line was removed and access to the goods lines was effected from pointwork at the Bangor end of the island platform. Access to the lower yard was still from the same point, but the connection to the 'up' line at the far end of the site was removed, creating a long spur off which the lower yard access was made. The two-arm signal on the island platform was removed, replaced by a single arm starting signal for the local platform face. The Bangor bay and excursion platform were disconnected at the same time. The track to Llanwnda was left *in situ* although beyond that it was dismantled, the work being carried away by Pwllheli shed workings. The signals at the 'down' platform and local platforms were replaced by posts with single arms.

After the investiture of Prince Charles on 1st July 1969, the remainder of the Afonwen line was dismantled, and the final closure was only months away. Freight traffic was withdrawn on 4th August 1969 and the passenger trains were withdrawn from 5th January 1970. Due to the fire on the Britannia bridge, the line was re-opened to freight traffic from 15th June 1970 until 5th February 1972 when the goods yard was used to offload freightliner traffic, which was then transported by road to and from Holyhead. There were two trains daily, one of which was conditional, but usually ran. Due to the intensive locomotive roster for

the freightliner trains, the shunting was left to an 0—6—0 diesel shunter which remained during the week at Caernarvon, the first locomotive to be allocated there on a regular basis for over forty years. The locomotive was based at Bangor, but only visited the depot at weekends for servicing and refuelling, the driver travelling to and from Bangor by bus. For most of the period the locomotive was No. 12 083. Containers were transhipped by two lorry-mounted cranes, which were semi-permanently mounted on a sleeper base. When the main line across the Menai Straits was finally re-opened, Caernarvon closed to rail traffic, the track being lifted and the site cleared for use as a car park.

THE LOCOMOTIVE DEPARTMENT

Details of the shed workings are somewhat obscure, particularly for the period before the First World War. However, some information has been gleaned first-hand from former cleaners.

In LNWR days Caernarvon was a sub-shed of Bangor, shed No. 21, and was classified as 21C, locomotives based here carrying Bangor plates. According to J. M. Dunn, the locomotive allocation at Caernarvon on 15th February 1921 was 8 small engines and 3 large engines, but unfortunately he failed to record details or numbers.

Apart from a Springs Branch mineral and a Crewe (North Staffs siding) freight, which ran all the year round, most of the workings were local, between Afonwen, Llanberis, Bethesda and Llandudno Junction. Increased summer passenger traffic after the grouping brought rostered turns to Liverpool, Manchester Exchange, and London Euston, the latter with two trips, one of which was the forerunner of 'The Welshman'. For the Euston turns, two of the three Claughtons, Nos. 6026/7/8, were

Photographs of Caernarvon shed are rare, only three views having come to light. This one, taken after the shed had closed, about 1936, was taken from the 'up and down' platform.   *W. A. Camwell*

based at Bangor for Caernarvon shed turns, whilst for local work the usual run of LNWR 2−4−2Ts, 0−6−2Ts and 0−6−0s of various permutations was provided. The Afonwen line had tender engines which were turned at either end of each trip, until the 4−6−2Ts were drafted into the area. Before the war, the Webb 0−6−2Ts were in evidence which, for heavier trains, were coupled in pairs bunker to bunker. With heavier traffic, Stanier locomotives were seen increasingly at Caernarvon, although this was after the shed had closed.

About 1928 there was a proposal to close Bangor shed and transfer the work to Caernarvon, Llandudno Junction and Holyhead. However, this was never taken very seriously because of the light engine mileage involved for working the Amlwch, Red Wharf Bay and Bethesda lines. Instead the decline in slate traffic caused Caernarvon shed to be closed on 14th September 1931, although it remained a signing-on point for some turns for several years, the shed facilities for fire cleaning and watering locomotives being used until the shed was demolished.

Caernarvon shed had a regular lodging turn before the First World War to Springs branch. The load called for a heavy duty locomotive, and No. 1231 of Springs branch was a regular performer on this turn. The view was taken from the shed entrance.   *Author's collection*

A closer view of the water tower. The mess coach was provided for the workmen who were on site for the re-signalling of the station and singling of the Menai Bridge line. *Author*

On the occasion of the 1911 Investiture at Caernarvon, due to the increase in traffic from within the Principality, it was decided to invoke the running powers agreed and use Cambrian crews, locomotives and rolling stock to work between Afonwen and Caernarvon on that day. Both Portmadoc and Pwllheli sheds were involved and four sets of men from Portmadoc and two from Pwllheli were afforded route-learning facilities prior to the event. They worked the entire special service running on that day as well as piloting the extra trains coming off the Cambrian. What locomotives and stock worked the branch was not recorded. Under reciprocal arrangements, which were never implemented on a regular basis, through running by Cambrian men and trains between Afonwen and Bangor were authorised, the LNWR having running powers to Penrhyndeudraeth and Pwllheli. The LMS and GWR inherited these arrangements and, although the LMS did run through trains on a regular basis to Pwllheli, and from about 1926 or 1927 to Portmadoc, with the 'Welshman', the GWR never invoked their side of the agreement. It was not until the 1950s that GWR engines began to appear at Caernarvon on the Land Cruise train that commenced at Criccieth and ran the circular route in the reverse direction through Barmouth to Corwen, up the Vale of Clwyd to Rhyl, where the train reversed. The locomotive went on Rhyl shed for servicing and turning before working along the coast to Caernarvon, on the Afonwen line and back to Criccieth. Pwllheli men and locomotives worked the trip, usually with '2251' class 0–6–0s and later British Railways Standard class '4s'.

During the First World War, three Cambrian Railways engines were loaned to Bangor for a short spell. They were 0–6–0 No. 73, 4–4–0 No. 85 and 4–4–0 No. 47, which arrived on 26th, 28th and 29th June 1917 respectively and in each case were put to work on the same or the next day. Their duties are believed to have included one or two trips over the Afonwen line before, according to the *Railway Magazine* for October 1917, they were sent on to Whitchurch LNWR.

PASSENGER

After the opening of the Afonwen and Llanberis lines, passenger traffic developed very slowly. There was little commuter traffic, and the only bulk movement of workers were to and from the slate quarries in the area. However, in many cases this was restricted to one journey each way once a week, the quarries providing barracks for the workers who lived in conditions of spartan hardship, from Monday to Saturday, travelling to work on the Monday morning and returning after the shift at midday on the Saturday. This practice finished after the First World War. Those living reasonably close to the quarries in most cases walked to work, not out of choice, but from financial hardship.

The Llanberis trains nearly all started and terminated at Caernarvon, and only one or two trains daily ran beyond the town. Latterly these were motor trains (push and pull) which, after the station was enlarged, used the Lanberis bay as no problems were experienced running round the stock. Certainly up to the time that motor trains were introduced, trains of four or five 6-wheeled coaches were usually hauled by Webb 2–4–2Ts. One of the regular locomotives was No. 620 which, after Llanberis shed was

The afternoon push & pull 'motor' train from Bangor drawing into the 'up and down' platform in November 1950. This working, in fact, was covered by No. 3 link at Bangor who used the unit on the Bethesda service. When that line closed for regular passenger services, the working from Bangor to Caernarvon ceased also. The locomotive was Ivatt 2–6–2T No. 41223. *Author*

closed, transferred to Caernarvon, moving out of the area after the grouping.

The Nantlle branch was worked by loco No. 2457 and a rake of four 6-wheeled coaches for many years, the locomotive performing shunting duties at Nantlle and Penygroes as required. The stock was stabled overnight at Penygroes, the locomotive running out from Caernarvon each day. At weekends the stock was worked empty to Caernarvon for servicing. A motor train unit was substituted quite early on, but the same procedure was adhered to. On both branches, the locomotive of the motor train units were at the 'down' (Llanberis or Nantlle) end. At one

stage steam railcars were tried on the Nantlle and Llanberis branches but they do not seem to have been successful and in any case a locomotive was still required to handle freight traffic. There is also in Gwynedd County Archives a picture of a petrol electric drive railcar in the Nantlle bay at Penygroes. The quality of the picture is poor and, although labelled as a 'steam' railcar, the radiator mounted on the roof denies this. It is also presumed that it was tried on the Llanberis branch.

Afonwen line trains usually worked from and to Bangor or beyond although some workings did start or finish at Caernarvon, the pattern remaining largely unchanged over

In February 1939, 4–6–0 class '5XP' No. 5515 was named *Caernarvon* at a small ceremony at the 'up and down' platform by the civic dignitaries. Details of the ceremony are unrecorded, and all that survive are three photographs. The locomotive was stabled for a short while in the Bangor bay, where this view was taken. *Author's collection*

The signalling diagram for Caernarvon No. 1 signal box showing the track and signal layout. The drawing was dated 1924 and shows the original spelling of 'Carnarvon' which was altered in 1925 to include the 'e'. The release crossover in the bay platform was worked locally by the fireman or platform staff. This crossover had been removed in 1938 but the diagram remained unchanged for many more years.

Author's collection

No. 42156, still with early BRITISH RAILWAYS large lettering on the side tanks, and matching numbers on the bunker, coasts past Caernarvon No. 1 signal box with the 3.15 p.m. S.O. Bangor to Pwllheli trip in July 1953. Behind the regular circuit stock are three extra coaches for store at Pwllheli. The disc signal in the foreground protected the goods line whilst the former shed road came off the left-hand side of the picture.

Author

The cattle pens located in the upper yard were not used so frequently after the First World War although they remained in use until the withdrawal of freight services. From about 1963 the sidings and pens were used for washing out cattle trucks from Holyhead whic which were stored at Caernarvon until required for the Irish traffic. *Author*

Looking across the excursion platform, used on this occasion in 1964 to store cattle trucks from Holyhead awaiting washing out.
Author

the years. Some 'up' trains used the 'down' platform which, like the local platform, was signalled for two-way working. Trains terminating at Caernarvon from Bangor usually ran into the Bangor bay, where the locomotive was released via the crossover and the excursion platform. With the deployment of motor trains just before the Second World War, some of the trains that terminated or started at Caernarvon worked through services, albeit unadvertised, from Caernarvon to Bethesda, or Llandudno Junction. It is believed that one rostered turn involved the unit working from Caernarvon to Bethesda, Bethesda to Amlwch, and back to Bethesda before returning to Caernarvon. After the war, stock from the last train from Bangor to Caernarvon was stabled in the Bangor bay. As the run round facility was no longer there, this train pulled into the 'up and down' platform, the loco ran round via the local line, pausing at the Bangor end of the platform to take water, coupled onto the stock and drew it clear of the platform before setting back into the bay and uncoupling. The locomotive then ran light engine to Bangor. The stock was used the next morning for the 6.50 a.m. to Llandudno, the locomotive travelling light engine from Bangor at 6.00 a.m. It is believed, but not confirmed, that this was part of a Caernarvon guard's rostered turn at one stage. In 1957 a DMU took over this working and was stabled in the Bangor bay, the driver travelling back to Bangor by bus. The early turn driver came out on the Pwllheli trip the next

morning. However, the practice only lasted one winter season, reverting to locomotive hauled stock for several years, before the DMU rostering became more intense. This time, however, the unit worked back empty stock to Bangor.

The wooden excursion platform (platform 6) was only used in peak summer but saw little use after the First World War. When the crossover was removed, it became a spare siding where stock was washed. With the loading ramp having flaps, it was also sometimes used for loading or unloading cars from end-door vehicles. The only time I can recall it being used for this purpose was when King George VI visited Caernarvon in 1947 and the Royal Daimler was loaded into a van. When a circus visited the town a few years later, the animals, particularly elephants, were apparently carried in end-door stock which was also unloaded at this point.

The crossover in the Bangor bay was hand-operated by the fireman or station staff, a locking bar being controlled from No. 1 signal box (lever 26) and the exit protected by signals.

During the day local carriage stock was cleaned out in the excursion platform. These two cleaners were photographed there in 1939.
Author's collection

The island platform, taken from an Afonwen train entering the 'up and down' platform on 10th May 1949. An LMS lorry can be seen in the goods shed and the cattle trucks in evidence on the back road of the goods lines are awaiting cleaning out. *Eric Russell*

For some reason very few passenger trains on regular services used the local platform, the 'up and down' platform being the most intensively used, although most 'up' trains used the island 'up' platform. Excursion trains seemed to use the local platform, and Land Cruises returning to Rhyl and Llandudno stopped there to take on water, as did the Cambrian Radio Cruise and the Welsh Chieftain, which commenced at Criccieth and ran the route in the reverse direction. It was the only train known in later years to use the local platform regularly in the Afonwen direction. The Llanberis excursion, known as 'The Snowdonian', ran through the 'up and down' platform, pausing to pick up

The station exterior as seen from the station yard on 16th July 1954. The canopy over the entrance to the booking hall was removed at the same time as the construction of the new island platform shelter and the brick exterior of the building was given a cement rendering.

J. J. Davis

The 'up and down' platform from the footbridge steps, looking towards Bangor in June 1952.

British Railways

the staff from No. 2 box. The locomotive and observation car, or sometimes a two-coach articulated unit, when it was part of the train formation, worked back to Caernarvon and pulled into the local platform where the locomotive took on water, before running round the coach or coaches via the 'up and down' platform. It then pulled on to the Llanberis line and set back into the Llanberis bay. After the closure of the Afonwen and Llanberis lines to all traffic and the singling of the line to Bangor, the local platform came into regular use on summer Saturdays for the Butlin's traffic. Passengers crossed over the footbridge to leave the station and board waiting Crosville buses. When this traffic was cut back to Bangor, the local platform ceased to be used altogether and the footbridge was boarded up.

FREIGHT

Traffic built up steadily from the opening of the line and, with the connections to Llanberis and Afonwen, slate and timber were the mainstay of outgoing traffic. In fact the slate traffic provided much of the freight workings up to the time of the depression, although the decline had commenced before the First World War, with some increase of traffic during the war. The general strike of 1926 created

problems for many of the smaller slate quarry owners and during this period they turned to road transport in an effort to maintain trade but never returned to using the railway afterwards. Some quarries, mostly the larger units, remained faithful, but they too fell victim to the depression and these two factors were partly responsible for the closure of the locomotive shed. What traffic remained was inward and fairly constant, with coal being the main commodity.

The Second World War generated some new traffic, usually linked to military uses, such as the bomb department at Llanberis, but this fell away on cessation of hostilities and general traffic continued the slow decline with the increased use of lorries. The remaining traffic was sorted at Caernarvon yard and, until the withdrawal of certain types of freight, kept the goods shed and yard busy. In direct contrast, traffic for an oil store in the lower yard built up steadily. For many years, two companies had five tanks between them, located on the station site, but increased demand caused large capacity storage tanks to be constructed on harbour land between the dock and the lower yard. The petroleum traffic was lost to shallow draught tankers that carried in bulk from Ellesmere Port along the coast. It had been intended to develop the rail traffic, but the maritime lobby was very strong, and despite the effort in

The 'up and down' platform, taken from the Bangor end of the buildings and looking towards No. 2 signal box and Afonwen in June 1952.
British Railways

The island platform, looking towards Bangor, again in June 1952.

British Railways

keeping the shipping lane dredged, their argument proved more convincing.

There had always been sufficient work to justify a shunting locomotive at Caernarvon from early morning until late afternoon for five days a week, and a half day on Saturdays and this continued right up to the end of steam. Two turns were involved from Bangor. At one time the locomotive came out with the first turn and the relieving crew travelled to Caernarvon by train or bus. The relieved men returned the same way. Latterly the early turn crew returned with the locomotive to Bangor, handing over to the afternoon men, who returned to Caernarvon light engine. Locomotives used for the 'Caernarvon shunt' included LNWR 0—6—2Ts, L & Y 0—6—0s, Class 3 0—6—0Ts, Stanier 2—6—2Ts, Ivatt 2—6—2Ts and Stanier or Fairburn 2—6—4Ts. Other shunting work was done by the Afonwen goods, or the Llanberis or Nantlle freight trips which ran daily. It was possible in the 1950s to see four freight turns at work in the yard at the same time.

Before and immediately after the grouping, Caernarvon shed had a regular turn to Springs Branch with a minerals train, mainly slate. It was a lodging turn and departed from the lower yard at 10.00 p.m. Springs Branch provided the locomotive, usually a 'G1' or a 'G2' class 0—8—0, and the train was always heavily loaded. From about 1925 or 1926 this working was cut back to Mold Junction, and ceased to be a lodging turn, the crew working back with a through freight to Caernarvon. Another working, also a lodging turn,

ran to Crewe (North Staffs. Sidings), returning with a passenger working to Chester the following day, running light engine to Mold Junction and then working a freight back to Caernarvon.

The yard shunter always performed any transfer of wagons from the upper to the lower yard, although workings were generally limited to two or three times a day. The goods shed was always very busy with staff at work from 6.00 a.m. until 6.00 p.m. for six days a week. This continued until the late 1950s. There were up to six railway-owned lorries based at the shed until about 1956 when the numbers were diminished. In addition to covering work from Caernarvon, they also performed the country lorry service and were a familiar sight in the neighbourhood. There was also a road wagon shunter based at the shed for several years which spent some of its time in the lower yard and the remainder shunting wagons from Quay siding, by the harbour. This was necessary because locomotives were not permitted to shunt outside the company's boundary after about 1953. Prior to this, it is understood that locomotives did shunt the harbour as required but no photographic evidence to support this has yet come to light. Before the advent of the company lorry, horses were in evidence and the stables were located alongside the Llanberis bay, with access to the station yard.

The shunting of Quay sidings was generally performed by the yard shunter propelling up to 15 wagons and a brake van down the Afonwen line. The brake van was detached

No. 42417 of Bangor shed stands at the 'up and down' platform with the 4.04 p.m. Bangor to Afonwen working on 2nd April 1956, before removal of the footbridge cover.
W. A. Camwell

Looking along the 'up and down' platform towards Afonwen, this 1960 view shows No. 2 signal box, the starter signals for the 'up and down' and the local platforms, and the goods shed beyond.
G. H. Platt

The 10 mph restriction in front of the box indicated the severity of the pointwork where the Llanberis and Afonwen lines diverged. Reading from right to left are the 'up and down' platform face, the local platform, also worked in either direction, the 'up' line, the goods line and to the left of that the upper level storage sidings. *Author*

Caernarvon No. 2 signal box stood at the 'down' end of the 'up and down' platform and controlled the Llanberis and Afonwen line movements. This 1952 study shows the Llanberis bay line behind the box. The station nameboard was replaced shortly after the photograph was taken, with an enamel one of standard British Railways pattern. *Author*

The matching signalling diagram for Caernarvon No. 2 box, also dated 1924. The track pattern remained unchanged until the Afonwen and Llanberis lines closed, but the signal gantry shown was replaced in 1939 by a simpler structure located 80 yards further from the box.

Author's collection

This LNWR gantry controlling entry to the station from the south, spanned the two parallel single lines from Afon Wen and Llanberis respectively. Shown here in 1938, by 1947 it had been replaced by the simpler version featured on page 70.

G. H. Platt

2—6—4T No. 2258 pulling on to the Afonwen line in 1947. The corrugated iron structure on the right of the picture is part of the Crosville depot.

G. H. Platt

on the Afonwen line and the vans or wagons were shunted outside the railway property across the harbour road. There were several warehouses along this road including food wholesalers and small engineering works. The trip was timetabled and the crew had to be in possession of the Caernarvon to Dinas staff. On completion, the train and brake returned to Caernarvon goods yard. In addition, the returning Nantlle goods was timetabled to stop at Quay sidings and pick up any wagons for Caernarvon and beyond.

The same arrangement was in force for Seiont siding on the Llanberis line, up to 15 wagons being propelled a mile and a quarter down the line to Seiont sidings. There was the added precaution that such a shunt had to be performed during daylight and in clear weather only.

Until the late 1950s, Caernarvon retained three guards workings, a left-over arrangement from the days when the station had many more crews based there. The three duties were not specifically freight turns and were interlinked with the guards' duties from Bangor. Eventually the work was transferred to Bangor, but it is interesting that they lasted twenty years after most of the facilities were transferred. The work included the early morning freight from Caernarvon to Afonwen, changing vans with a Bangor guard and working the first Pwllheli passenger trip back to Bangor, returning to home station 'on the cushions'. A second working involved a through working to Llandudno Junction and returning with the 8.35 p.m. passenger to Caernarvon, and the third, which is not known for certain, is believed to have covered the Llanberis freight working as part of the duty.

Latterly traffic declined and the mainstay of the yard was the coal traffic, with some agricultural produce and food stock. With the rearrangement of livestock handling at Holyhead, cattle trucks were delivered to Caernarvon where they were cleaned and stored until required. They were then worked as specials to Holyhead.

A pre-war view taken inside No. 2 box.   *Author's collection*

CAERNARVON

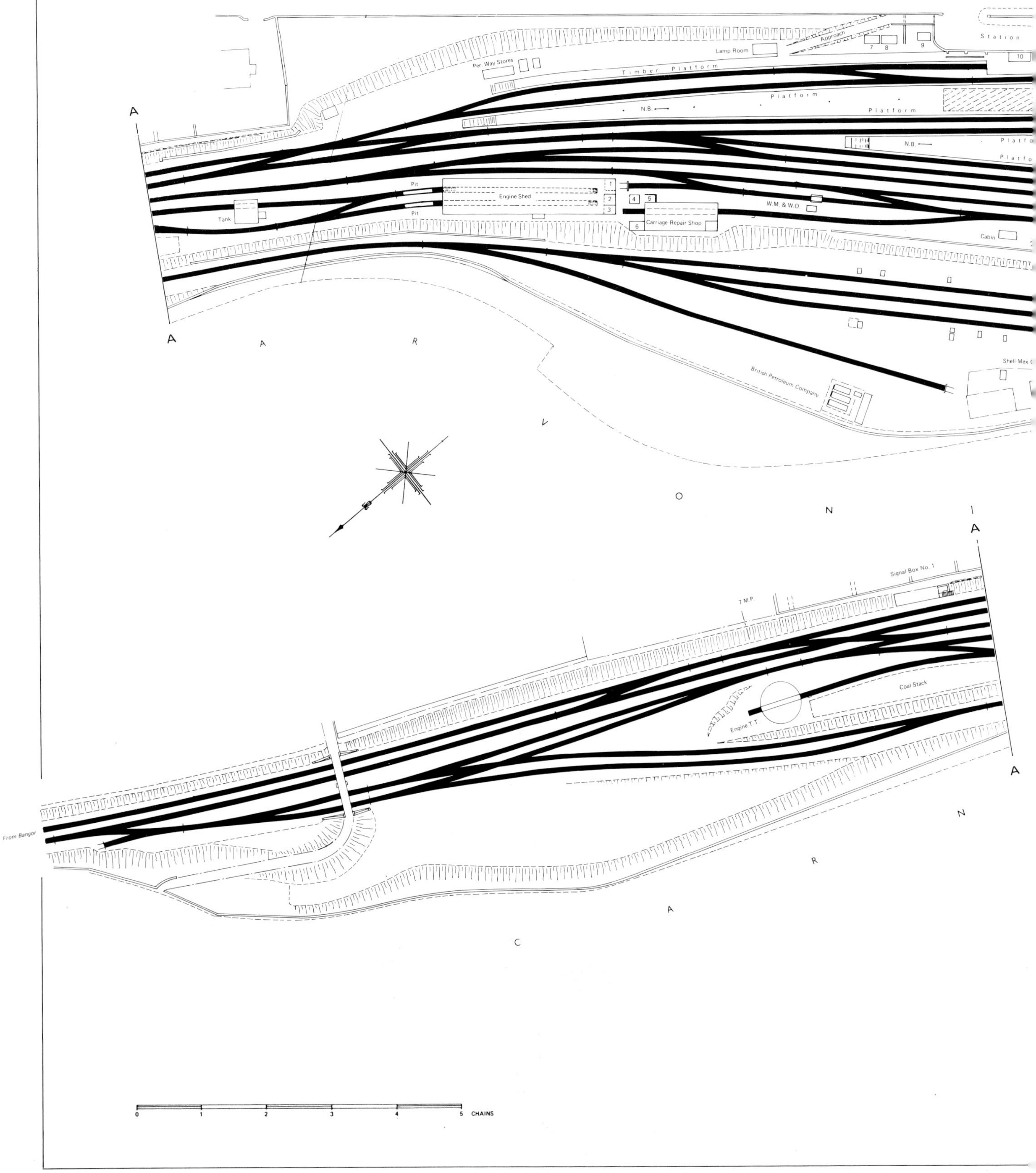

Station

Approach

Lamp Room

Per. Way Stores

Timber Platform

N.B.

Platform

Platform

N.B.

Platform

Platform

Pit

1

Engine Shed

2

4

5

3

Tank

Pit

6

Carriage Repair Shop

W.M. & W.O.

Cabin

A

A

A

R

V

O

N

British Petroleum Company

Shell Mex

Signal Box No. 1

7 M.P.

Coal Stack

Engine T.T.

From Bangor

A

A

N

R

A

C

0 1 2 3 4 5 CHAINS

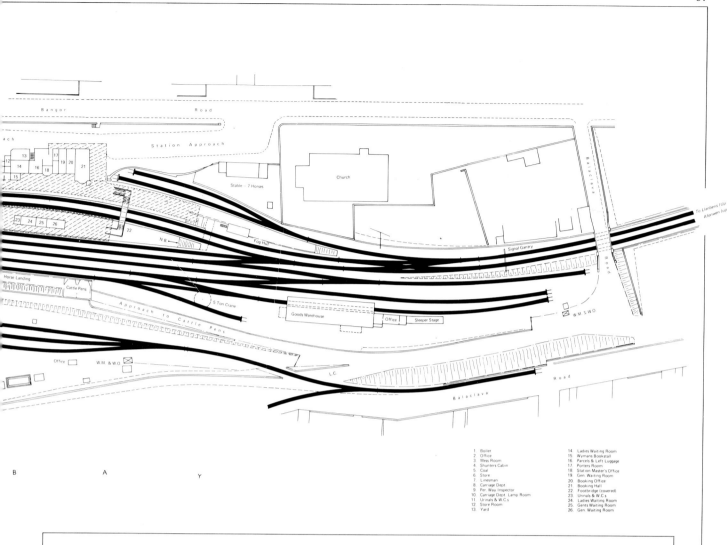

Bangor   Road

Station   Approach

Church

Stable - 7 Horses

N.B.

Fog Hut

Balaclava   Road

To Llanberis (Up & Down)
Afonwen (Up & Down)

Signal Gantry

Horse Landing

Cattle Pens

5 Ton Crane

Approach to Cattle Pens

Goods Warehouse

Office   Sleeper Stage

W.M. S.WO

Office   W.M. & W.O.

L.C.

Balaclava   Road

B   A   Y

1	Boiler	14	Ladies Waiting Room
2	Office	15	Wymans Bookstall
3	Mess Room	16	Parcels & Left Luggage
4	Shunters Cabin	17	Porters Room
5	Coal	18	Station Master's Office
6	Store	19	Gen. Waiting Room
7	Linesman	20	Booking Office
8	Carriage Dept	21	Booking Hall
9	Per Way Inspector	22	Footbridge (covered)
10	Carriage Dept. Lamp Room	23	Urinals & W.C.s
11	Urinals & W.C.s	24	Ladies Waiting Room
12	Store Room	25	Gents Waiting Room
13	Yard	26	Gen. Waiting Room

UP DIRECTION towards Bangor

Distance from Griffiths'
Crossing: 1 mile 1638 yards

Running time:
   passenger trains   5 minutes
   freight trains   8 minutes

Intermediate siding: Parkia. 1 mile 1500 yards

Gradient leaving station: 1:600 rising

Next signal box from
Caernarvon No. 1 box
excluding Port Dinorwic box: Port Siding. 5 miles 972 yards

Caernarvon No. 2 box to
Caernarvon No. 1 box: 442 yards

DOWN DIRECTION towards Afonwen

Distance from Dinas
Junction: 3 miles 271 yards

Running time:
   passenger trains   10 minutes
   freight trains   20 minutes

Intermediate siding: Quay. 860 yards

Gradient leaving signal box: 1:600 falling

Token colour: Red

Token type: Large staff

Staff instrument located in Caernarvon No. 2 signal box.

GOODS YARD.

Upper Yard

Sidings access – from No. 1 end by crossover from down line
                              outside No. 1 box
                    from No. 2 end by three way point to goods
                    line by No. 2 box

Exit   from No. 2 end by three way point to Afonwen
                    or Llanberis line
                    from No. 1 end by goods avoiding line and to
                    extreme end past footbridge.

Lower yard

Access and exit from No. 1 end extreme end past footbridge

Shunter on duty from 4.00 a.m. until 10.00 p.m. up till 1950s.
Then until 7.15 p.m. SX.

Trip locomotives shunted as required – Afonwen freight,
Llanberis freight, Nantlle freight and afternoon Afonwen
freight.
When not working, locomotive stands outside shunter's cabin
in upper yard.

Usual locomotive for yard shunt.

   Up to 1950   LNWR 0–6–2T
   after 1950   L & Y 0–6–0 or Stanier 2–6–2T
                               Ivatt 2–6–2T
                               Stanier 2–6–4T
                               Fowler 0–6–0T

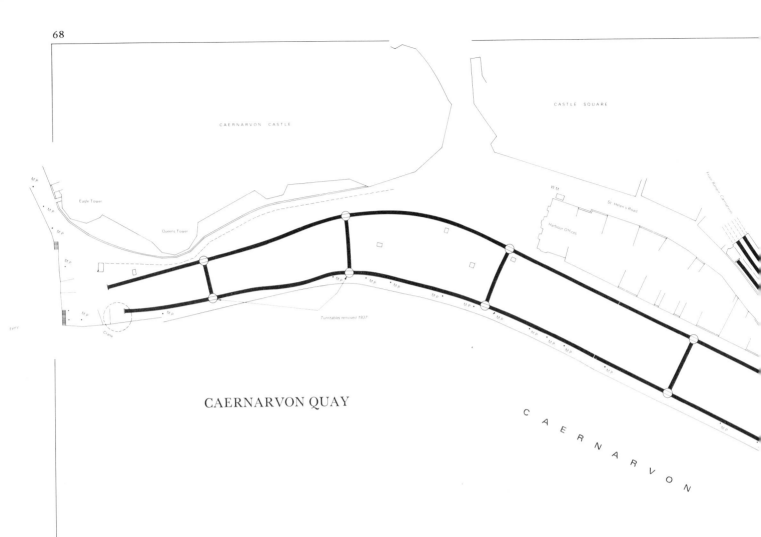

CAERNARVON QUAY

CASTLE SQUARE

CAERNARVON CASTLE

CAERNARVON

The southern end of Caernarvon tunnel, looking towards the station, with the two-lever frame controlling entrance to the harbour and quay sidings in the foreground. *Author*

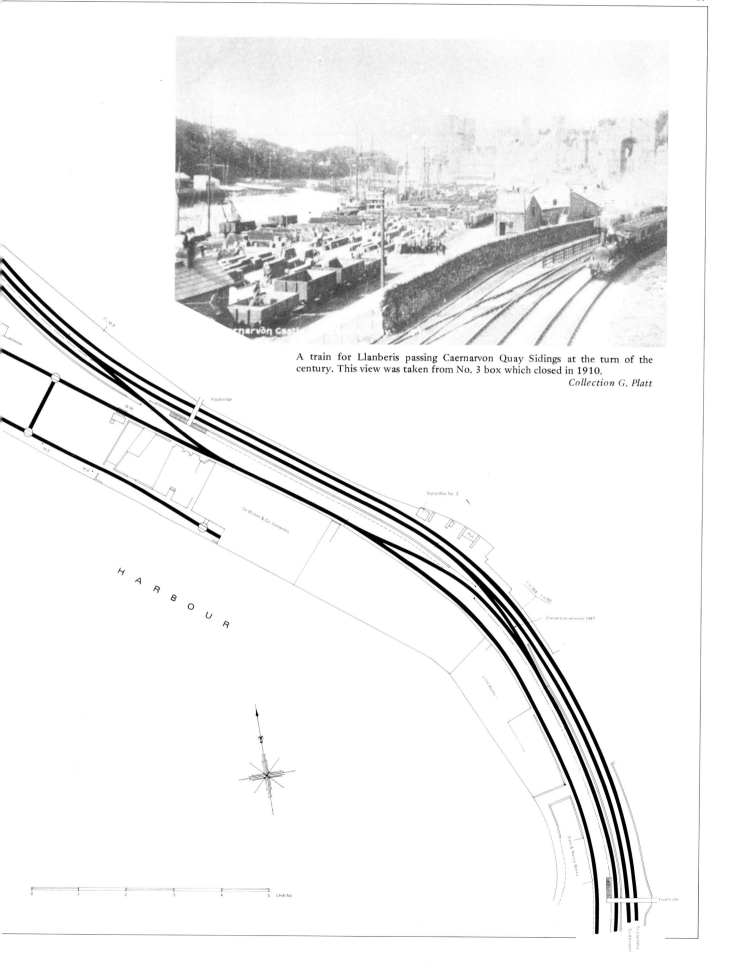

A train for Llanberis passing Caernarvon Quay Sidings at the turn of the century. This view was taken from No. 3 box which closed in 1910.

Collection G. Platt

Fairburn 2—6—4T No. 42078, working bunker first, pulls out of Caernarvon tunnel with a Bangor to Pwllheli turn in 1965. Notice the cars straddling the private track alongside the road. Despite the newly ballasted appearance of the Llanberis line, services had been withdrawn and demolition was but weeks away.

Author

Left: Looking down the grade towards Llanberis and Afonwen in 1966. The track dips sharply to pass underneath Turf Square before climbing briefly to Caernarvon tunnel, which passes underneath Castle Square. *Right:* Access to the quay sidings and harbour lines was off the Afonwen line through the gateway, and across a minor road. This was the site of the former Carnarvonshire and Carnarvon & Llanberis Railway termini prior to the opening of the Carnarvon Town line under Castle Square. There was once a crossover and run round loop here, with a signal box controlling train movements.

Author

No. 42157 returns down the grade to Caernarvon with the Llanberis goods, in June 1952. The quay line leading off to the right of the picture is visible between the two telegraph posts.

Author

DINAS JUNCTION

To Afonwen

To Rhyd-ddu

North Wales Narrow Gauge Railway

3 M.p.

SP

SM House

Platform

Platform

Old Refreshment Rooms

Mess Room

Transhipping Shed

Latrines

Turntable Tip

North Wales Narrow Gauge Railway

P L Hut

1 2 3
4 5 6 7 8

1 Booking Office & Station Master's Office
2 Booking Hall & Waiting Room
3 Booking Office
4 Lamps
5 Signal Box
6 Coal
7 Ashes
8 Waiting Room

A   A

Tran

Dies

3 M.p.

End of siding 991 yds

From Caernarvon

CHAINS

0   1   2   3   4   5

The 'down' and 'up' platforms, looking towards Afonwen in 1934-6.

Lens of Sutton

Dinas Junction

Apart from the temporary stations on the former Carnarvonshire Railway, which were closed when the connection was made with the L & NWR station at Caernarvon, Dinas Junction was the first station between Caernarvon and Afonwen and also the first token interchange point.

The Carnarvonshire Railway opened the station here in September 1877, the same year as the North Wales Narrow Gauge Railway opened. The narrow gauge line generated some traffic, but there were few passengers otherwise and it is surprising it lasted as long as it did. The growth of traffic over the line brought about the extension of the passing loop in 1893 and again after the Second World War, to enable ten-coach trains to cross. Freight dwindled with the closure of the slate quarries, and it fell to nothing with the demise of the Welsh Highland Railway in 1937. Up to the early 1930s, a short working from Caernarvon shunted the yard daily, spending just over an hour there, before returning. Latterly the sidings were used as a crippled wagon store. Whilst they were taken out some time prior to closure of the line, the crossing loop remained in use until the end.

In the immediate post war days, and for the successive ten years, the signal box was kept busy, especially on Saturdays in the peak holiday season, trains crossing throughout the day, from about 7.30 a.m., and there was little time for anything other than the business in hand. Occupation of the section between Dinas Junction and Groeslon, the

Distance from Caernarvon:	3 miles 271 yds up direction. Next token point.
Distance from Groeslon:	1 mile 1121 yds down direction. Next token point.
Distance from Llanwnda:	913 yards
Running time from Dinas Junction	
up direction	
passenger trains	8 minutes
freight trains	12 minutes
down direction	
passenger trains	3 minutes to Llanwnda
freight trains	3 minutes to Llanwnda
Intermediate crossings:	
up direction	Pant Crossing — 1 mile 1253 yds
down direction	Glanrhyd Crossing — 389 yds
Intermediate sidings:	
up direction — Quay sidings — 2 miles 1540 yds	
Gradient leaving station:	
up direction	level to loop then falling
down direction	rising
Single Line Tokens	
Dinas Junction-Caernarvon No. 2 — Large staff coloured red	
Dinas Junction-Groeslon — Key token coloured blue	

next station south, was authorised by a key token. This was normally housed in a pouch attached to an aluminium hoop. A large electric train staff was used for the Caernarvon No. 2 to Dinas Junction section. It was difficult for footplate crews to exchange tokens on the move, particularly in the darkness of early morning or on late turns. To be a signalman performing the exchange called for skill and not a little courage. Despite the requirements that trains slowed

From the road bridge over Welsh Highland Railway tracks, looking towards Caernarvon in 1934. The 'up' platform waiting room is on the left hand side of the photograph, with the LMS 'down' platform shelter in front of the Welsh Highland office. The tranship shed is in the middle distance, with the Snowdon Mountain Railway owned refreshment rooms beyond and the WHR station master's house on the extreme right.
F. M. Gates

The tranship sidings at Dinas Junction in 1910, looking from the 'up' end of the 'down' platform towards Afonwen. Note the broken slate between the narrow gauge tracks.
L & GRP, courtesy David & Charles

to about 10 miles per hour to effect the change, it was necessary for the signalman to hold an oil lamp in one hand, which illuminated the staff, and effect a release and grasp the other token in the same instant. I still have memories of Hugh Williams performing this feat at 5.00 a.m. on a bitter December morning, standing on the crumbling platform edge with snowflakes driving into his eyes while Bob 'Joy' Williams reduced speed to about 25 mph, desperately trying to make up time with the Afonwen Mails; the smack of the large staff as it hit the palm of his hand could be heard across the platform and above the noise of the wind.

Of course, not all exchanges were effected cleanly, and a nervous fireman who was less concerned about the outgoing token would at times drop it short. The problem of finding the staff in poor illumination have to be experienced to be appreciated, particularly because as soon as the train had cleared the platform, it was necessary to get back to the box and signal 'train entering section' to Groeslon. A platform lamp was always lit and hung on the old Welsh Highland Railway building, illuminating the spot where the signalman would stand. The hand lamp was essential to the exchange and from experience it was essential to keep at least one spare lamp ready and lit in the box.

However, this problem was only for 'down' trains, as all 'up' traffic had to pull into the loop, and the speed limit was observed to the letter. Token exchanges were always civilised in this direction, and conducted during darkness by the light of the signal box. Even so, it is on record that ten minutes were spent looking for the hoop one evening when a fireman developed a mean streak.

The box was always kept in a spotless condition, and the Webb frame was respectfully handled with the obligatory duster.

The station closed to all traffic officially on 10th September 1951 although there was a last flicker of passenger activity on 9th August 1963, when the Queen boarded the royal train for Criccieth. The 'down' platform was tidied up, and a six foot strip of tarmac laid, but there was no official ceremony.

No. 42261 climbs up the grade before levelling out at Dinas Junction with the 2.52 p.m. Bangor to Afonwen in 1952. The right-hand track, the headshunt for the station, was used as a crippled wagon store, freight services having been withdrawn the previous year.   *Author*

Llanwnda station, looking towards Afonwen, from the road bridge, with the Dinas Junction distant in the foreground. Around the turn of the century it was proposed to install a siding to serve a cattle dock to the left of the main line, but this was never implemented.

C. L. Mowat

Llanwnda

Llanwnda was opened as a temporary station by the Carnarvonshire Railway, and originally named Pwllheli Road. Access from the main Caernarvon-Pwllheli road was via the goods and coal yard for road vehicles, with a separate footpath for pedestrians. There were three buildings on the platform, the main structure being built of red brick with yellow brick quoins and string courses around the building.

Traffic was light. Passenger trains made conditional stops but the cost rarely justified the effort and freight traffic was little better. After a fruitless stop, when no-one alighted or boarded the train, one of the Bangor drivers was moved to comment that it was 'a bloody Hornby toy station — no life!' and in truth, there was a similarity, a small single storey structure, a short platform on a curve and a siding.

It remained open until the end, which was somewhat surprising with the reduction of traffic and several trains not stopping, particularly after the closure of Pant Glâs. Freight traffic was dealt with by the 'down' Afonwen goods and there was some parcels traffic which kept the station staff occupied. An early drawing shows an additional siding south of the platform, running up to the retaining wall of the road but no evidence has come to light that it was ever put in.

Distance from Dinas Junction:	913 yards up direction
Distance from Groeslon:	1 mile 208 yds down direction
Running time from Llanwnda	
up direction	
passenger trains	2 minutes
freight trains	3 minutes approx. not shown in timetable
down direction	
passenger trains	4 minutes
freight trains	10 minutes, varies according to year
Intermediate crossings:	
up direction	Glanrhyd Crossing — 524 yds
Gradient leaving station:	
up direction	1:104 falling
down direction	1:104 rising

Llanwnda was not a token station but an intermediate halt on the Dinas Junction to Groeslon section, the train token controlling access to the siding.

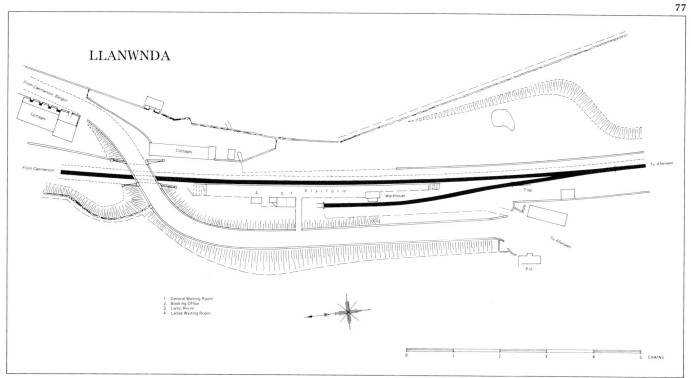

LLANWNDA

1. General Waiting Room
2. Booking Office
3. Lamp Room
4. Ladies Waiting Room

View from the Afonwen end of the platform, looking towards Caernarvon on 5th May 1961. The presence of the railway lorry on the platform was a regular sight, avoiding unnecessary handling of small freight over rough ground.

D. Thompson

The goods yard and shed at Llanwnda, taken from the yard and looking towards Afonwen. Coal was the only commodity off-loaded here, and deliveries rarely exceeded two wagons.

J. H. Moss

2—6—4T No. 42601 pauses at Groeslon station with an Afonwen train on 27th July 1963. The low height of the platform necessitated the provision of extra steps for the less agile.

A. Cooke

Groeslon

This was one of the original stations on the Carnarvonshire Railway, opening in 1866 following the official inspection. It was also a token exchange point, a crossing loop having been installed here from 1911. Passenger traffic was healthy throughout the line's existence as Groeslon was a convenient centre for several of the surrounding villages. Freight traffic was mainly inward, with coal being unloaded in the siding on the 'down' side, the points for which were operated by a two-lever ground frame locked by the Groeslon-Penygroes staff. Signals were controlled by an open air 18-lever frame located on the 'down' platform south of the buildings. It controlled the points at each end of the loop, and the signals which were interlocked with the hand-operated level crossing gates. The token equipment was housed in the station master's office.

There were two buildings on the 'down' platform, the main structure being of red brick, with slate roof. There was a similarity in construction to Llanwnda, with the same use of yellow brick decoration. The secondary building, of wooden construction with a sliding door, was mainly used as a store although it was designated as a goods shed on the official plans. The 'up' platform had a wooden shelter which was on the small side and little used. There was no footbridge, passengers crossing the line on the level at the Caernarvon end. The low platforms were of stone construction, with wooden extensions at the Afonwen end.

Distance from Dinas Junction:	1 mile 1121 yds, up direction. Next token point.
Distance from Penygroes:	1 mile 1682 yds, down direction. Next token point.
Distance from Llanwnda:	1 mile 208 yds, up direction. Next station.

Running time from Groeslon
up direction

passenger trains	3 minutes
freight trains	5 minutes

down direction

passenger trains	5 minutes
freight trains	7 minutes

Intermediate sidings:
down direction   Tudor Siding (private) Distance from Groeslon 1 mile.

Intermediate crossings:
down direction   Glynllifon.

Gradient leaving station:
up direction   1:61 falling
down direction   1:61 rising

Single Line Tokens
Groeslon-Dinas Junction — Key token coloured blue
Groeslon-Penygroes — Large staff coloured red

The token for Groeslon to Penygroes also controlled access to Tudor Siding.

Taken from the 'down' platform, looking towards Dinas Junction, this picture shows the 'up' platform shelter and crossing gates across the tracks. The 'up' platform was higher and did not need any portable steps.

J. H. Moss

The LMS operated an extensive road lorry service, and Groeslon was served by Penygroes-based lorries. It was not usual practice to permit the lorries onto the platform, as this involved some rather tricky handling for the driver. Nevertheless the staff do not appear too put out by their efforts as they pose beside the lever frame on the 'down' platform. The vehicle appears to be a Karrier van. *Author's collection*

The open air lever frame was located alongside the goods store on the 'down' platform. The indicators were mounted on posts behind the frame and the diagram behind the levers. The token equipment was located in the station master's office. *J. H. Moss*

The wooden extension to the 'up' platform is clearly seen in this view looking towards Afonwen. The goods siding on the 'down' side is just apparent here.

J. H. Moss

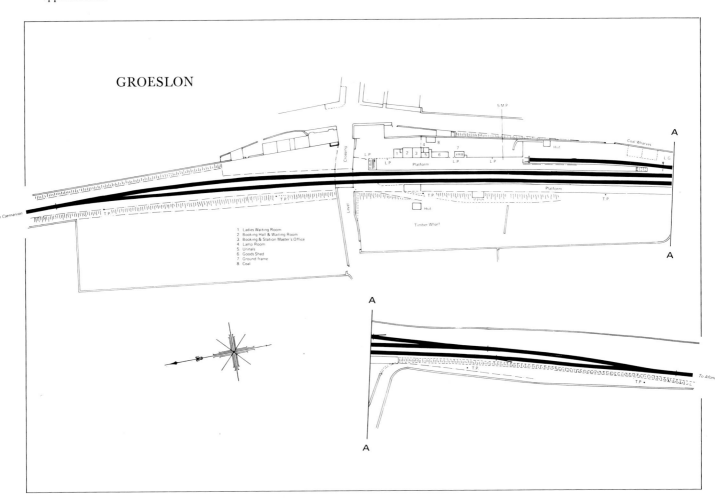

Looking towards Afonwen on 8th August 1932, with the Nantlle branch bay platform to the left and the goods yard on the right.

L & GRP, courtesy David & Charles

Penygroes

Penygroes was the largest intermediate station on the Afonwen branch and junction for the branch to Nantlle which turned off to the east. It was also a token exchange point with a crossing loop and signal cabin, of brick and timber construction, with a slate roof, housing a standard Webb pattern lever frame and the token instruments. The frame had 33 levers, latterly with 4 spare. The box was located on the 'down' side just off the Afonwen end of the platform.

The main station buildings were located on the 'down' platform, and were more comprehensive than the others along the line. The structure, incorporating a station master's house, offices and waiting rooms, was built of red brick, with a slate roof, and boasted a small canopy. The 'up' platform was provided with a semi-open shelter of granite construction with yellow brick reveals and a slate roof. The platforms, of stone construction edged with concrete slabs, were of low height and portable steps were available. There was an open footbridge of standard design at the south end of the platforms and a trolley crossing by the signal box.

The climb out of Penygroes for Afonwen trains commenced immediately south of the station, and taxed engines and crews alike. Usually time was made up coming from Groeslon to allow the fire to be prepared for the assault (See the gradient profile opposite page 1).

The coal yard remained in use for some time after the line was dismantled, but with the construction of the

Dinorwic pumped storage scheme, gravel was supplied from Grianog quarry, about half way between Penygroes and Pant Glâs, and McAlpine's, the contractors, acquired the trackbed from Grianog crossing to Llanwnda to create a private roadway to carry the quantities of gravel needed. This kept the traffic off the public road and now the construction of the hydro-electric scheme has finished, it has

Distance from Groeslon:	1 mile 1682 yds up direction. Next token point
Distance from Brynkir:	5 miles 1069 yds down direction. Next token point
Distance from Pant Glâs:	3 miles 1304 yds down direction. Next station
Running time from Penygroes:	
up direction	
passenger trains	5 minutes to Groeslon
freight trains	7 minutes
down direction	
passenger trains	10 minutes to Pant Glâs
freight trains	14 minutes approx.
Intermediate sidings:	
up direction	Tudor Siding (private slate mill)
Intermediate crossings:	
up direction	Glynllifon 1 mile from Pengroes
down direction	Grianog 2 miles from Penygroes
Gradient leaving station:	
up direction	1:540 rising
down direction	1:540 falling
Single Line Tokens	
Penygroes-Groeslon — Large staff coloured red	
Penygroes-Brynkir — Key token coloured blue	
Penygroes-Nantlle — One engine in steam staff: Square coloured white with key.	

PENYGROES

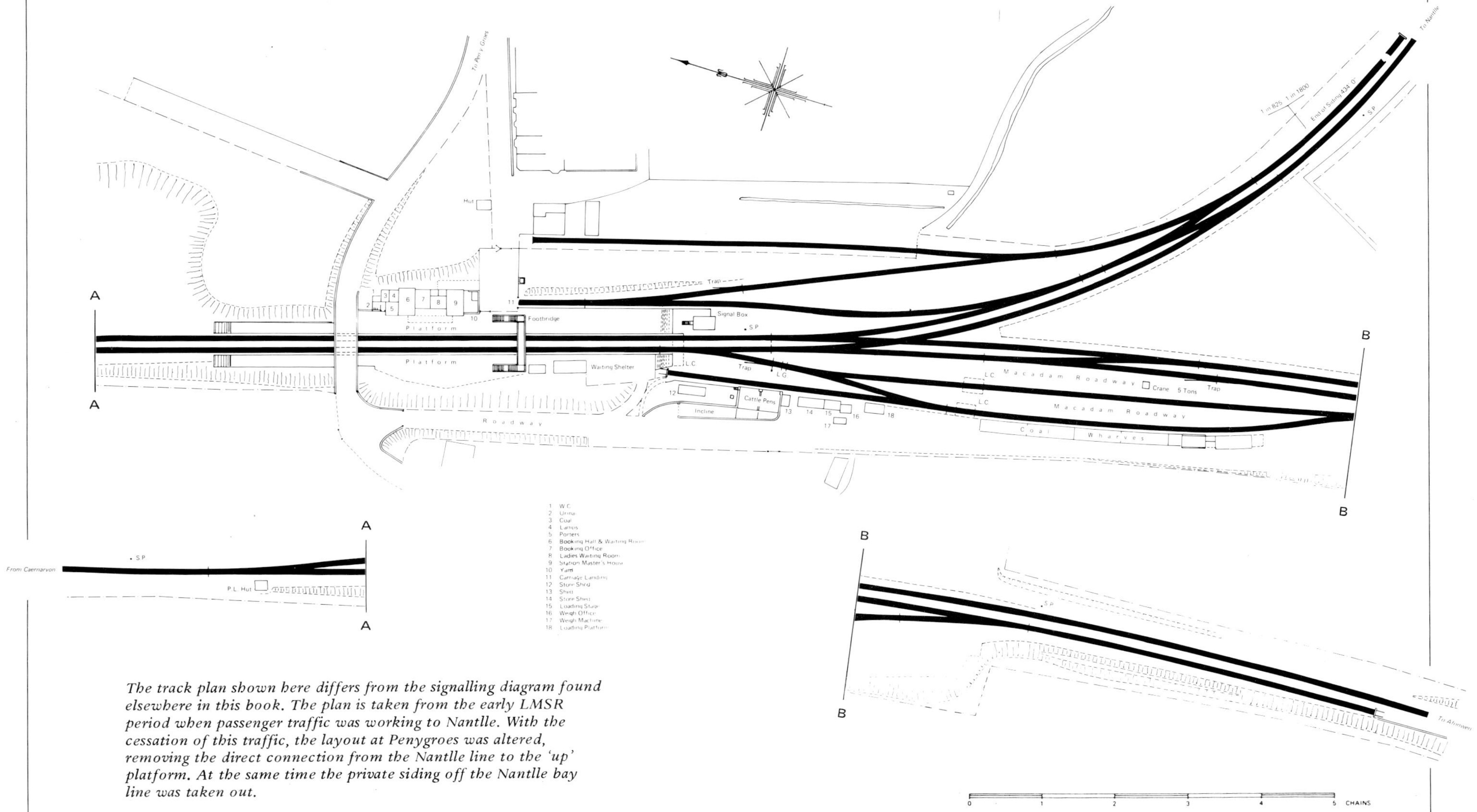

To Nantlle
1 in 825
1 in 1800
End of Siding 434' 0"
S P
To Pen y Groes
Hut
Trap
Signal Box
S P
Footbridge
Platform
Platform
Waiting Shelter
L C
Trap
L G
L C
Macadam Roadway
Crane
5 Tons
Trap
L C
Macadam Roadway
Coal Wharves
Cattle Pens
Incline
Roadway
1
2
3
4
5
6
7
8
9
10
11
12
13
14
15
16
17
18
A
A
B
B
A
A
B
B
From Caernarvon
S P
P.L. Hut
S P
To Afonwen
1 W.C.
2 Urinal
3 Coal
4 Lamps
5 Porters
6 Booking Hall & Waiting Room
7 Booking Office
8 Ladies Waiting Room
9 Station Master's House
10 Yard
11 Carriage Landing
12 Store Shed
13 Shed
14 Store Shed
15 Loading Stage
16 Weigh Office
17 Weigh Machine
18 Loading Platform
0
1
2
3
4
5
CHAINS

The track plan shown here differs from the signalling diagram found elsewhere in this book. The plan is taken from the early LMSR period when passenger traffic was working to Nantlle. With the cessation of this traffic, the layout at Penygroes was altered, removing the direct connection from the Nantlle line to the 'up' platform. At the same time the private siding off the Nantlle bay line was taken out.

The main buildings were located on the 'down' platform as this view taken about 1924 shows. The footbridge was little used, most passengers preferring to walk across the tracks, despite it being an offence. The Nantlle bay is beyond the footbridge. *C. L. Mowat*

been proposed to use the track bed as a cycle track. McAlpine's demolished the buildings at Penygroes and Llanwnda although the road overbridge spanning the line at the station is still intact.

The village had developed with the demand for slate which was inevitably the main traffic. Before the last war it was common practice for all 'up' freight trains to clear Penygroes yard of loaded wagons, bring them down to Caernarvon, where they would be marshalled into trains. There was some livestock, but little else. Inward traffic was the usual coal and sundries, with some timber traffic before 1904 to mines in Drws y Coed, beyond Nantlle. However, this involved road haulage from Nantlle yard, and it was quicker and probably cheaper to use the North Wales Narrow Gauge Railway to Rhyd Ddu. The mines were reputed to have been worked out by 1904.

With the dramatic decline of the slate traffic in the 1930s the importance of Penygroes as a railway junction diminished. The passenger service on the Nantlle line ceased and the freight traffic dwindled, and with it the need for a shunter being on hand there. Nevertheless traffic did persist until the 1960s.

Penygroes was connected by the railway telephone circuit A957 with the call sign of dash, dot. The telephone was located in the signal box. In addition the Grianog crossing could only be contacted by Penygroes station box, and Pant Glâs level crossing could only be called by Penygroes station box or Brynkir office. As is the habit on local telephone circuits, if the buzzer went and things were slack, everyone picked up the receiver and listened in. That

is, except Grianog and Pant Glâs, who remained in ignorance.

For 'up' trains there was a restriction between the 9 and 8 mileposts of 40 mph and between the 7¾ and 7¼ mileposts of 20 mph, due to the falling gradient.

The station staff pose, with mascot, on the 'down' platform in the shade of the canopy. *Author's collection*

The footbridge and road overbridge, looking towards Caernarvon.   *J. H. Moss*

The garden behind the 'up' platform at Penygroes frequently merited prizes and commendations. The station name was picked out in grass letters.   *Author's collection*

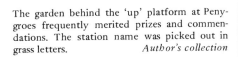

Another view of the main building, taken from the 'up' platform.   *J. H. Moss*

Looking towards Afonwen shortly after the line closed to all traffic.

Author

A general view of Penygroes taken from the goods yard access on 30th August 1961. The station's neat appearance reflects how the station staff took a pride in their work.

T. J. Edgington

A hazy but atmospheric winter view of Pant Glâs. The siding beyond the crossing was lifted just after the war, in 1947.   *Author's collection*

Pant Glâs

The station at Pant Glâs was authorised in December 1869 after the line had been opened. Traffic was slight at all times but it remained open to passenger traffic until January 1957, the freight service having been withdrawn two years earlier. It is somewhat surprising it lasted as long as it did, being located some distance from the village which was on the Penygroes to Portmadoc road.

The platform, faced with timber and infilled with stone, was very short, being just 220 feet long. The buildings were similar to the Welsh Highland design at Dinas, although the lamp room was a somewhat flimsy affair, replaced about 1956. The level crossing had a hand-operated pair of gates interlocked with the signals, which were controlled by a four-lever frame mounted on the platform between the building and the lamp room.

The drawing shows a small waiting room by the level crossing, but no information has been discovered about this structure which is believed to have been demolished before 1930.

Distance from Penygroes:	3 miles 1304 yards up direction. Next token point
Distance from Brynkir:	1 mile 1525 yds down direction. Next token point.

Running time from Pant Glâs
up direction

passenger trains	9 minutes
freight trains	14 minutes approx.

down direction

passenger trains	3 minutes
freight trains	5 minutes approx.

Intermediate crossing:
up direction	Grianog

Gradient leaving station:
up direction	1:270 rising
down direction	1:270 falling

Station intermediate in Penygroes-Brynkir token section.

Approximate length of station from limits — 660 feet
Approximate width of station at widest points — 160 feet (including station master's house).

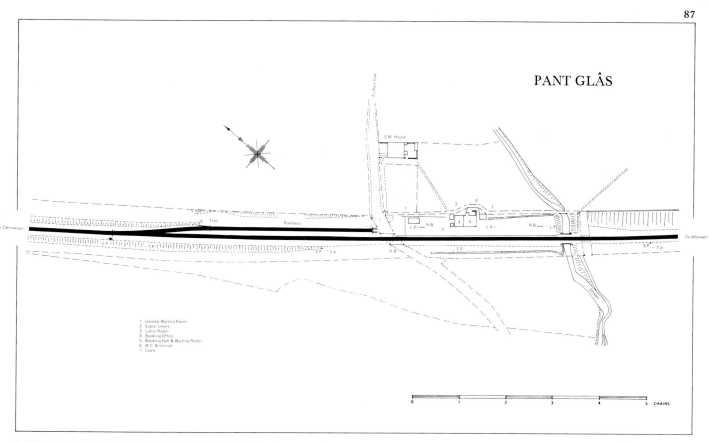

PANT GLÂS

1 General Waiting Room
2 Signal Levers
3 Lamp Room
4 Booking Office
5 Booking Hall & Waiting Room
6 W.C. & Urinals
7 Coals

0   1   2   3   4   5 CHAINS

Pant Glâs was somewhat isolated and exposed to the elements, as this photograph shows. Drifting was one of the winter problems, and the clearance gang are digging the signal wires free. The frame was located on the platform. The view is looking towards Afonwen. *Author*

A DMU trundles past Pant Glâs on its way to Pwllheli. The old structure of the station is shown clearly, and is similar to the design of those used on the North Wales Narrow Gauge Railway, latterly the Welsh Highland Railway, which ran from Dinas Junction. *W. A. Camwell*

Pant Glâs station was never well patronised and the small station building was more than adequate for the traffic. There was a goods siding located north of the level crossing, but this was rarely used and was removed some time before the line closed. *H. C. Casserley*

The gates on the Caernarvon side of the station were normally left across the tracks and opened for trains. This view shows the setting shortly before the line closed to all traffic. The upper quadrant signal replaced that shown on page 86 about 1952. *J. H. Moss*

No. 80090 pulls into the 'down' platform with a Bangor-Afonwen working. The porter signalman brings the train staff from the office, where the instruments are kept. The lever frame can just be seen between the two buildings.

W. A. Camwell

Brynkir

Brynkir opened to traffic on 2nd September 1867. The crossing loop was extended in 1893 and again in 1947 to accommodate the ten-coach trains which were using the line. Located in the centre of the village, it was always a busy station with a good livestock traffic. General merchandise and coal were also carried regularly. The 'down' platform was the location of the main buildings, with a brick-built office and waiting room, a separate ladies' waiting room and the lever frame between. There was a small wooden goods shed alongside and, at the Caernarvon end, a cylindrical water tank mounted on brick columns. The goods yard was located on the 'down' side behind the platform, one of a pair of sidings leading off from this line serving cattle pens. For many years a camping coach was located beyond the pens, protected by having the connecting rails removed.

The 'up' platform was open to the elements and was equipped with a shelter and a seat, There was a water column at the Caernarvon end.

The token equipment was located in the station master's office. Again the platforms were of low height and supplemented by portable steps.

Distance from Penygroes:	5 miles 1069 yards up direction; next token point
Distance from Pant Glâs:	1 mile 1525 yards up direction; next station
Distance from Llangybi:	3 miles 1207 yards down direction; next token point
Distance from Ynys:	1 mile 1694 yards down direction; next station

Running times from Brynkir:
up direction
 passenger trains — 5 minutes
 freight trains — 7 minutes approx.
down direction
 passenger trains — 3 minutes
 freight trains — 5 minutes approx.

Intermediate crossing:	*down direction* — Ynys station
Gradient leaving station:	*up direction* 1:100 rising
	down direction 1:100 falling

Single Line Tokens:
 Brynkir-Penygroes — Key token coloured blue
 Brynkir-Llangybi — Large staff coloured red

Main (down) platform length	380 feet
Up platform length	380 feet

Brynkir station was frequently used for crossing trains, especially on Saturdays when the Butlin's specials ran. Here 42156 and 42663 wait for the staff with a return ECS working in 1952.

Author

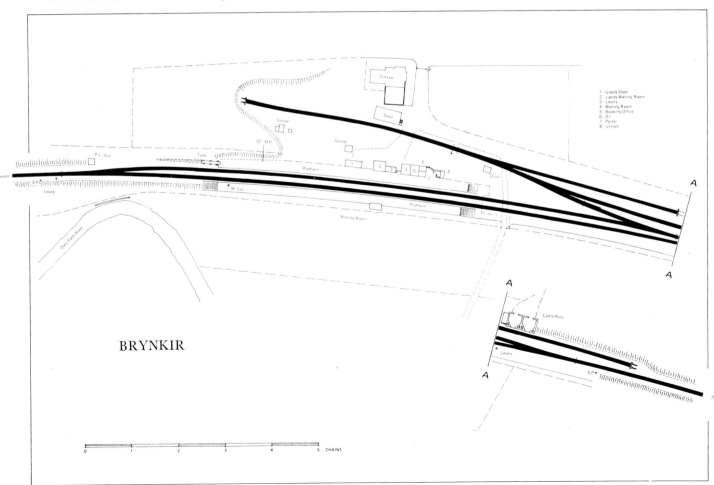

BRYNKIR

A fine view of the platforms at Brynkir, looking towards Afonwen, taken from the top of the water tank on the 'down' platform. The 'up' platform is neatly set out, but again was a bleak place at the best of times. The goods yard was generally busy, with a livestock market held weekly.
British Railways

The main building at Brynkir was located on the 'down' side. The platform was low in height and steps were much in evidence.
British Railways

The road access to Brynkir station showing the goods siding slightly raised in the
middle foreground. The station master's
house is just visible on the right-hand edge
of the picture.   *Author*

The goods siding ran across the forecourt,
over the access road, and into a small yard
behind the 'down' platform. This corrugated iron store and platform were located
just before the road crossing.   *J. H. Moss*

No. 42460 pulling into Brynkir with an Afonwen-Bangor local train in 1952. Notice the cattle pens with a camping coach
beyond, and the van in a short siding.

Author

Ynys station, shown here looking towards Afonwen, never appeared to do much business, but it survived to the end and even acquired a replacement bus for a few years.

C. L. Mowat

Ynys

One of the smaller stations on the line, Ynys opened in July 1872 and, despite its small size and out of the way location, remained open until the line closed. One of the conditions for closure was that a replacement bus service was provided, and Crosville Motor Services Ltd. based a minibus at their Pwllheli depot to cover this requirement. It survived about three seasons before the service was withdrawn.

The platform was again of low height and the buildings were of timber construction apart from the station master's house which adjoined the platform. A small 4-lever frame was located on the platform and controlled signals which were also interlocked with the hand-operated crossing gates. The indicators were located in a cabinet behind the frame and can be seen in one of the photographs.

There was one little used siding located on the 'down' side. Access was from a facing point in the 'down' direction, locked by a key on the train staff, freight trains from Afonwen to Caernarvon consequently calling as required.

Distance from Brynkir:	1 mile 1694 yards up direction; next token point
Distance from Llangybi:	1 mile 1273 yards down direction; next token point
Running time from Ynys:	
up direction	
passenger trains — 4 minutes	
freight trains — 7 minutes approx.	
down direction — Rhosgill Bach	
passenger trains — 4 minutes	
freight trains — 4 minutes approx.	
Intermediate crossing:	*down direction* — Rhosgill Bach
Gradient leaving station:	*up direction* 1:60 rising
	down direction 1:60 falling
Station intermediate in the Brynkir-Llangybi token section.	
Main (up) platform length	260 feet construction — timber

The station master's house at Ynys, adjacent to the level crossing.

Author

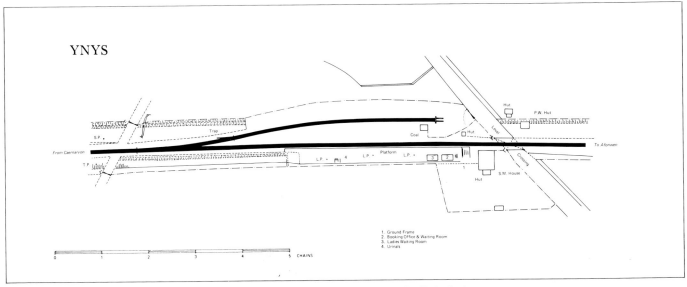

YNYS

1. Ground Frame
2. Booking Office & Waiting Room
3. Ladies Waiting Room
4. Urinals

The introduction of DMUs did little to increase traffic from Ynys as there were only a couple of houses near to the station. Again the lever frame was situated alongside the station building. *J. S. Gilks*

Ynys was one of the smaller halts on the Afonwen line, but always presented a smart appearance. The buildings were always kept clean and the level crossing gates pristine white. This view shows the corner of the station house, with the small lever frame located between the nameboard and the wooden building. This view is looking towards Caernarvon.

J. H. Moss

No. 41236 at the 'down' platform with an Afonwen train.

W. A. Camwell

Llangybi

Llangybi station was authorised in December 1869 and was initially a simple halt with a siding on the 'up' side. A loop and another platform were provided in the period 1914-15 when it became a staff section. According to Baughan, it was the 'up' platform which was provided at this date, but loco men from Bangor disagree. The loop was extended in 1947 to accommodate the ten coach trains, and, apart from the removal of the siding in 1938, the station remained unchanged until the line closed. Because of its isolated location, two pairs of cottages were provided for the staff.

The station buildings were all located on the 'up' platform, and included a standard Crewe signal hut, an office which bore a slight resemblance to Pant Glâs, a ladies' waiting shelter and a urinal. The 'down' platform was an inhospitable place to wait on wet days as it was devoid of all shelter.

The token equipment and the telephone were located in the office, not the cabin. The platforms were 380 feet in length and the line was crossed by passengers on the level across the walkway over the tracks.

Distance from Ynys:	1 mile 1273 yards up direction; next station
Distance from Brynkir:	3 miles 1207 yards up direction, next token point
Distance from Chwilog:	1 mile 542 yards, down direction; next token point

Running time from Llangybi:
up direction
    passenger trains — 4 minutes to Ynys
    freight trains — 10 minutes
down direction
    passenger trains — 3 minutes to Chwilog
    freight trains — 5 minutes

Intermediate crossing:	*up direction* — Rhosgill Bach 1 mile 49 yards
Gradient leaving station:	*up direction* 1:182 rising *down direction* 1:182 falling

Single Line Tokens
    Llangybi-Brynkir — Large staff coloured red
    Llangybi-Chwilog — Key token coloured red

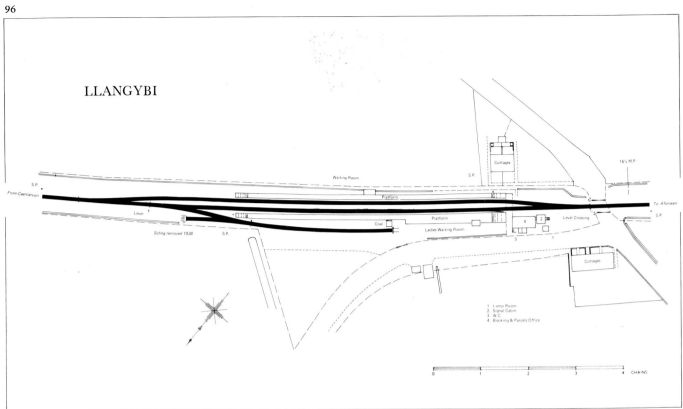

LLANGYBI

From Caernarvon

To Afonwen

16¼ M.P.

S.P.

S.P.

S.P.

S.P.

Waiting Room

Platform

Platform

Ladies Waiting Room

Lever

Coal

Cottages

Cottages

Level Crossing

Siding removed 1938

1 Lamp Room
2 Signal Cabin
3 W.C.
4 Booking & Parcels Office

4   2

3   1

0   1   2   3   4   CHAINS

A DMU for Bangor to Pwllheli pauses at Llangybi on 22nd May 1962.

J. S. Gilks

This view, taken a short distance down the line, shows the whole station including the railway owned houses. A DMU, still new, waits to cross an Afonwen train on 27th June 1956. *H. C. Casserley*

A closer view of the signal cabin, looking towards Caernarvon. The 'down' platform was devoid of shelter. The siding behind the 'up' platform was removed in 1938 due to lack of traffic.

D. Thompson

The station offices were grouped with the signal box at the Afonwen end of the station south of the 'up' platform. The main building was similar in construction to Pant Glâs apart from the entrance door. Beyond the platforms was a level crossing, hand operated. Note the surviving ex-LNWR lower qudrant starting signal at the end of the 'down' platform. *J. H. Moss*

98

Despite being a token exchange station, Chwilog had only one platform face and no crossing facilities were provided. The goods yard was small but there was a considerable volume of traffic of one sort or another. In 1958 the platform was rebuilt, and this photograph, taken on 16th October, shows the result of one sort or another. The passenger traffic was steady throughout the year. In 1958 the platform was rebuilt, and this photograph, taken on 16th October, shows the result soon after completion.

British Railways

No. 80090 pulls into Chwilog station with a Bangor-Afonwen working.   *W. A. Camwell*

Chwilog

Opened 2nd September 1867, Chwilog was a large station when compared with Llangybi, Brynkir and Groeslon and was centrally located in the village. Although it was a token exchange point, there was no provision for trains to cross and passenger trains were expressly forbidden to do so. On rare occasions a freight train would be set back into the yard and the staff was surrendered to enable a passenger train to work through, but such happenings were avoided wherever possible by control. The token equipment was located in the station master's office. The signals were interlocked with the level crossing gates, which were again hand-operated, and the indicators were located on a small post behind the lever frame at the 'down' end of the platform. The platform itself was on the 'up' side. The imposing station building was of red brick, with a slate roof, and incorporated the station master's house. The other structures on the platform were made of wood and corrugated steel sheet.

The yard was located to the east of the platform. There were two sidings and a headshunt serving a goods shed and coal wharves. The shed was privately owned by the local Farmers Association who had a considerable traffic. For many years milk was despatched daily by special train to Hanson's dairy in Broad Green, Liverpool, and live cattle movements were frequent. In addition, farm equipment and fertilizers were also brought in, and, of course, the usual coal traffic. Cattle were loaded at the lower sidings south of the level crossing, where pens and feeding facilities were provided. The station was busy right up to the closure of the line.

Distance from Llangybi:	1 mile 542 yards up direction; next token point
Distance from Afonwen:	1 mile 226 yards 'down' direction; next token point
Running time from Chwilog:	
up direction	
passenger trains — 4 minutes to Llangybi	
freight trains — 10 minutes	
down direction	
passenger trains — 3 minutes to Afonwen	
freight trains — 5 minutes	
Gradient leaving station:	*up direction* 1:60 rising
	down direction 1:60 falling
Single Line Tokens	
Chwilog-Llangybi — Key token coloured red	
Chwilog-Afonwen - Key token coloured blue	

CHWILOG

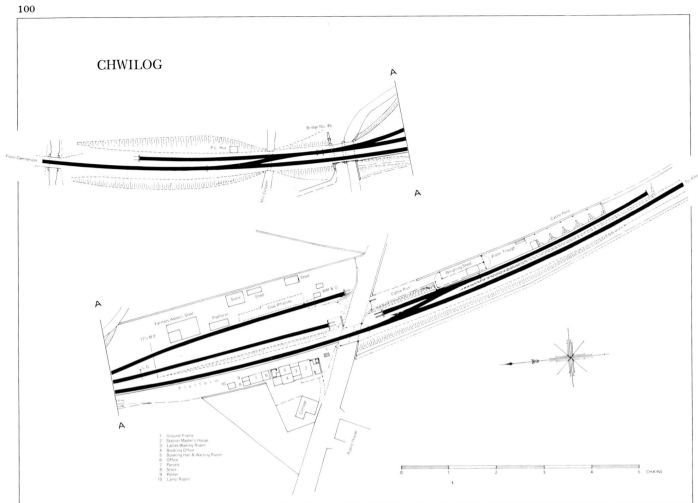

1. Ground Frame
2. Station Master's House
3. Ladies Waiting Room
4. Booking Office
5. Booking Hall & Waiting Room
6. Office
7. Parcels
8. Store
9. Porter
10. Lamp Room

Nos. 41200 and 45144 from Bangor coast down the gradient immediately south of Chwilog station with an ECS working to Penychain. The siding for the cattle pens is on the right.

J. W. T. House

Another view looking towards Caernarvon, this time from inside the track south of the station on 27th June 1956. The small frame controlling access to the sidings can be seen on the left hand lower side of the photograph. *H. C. Casserley*

This six lever platform frame, controlling the signals only, was located close to the level crossing. The keys for locking the crossing gates and releasing the siding points can be seen inserted in the locks behind the levers. *G. H. Platt*

The absence of wagons in this view looking towards Afonwen is deceptive as here at least the yard was usually busy.

J. H. Moss

The main station building at Chwilog was an imposing structure incorporating the station master's house.

J. H. Moss

Taken from the platform and looking back towards Caernarvon. The staff continued the tradition of well-kept station gardens and here they picked out the station name in stones, painted over with whitewash.

J. H. Moss

The LMS used the 'up' side passenger loop face for most of its arrivals and departures, but not exclusively. Weary loco crews dropped clinker and ash on the boundary side of the 'up' goods loop in the foreground. The station master's house on the left is now the only evidence that there was once a station here.

J. H. Moss

Afonwen

Authorised by Act of 22nd July 1861, the Aberystwyth & Welsh Coast Railway, which was duplicated from Portmadoc to Afonwen by the Carnarvonshire Railway, was completed and inspected by Captain Tyler in March 1867. Carnarvonshire Railway services commenced from Pant, near Caernarvon, to Afonwen on 2nd September 1867 and, until the Cambrian Railways services began a month later on 10th October, extended their operations to Criccieth, Portmadoc and Penrhyndeudraeth. The earliest services were worked by Cambrian Railways locomotives until the Carnarvonshire Railway acquired their own motive power. Running powers under reciprocal agreement continued until 1870 when it was cancelled.

The LMS had no station of its own at Afonwen but used the north face of an island platform on the 'up' side of the GWR station. However, this was not an exclusive arrangement, the GWR making use of whichever platform suited their needs, although they usually kept to the south face for 'up' trains wherever possible. There were no freight handling facilities, the sidings provided being merely for re-marshalling and exchange of traffic between the two companies. LMS freight trains would enter the sidings via the goods line which ran parallel to the LMS platform. The locomotive then uncoupled and performed any servic-

ing necessary before attaching to the brake van and proceeding to the 'down' main line in the station. It would then set back into the siding south of the 'down' line and deposit the brake van on the secondary siding. The wagons were sorted by the GWR staff, whilst the LMS crews coupled up, attached the brake van and waited to return to their own line, this practice continuing well after nationalization. Passenger trains from the LMS to Penychain and Pwllheli on a quick turn round usually used the GWR 'up' platform face, running round the train on the 'down' line if clear, and the LMS line if not. On peak Saturdays in the 1950s, with many Butlin's specials, a traffic controller was on the platform to sort out any problems that might arise.

STATION WORKING

The LMS line was single track, the token equipment being located in the signal box on the 'down' platform. Whilst the GWR line came under the control of Oswestry, LMS linesmen had access to their equipment for servicing and maintenance. There were no LMS staff based at Afonwen.

Between the two World Wars, traffic built up and in the holiday period there were close on a hundred train movements daily in the high summer season. The GWR sections on either side of the station were also single line, to Criccieth in the east, 3 miles 21 chains, and to Pwllheli in the west, 4 miles. After the 1939-45 war, the track was doubled

At the parting of the ways, 2–6–4Ts Nos. 42260 and 42461 commence the climb to Chwilog with an ECS from Penychain to Llandudno Junction in 1952. The working of two locomotives both bunker first, as shown here, was rather unusual. The third coach is of vintage stock.

Author

An afternoon freight train from Caernarvon pulls into the back road at Afonwen headed by No. 42628. The load is typical. This picture was taken in front of the railway cottages in 1952.

Author

On Saturdays, Bangor No. 3 link had a turn which involved working a trip to Amlwch and return followed by a trip to Afonwen. At this time the line was restricted to class 2 locomotives and the Ivatt 2–6–2Ts were able performers on this work. The locomotive stabled the Amlwch line stock at Bangor and took over a four coach set from Llandudno Junction. It was the practice to work bunker first over the Amlwch line and consequently the outward trip to Afonwen was also run bunker first. Here Hugh Jones starts out of Afonwen on the last leg of his shift with the 7.05 p.m. to Bangor, with No. 41223 pulling out of the GWR 'up' platform. *Author*

between Afonwen and Penychain, where Butlin's had their holiday camp, the new line being brought into use in 1947.

The LMS worked through to Pwllheli with certain turns, but these were few in number and generally kept to one or two trains at off-peak times. The LMS made use of the turntable at Afonwen, until it was taken out of use, a move which prompted a greater use of tank engines to and from Bangor. Those trains that did work through to Pwllheli were eventually able to use the turntable at Pwllheli East, but this still entailed some tender first running. The publication entitled 'Instructions to LMS Servants when working over the Great Western Railway' covered all details. This publication was revised from time to time. Reference to the Afonwen to Pwllheli section appeared in an issue dated 1932. Bangor No. 2 link provided most of the relevant trips. There was some resistance to the through running, in particular by Portmadoc shed, which provided many locomotives and crews to work LMS stock through to Pwllheli or Portmadoc. The rostered turns at Bangor were rearranged after the war to enable men from the top three links to work regularly over the line, and with nationalization in 1948 the through running increased. Ironically, there had been a long-standing agreement with the LNWR and the Cambrian to enable Portmadoc men to work through to Caernarvon, although it was not implemented until the establishment of the Land Cruise trains. These commenced the circuit at Criccieth and returned via

Corwen, Rhyl and the coast, before taking the Afonwen line back home.

The traffic movements at Afonwen provide a fascinating study and to this end, the train movements for both companies in the high summer of 1954 are listed on page 114. As mentioned, the LMS used the north face of the island platform for arrivals and departures, running round sometimes via the main 'up' platform, if water was to be taken from the column, before completing the run round. In 1938, for instance, the 10.18 a.m. arrival (9.00 a.m. ex-Bangor) did this regularly, due to occupation on the 'down' line. Sometimes the stock would be drawn into the exchange sidings, and the 10.40 a.m. to Bangor would depart from the 'up' platform. The more usual practice was to take water from the LMS tank, which was located behind the 'down' platform. The GWR also had a tank here, and the turntable used to be located beyond the two tanks, on the seashore.

Access to Afonwen station was along an unmade road. It was little used, the majority of locals being staff who lived in railway houses close by. Access from the track was over a footbridge to the Pwllheli end of the island platform. The main buildings and offices were on this platform together with a small licensed premises, dependent entirely on the railway for its trade. For most of the year this was provided by train crews from Bangor with layover time. The proprietress died some years before the station closed, and no one was willing to take over the business.

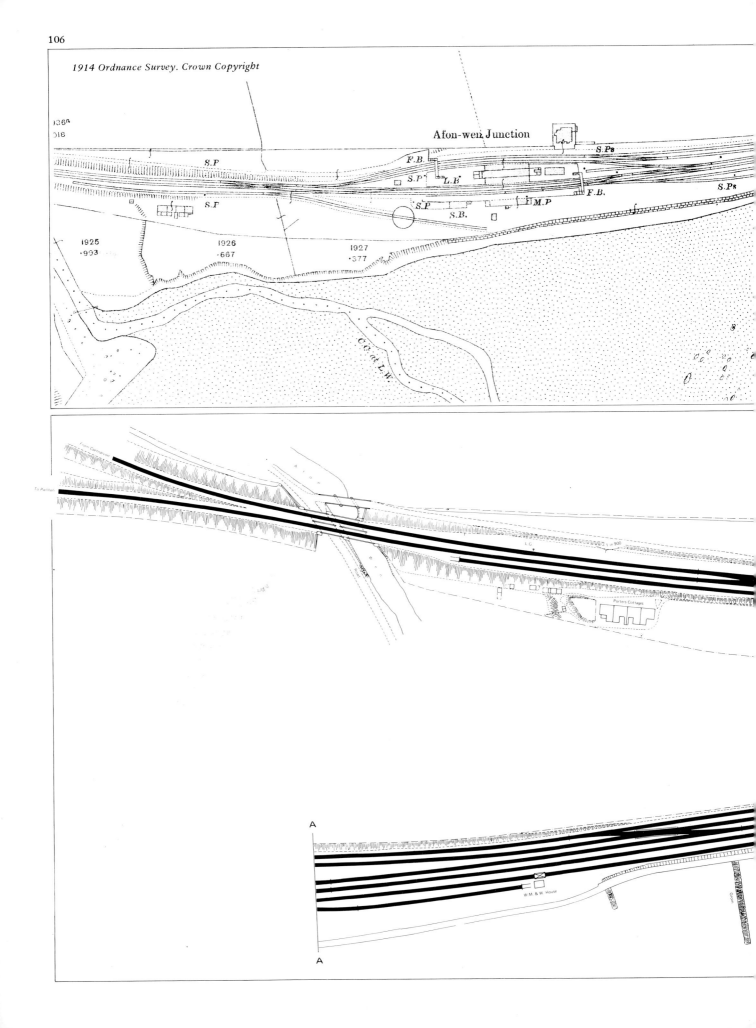

1914 Ordnance Survey. Crown Copyright

Afon-wen Junction

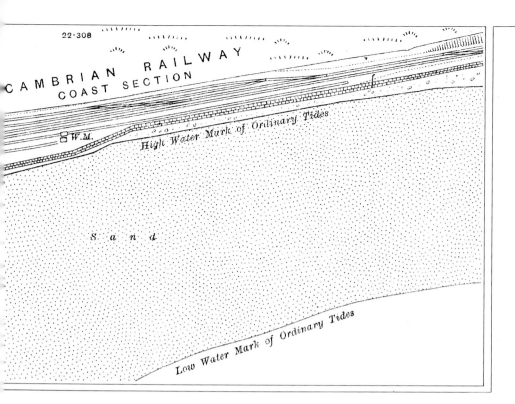

AFONWEN

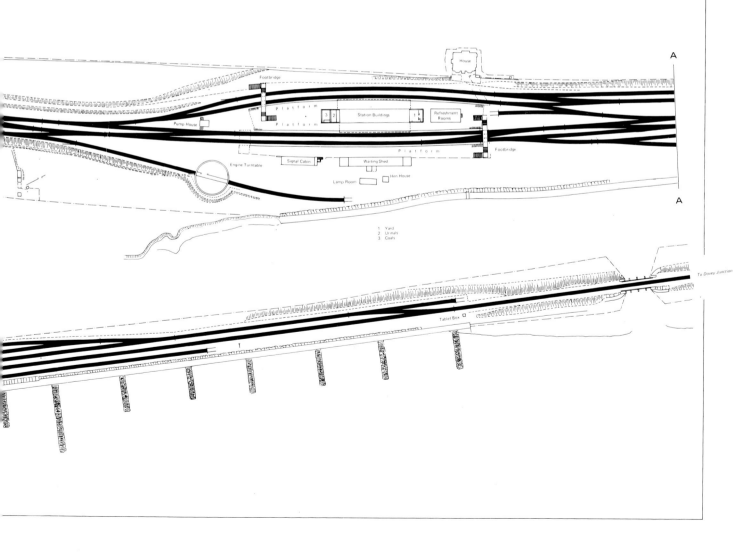

Nos. 40087 and 45417 pull in to Afonwen with a Huddersfield to Penychain Saturdays Only working, composed of Eastern Region stock. This returned as an ECS working later the same day to Llandudno Junction by the same locomotives as part of the normal Bangor diagram. The 2—6—2T in the distant left is standing in the ashpit road.

J. W. T. House

Once the LNWR tanks were withdrawn from all but the lightest of duties, their place on the Afonwen turns were taken initially by 2—6—2Ts of Fowler and Stanier designs. The layout of the cab on the Stanier version was appreciated by the crews, but this was tempered by the class's inability to work to their nominal loading capacity and generate enough steam. For a while Bangor crews struggled with several of this breed, but eventually they were replaced by 2—6—4Ts, much to the train crews' relief. In 1949, however, there were several 2—6—2Ts in evidence, and here No. 40087 waits at the 'up' platform face with the 10.50 a.m. return working to Bangor. *Eric Russell*

Taken from the footbridge which linked the station to the track from the village, this view shows the lines to Pwllheli and Chwilog. The cottages on the far side of the tracks were for station staff.

J. H. Moss

The 'down' platform was a very basic affair, open to the elements, although fortunately with its back to the sea. Access from the island platform was by another footbridge at the Criccieth end. This was an open structure, and on a cold or wet day, a major obstacle to overcome if one wanted to get to the 'down' platform. The signal box was located at the Pwllheli end of the same platform.

LMS freight traffic ran into exchange sidings at the east end of the station. The sorting was undertaken by the GWR men. Until the Second World War, there were three freight trains daily from Caernarvon or Menai Bridge, the first arriving just before 7.00 am. This locomotive would work back passenger with through coaches from Portmadoc and Pwllheli to Euston, which worked forward from Bangor as 'The Welshman'.

The LMS passenger train marshalling instructions relating to these workings were precise. In 1934 these were listed as the 7.50 am Afonwen to Liverpool (Lime Street); the 10.48 am Afonwen to Bangor and Euston; and the 1.45 pm Afonwen to Llandudno Junction and Liverpool. Local traffic working was not listed in the marshalling instructions books but nevertheless were set out in detail. The listed workings in 1954 were the through workings from Portmadoc and Pwllheli which formed 'The Welshman'.

There was a permanent speed restriction through the station platforms of 30 mph, whilst the LMS trains were restricted to 10 mph when entering their platform. Locomotives required to stand for any length of time were usually placed on the turntable road behind the 'down' platform, where there was provision for dropping ash and clinker.

Trains with a short layover time were allowed to clean their fires and drop ash at two points, one on the back road north of the LMS platform road and level with the footbridge connecting the island platform and the dirt road. The other disposal point was in the exchange sidings east of the platform, again off the back road. There was no separate provision for train crews to have their refreshment and the usual practice was to go to the refreshment room, or stay on the footplate.

Distance from Chwilog: 1 mile 226 yards up direction; next token point

Running time from Afonwen:
up direction
    passenger trains — 3 minutes
    freight trains — 7 minutes

Gradient leaving station: 1:280 rising

Single Line Token
    Afonwen-Chwilog — Key token coloured blue

Main island platform length: 325 feet

Down platform length: 355 feet

Signalling was the responsibility of the GWR who provided the equipment. Inter-company contact was effected by the telephone circuits, and the LMS circuit number A957 Caernarvon to Afonwen could be linked to the GWR circuit number 329. Signalmen had to report to Chester control, the arrival and departure of all freight and special ECS workings to and from the Caernarvon line. The telephone circuit exchange at Caernarvon effected the connection.

The Radio Land Cruise was a popular post-war innovation and in 1954 there were three trains daily on Tuesday to Thursdays on the circuit. Two worked back along the coast in the afternoon and paused briefly at Afonwen for water before commencing the climb to Caernarvon. Here No. 46428, based for the summer at Rhyl, is being topped up with water. It is in the 'up' side passenger loop, normally used by Bangor & LM Region trains. The two workings in this direction were crewed by Rhyl men throughout, as they had learned the road over Western Region tracks, thus eliminating the need for pilotmen. However, it is believed that only four sets of men could sign for the road. *J. H. Moss*

The 'down' main platform at Afonwen displays much bustle as passengers leave a Western Region working from Barmouth to make their way to the footbridge and over the tracks to the LM Region train for Caernarvon and Bangor, just visible in the main 'up' platform.

Eric Russell

The 'down' platform shelter and signal box, taken from the 'up' island platform, looking towards Pwllheli on 31st July 1962. *J. J. Davis*

The east end of Afonwen station, looking towards Portmadoc in 1960, with a train from Bangor in the LMS platform 3. Another ECS train is in the 'down' sidings with more carriage stock visible in the 'up' side sidings. The refreshment room adjacent to the foot-bridge was still in use at this time. *G. H. Platt*

A GWR permanent way inspection trolley stands at the western end of the 'up' platform at Afonwen. This photograph was taken before the second war. *Author's collection*

From the footbridge looking towards Portmadoc in 1936 with the afternoon freight standing in the machine siding awaiting departure.

G. H. Platt

GWR 2—6—2T No. 5570 pulling in to the 'down' main platform with a Portmadoc to Pwllheli freight in 1949. This train was scheduled to shunt for about an hour before resuming its journey. Once the brake van had cleared the points in the foreground the train set back, the van being left in the right hand siding. The stock would then be sorted so that Caernarvon line stock could be picked up by the afternoon freight from Menai Bridge. The Pwllheli freight would also collect any traffic left by the early morning freight from Caernarvon, usually empties, to be delivered to Pwllheli. Quite often there would be insufficient time to complete all the shunting, and some of the work was left for the afternoon freight turn to complete.

Eric Russell

LMR AND WR TRAFFIC MOVEMENTS AT AFONWEN STATION
Saturdays Only, 14th June to 19th September 1954
based on traffic survey taken on 24th July 1954

Reporting	Time	FROM	TO	arrive	depart	Region	Coaches	Circuit	Stock Formation, notes, etc	Stock disposal	Loco	Pilot	M.P.D.
	5.35	Pwllheli	Dovey Jn	pass	5.46	WR	4	32	Van 3rd, 3rd, Compo, Van 3rd.	works 8.14am Aberystwyth	4560		Pwllheli
	4.35	Bangor	Afonwen	5.39		LMR	8	327	6 corr. + 1–BG (Pwllheli) + 1–BG (Portmadoc)	works 6.37am Manchester Ex.	42588		Bangor
	6.00	Pwllheli	Portmadoc	6.11	6.25	WR	5	27d	Van 3rd, 3rd, Compo, 3rd, Van 3rd attatch 1–BG Manchester – Portmadoc	works 6.55am Barmouth	9004		Pwllheli
	6.03	Portmadoc	Pwllheli	6.18	6.25	WR	2	37	Br. 3rd, Compo.	works 1/35pm Portmadoc	2202		Portmadoc
							1	38	Br. Compo				
							1		attatch 1–BG Liverpool – Pwllheli	works 3/30pm to Euston			
W494		Afonwen	Manchester Ex		6.37	LMR	6	327	reformed at Bangor to 11 (+ circuit 328)	works 11.25am M/c. – Llandudno	42588		Bangor
	5.30	Bangor	Pwllheli	6.55	7.09	LMR	3	1232	Lav. set N.C.	works 8.10am Llan. Jn	42415		Bangor
							2	1982	TK				
freight	5.28	Caernarvon	Afonwen	7.25		LMR			Loco to Pwllheli East for ECS circuit 338	brake van to down side siding 2	42178		Bangor
ECS	7.30	Pwllheli	Afonwen	7.42		LMR	3	1232	Lav. set N.C.	works 8.10am Llandudno Jn	42415		Bangor
							2	1982	TK				
	7.15	Pwllheli	Paddington	pass	7.43	WR	9		Van 3rd, 3–3rd, Compo, 3–3rd, Van 3rd	as required Paddington.	7806		Portmadoc
LE		Afonwen	Pwllheli East	7.45		LMR			to collect ECS for 8.45am W164		42178		Bangor
2xLE	6.30	Bangor MPD	Penychain	7.50	8.12	LMR			to work & assist 8.45am Penychain – Stoke	take water on turntable road	42455	40086	Bangor
	7.40	Pwllheli	Dovey Jn.	7.52	7.58	WR	5	25	Van 3rd, Compo, 3rd, Van 3rd + 3rd.	works 11.05am Barmouth	2202		Pwllheli
	7.40	Portmadoc	Pwllheli	7.57	8.02	WR	5	30	Van 3rd, 3rd, Compo, Van 3rd.	works 11.30am Wrexham	9004		Pwllheli
		Afonwen	Llandudno Jn.		8.10	LMR	2	1982	TK	works 11.35am Bangor	42415		Bangor
							3	1232	Lav. set N.C.				
LE	7.18	Bangor MPD	Afonwen	8.30		LMR			to work 11.12am Manchester Exch.	to turntable road.	42444		Bangor
W164	8.45	Penychain	Stoke on Trent	8.48	9.02	LMR	10	338	RSD. not specified. Set alternates with 375	works 3/34pm ECS to Crewe.	40086	42455	Bangor
LE	7.25	Bangor MPD	Afonwen	8.49		LMR			to work 9.56am Manchester W138	take water on turntable road	42157		Bangor
LE cpld.	7.25	Bangor MPD	Afonwen	8.49		LMR			to Portmadoc LE to work 9.55am Euston		40130		Bangor
	8.45	Pwllheli	Birkenhead	pass	8.58	WR	5	29	Van 3rd, 3rd, Compo, Van 3rd.	work 5/07pm Barmouth	6371		Pwllheli
ECS	7.20	Llandudno Jn. C.S.	Penychain	9.20	9.40	LMR	10	RSD	to work 10.50am Penychain – Liverpool	to up side back road	41223	42416	Bangor
	6.50	Machynlleth	Pwllheli	pass	9.36	WR	5	27	Van 3rd, 3rd, Compo, 3rd, Van 3rd.	store till Monday 10.25am	78000		Machynlleth
ECS	7.50	Llandudno Jn. C.S.	Afonwen	9.42		LMR	10	748	to work 11.25am Penychain – Warrington	stock to up side sidings	41239	42460	Bangor
W138	9.40	Penychain	Manchester Ex.	9.43	9.56	LMR	10	339	stock from Pwllheli East. 42178 to assist	2/20pm ECS to Monton Green	42157	42178	Bangor
	9.35	Pwllheli	Paddington	pass	9.53	WR	8		Van 3rd, 2–Compo, 4–3rd, Br. Compo (Pilot loco 78002 Portmadoc–Machynlleth)	as required Paddington	2233		Portmadoc
W100	9.55	Portmadoc	Euston (A/wen)	10.10		LMR	4	RSD	B.R. Standard Stock.	work forward 10.25am Euston	40130		Bangor
W100	10.00	Pwllheli	Euston (A/wen)	10.10		LMR	3	RSD	B.R. Standard Stock.	work forward 10.25am Euston	4575		Pwllheli
W100		Afonwen	Euston	10.25	10.25	LMR	7	RSD	B.R. Standard Stock	works 11.15am Monday	40130		Bangor
	10.08	Pwllheli	Swansea	pass	10.22	WR	8		Van 3rd, 4–3rd, 2–Compo, Br. Compo	as required Swansea.	6378		Pwllheli
	9.00	Bangor	Afonwen	10.20		LMR	6	330	6 corr. not specified	works 10.45am Liverpool	42588		Bangor
	8.05	Machynlleth	Pwllheli	10.36	10.40	WR	4	24	Van 3rd, 3rd, Compo, Van 3rd.	works 12/45pm Birkenhead	9000		Pwllheli
cpld.		Afonwen	Pwllheli		10.40					after working 10.00am Euston		4575	Pwllheli
	10.25	Pwllheli	Dovey Jn.	10.37	10.41	WR	6	27a	Van 3rd, 3rd, Compo, Van 3rd. + 3rd	works 1/35pm Pwllheli	78000		Machynlleth
ECS	9.15	Bangor	Afonwen	10.43		LMR	11	RSD	to work 12/05pm Penychain – Liverpool	stock to Up Side sidings	40102	41200	Bangor
ECS		Afonwen	Penychain		10.45	LMR	10	748	to work 11.25am Penychain – Warrington	from Up Side sidings	42460	41239	Bangor
W454		Afonwen	Liverpool		10.45	LMR	6	330	strengthened to 11 at Bangor (+circuit 348) (Loco & crew working changed this day only: normally works 11.12am M/cter)	works 3/20pm ECS to Edge Hill	42444		Bangor
W142	10.50	Penychain	Liverpool	10.53	11.03	LMR	10	RSD	not specified. Corridor stock	ECS to Edge Hill.	42416	41223	Bangor
		Afonwen	Manchester		11.12	LMR	6	335	not specified. Stock from Down side sidings (Loco & crew working changed this day only: should work 10.45am Liverpool)	works 4/30pm M/c. – Llandudno	42588		Bangor
	11.10	Pwllheli	Birmingham	pass	11.23	WR	8		Van 3rd, 2–3rd, Compo, 2–3rd, Van 3rd.	as required Birmingham Snow Hill	2289		Portmadoc
W318	11.25	Penychain	Warrington	11.28	11.40	LMR	10	748	not specified. Corridor stock	works ECS to Grange Lane	42460	41239	Bangor
	7.03	Wrexham	Pwllheli	11.40	11.44	WR	3	31	Compo, Van 3rd, 3rd.	works 5/25pm to Chester	5319		Portmadoc
	11.30	Pwllheli	Wrexham	11.42	11.43	WR	5	30	Van 3rd, 3rd, Compo, Van 3rd.	works 12/25pm Pwllheli, Monday	2217		Pwllheli
ECS		Afonwen	Penychain		11.47	LMR	11	RSD	to work 12/05pm Penychain–Manchester	stock from Up Side sidings	41200	40102	Bangor
freight	8.20	Barmouth	Pwllheli East	12/00	12/10	WR					9013		Portmadoc
freight	11.40	Pwllheli East	Portmadoc	12/00	12/07	WR					9020		Pwllheli
W144	12/05	Penychain	Manchester	12/08	12/19	LMR	11	RSD	not specified. Corridor stock	Crewe to advise at Manchester	40102	41200	Bangor
W311	8.05	Manchester Ex.	Penychain	12/14	12/23	LMR	10	879	not specified. Corridor stock	works 12/37pm ECS to Llan. Jn.	42418	41212	Bangor
W325	8.15	Manchester Ex.	Penychain	12/38	12/45	LMR	10	367	not specified. Alternates with circuit 339	1/17pm ECS to Pwllheli East	42455	42233	Bangor
ECS	12/37	Penychain	Llandudno Jn.	12/40	1/05	LMR	10	879		RSD Crewe to advise disposal	42418	41212	Bangor
	11.23	Bangor	Pwllheli	12/52	1/02	LMR	3	1311	3 coach set. N.C.	works 1/45pm Pwllheli–Bangor	42415		Bangor
W355	10.15	Warrington	Penychain	1/26	1/36	LMR	10	928	E.R. stock. Huddersfield–Warrington w/f.	works 4/00pm ECS to Llan. Jn.	42178	40086	Bangor
	7.50	Birkenhead	Pwllheli	1/37	1/45	WR	4	24a	Van 3rd, Compo, 3rd, Van 3rd.	works 3/45pm Pwllheli–Dovey Jn.	7310		Pwllheli
W399	9.35	Liverpool	Penychain	1/43	1/53	LMR	12	RSD	not specified. Corridor stock.	works 2/20pm ECS to Holyhead	42175	40130	Bangor
	1/35	Pwllheli	Portmadoc	1/47	1/50	WR	2	37	Compo, Br. 3rd.	works 6.03am Monday	9013		Portmadoc
	1/45	Pwllheli	Bangor	1/57	2/07	LMR	3	1311	3 coach set. N.C.	works 3/55pm Bangor–Amlwch	42415		Bangor
	12/45	Bangor	Pwllheli	2/00	2/10	LMR	3	715	3rd, Compo, Van 3rd.	works 3/30pm Pwllheli–Llan. Jn	42444		Bangor
							3	1220	Lav. set N.C.	works 3/30pm Pwllheli–Llan. Jn			

LMR AND WR TRAFFIC MOVEMENTS AT AFONWEN STATION *continued*

Reporting	Time	FROM	TO	arrive	depart	Region	Coaches	Circuit	Stock Formation, notes, etc.	Stock disposal	Loco	Pilot	M.P.D.
2xLE	2/05	Penychain	Bangor MPD	2/08	2/20	LMR			after working 9.35am L/pool – Penychain		40130	42175	Bangor
ECS	2/20	Penychain	Holyhead	2/23	2/40	LMR	12	RSD	Reverses at Bangor. Holyhead loco & crew.	works 4/00pm Chester Sunday	42233	42455	Bangor
	11.00	Ruabon	Pwllheli	pass	2/36	WR	7	35	Van 3rd, 3-3rd, Compo, 3rd, Van 3rd.	works circuit 27 in week	7313		Pwllheli
W467	1/30	Llandudno Jn.	Penychain	3/20	3/30	LMR	6	375	not specified. Corridor stock	works 4/15pm ECS to Afonwen	42157		Bangor
	3/30	Pwllheli	Bangor	3/42	3/50	LMR	3	1220	Lav. set N.C.	works 5/40pm forward to Llan. Jn	42444		Bangor
							3	715	Van 3rd, Compo, 3rd.	works 5/40pm forward to Llan. Jn			
							1		BG. Pwllheli-Euston on W160	works 9/15pm forward to Crewe			
	1/35	Dovey Jn.	Pwllheli	3/45	3/50	WR	6	27a	Van 3rd, 3rd, Compo, 3rd, Van 3rd. + 3rd	works 6/40pm Pwllheli-Portmadoc	2271		Machynlleth
	3/45	Pwllheli	Dovey Jn.	3/58	4/00	WR	4	24a	Van 3rd, Compo, 3rd, Van 3rd.	works 7/13pm ECS to Machynlleth	9000		Pwllheli
ECS	4/00	Penychain	Llandudno Jn.	4/03	4/15	LMR	10	928	E.R. stock	works forward to Leeds as req'd.	40086	42178	Bangor
	11.05	Birmingham S.H.	Pwllheli	4/14	4/15	WR	8		Van 3rd, 2-3rd, 2-Compo, 2-3rd, Van 3rd.	store Pwllheli for 11.10am Sat.	2289		Portmadoc
ECS	4/15	Penychain	Afonwen	4/18		LMR	6	375	store Up Side sidings	works 7/05pm Afonwen-Bangor	42156		Bangor
	3/15	Bangor	Afonwen	4/34		LMR	3	1230	Lav. set N.C.	works 5/14pm Afonwen-Bangor	42588		Bangor
							2	2007	T	works 5/14pm Afonwen-Bangor			
	9.00	Paddington	Pwllheli	4/35	4/37	WR	9		Van 3rd, 3-3rd, Compo, 3-3rd, Van 3rd.	store Pwllheli for 7.15am Sat.	7802		Pwllheli
	4/30	Pwllheli	Portmadoc	4/41	4/45	WR	1	38	Br. Compo.	works 6.03am Monday	9009		Pwllheli
	10.20	Swansea	Pwllheli	pass	5/00	WR	8		Br. Compo, 2-Compo, 4-3rd, Van 3rd.	store Pwllheli for 10.08am Sat.	2298		Pwllheli
		Afonwen	Bangor		5/14	LMR	2	2007	T	spare at Bangor	42588	42157	Bangor
							3	1230	Lav. set. N.C.	works 7/45pm Bangor-Amlwch			
	4/00	Barmouth	Pwllheli	5/33	5/34	WR	4	25	Van 3rd, Compo, 3rd, Van 3rd.	works 7.40am Monday	4560		Pwllheli
	5/25	Pwllheli	Chester	5/36	5/38	WR	3	31	3rd, Van 3rd, Compo.	works 7.03am Monday	2271		Machynlleth
cpld	5/25	Pwllheli	Afonwen	5/36					to work 11.15am Euston-Afonwen-Portmadoc		2289		Portmadoc
W89	11.15	Euston	Afonwen	5/50		LMR	7	RSD	B.R. Standard stock	to Portmadoc & Pwllheli	42416		Bangor
	12.30	Birkenhead	Pwllheli	pass	5/53	WR	5	30	Van 3rd, 3rd, Compo, 3rd, Van 3rd.	works 8/15pm Pwllheli-Portmadoc	6337		Portmadoc
W89	11.15	Euston	Portmadoc		5/55	LMR	4	RSD	B.R. Standard stock	works 11.00am to Euston Monday	2289		Portmadoc
W89	11.15	Euston	Pwllheli		6/02	LMR	3	RSD	B.R. Standard stock	works 11.00am to Euston Monday	42416		Bangor
	10.50	Paddington	Pwllheli	pass	6/30	WR	6		Br. Compo, 3-3rd, Van 3rd.	works 9.35am Paddington Monday	78002		Portmadoc
LE	6/25	Pwllheli	Afonwen	6/35		LMR				works 7/05pm to Bangor	42416		Bangor
	6/40	Pwllheli	Portmadoc	6/57	6/58	WR	5	27a	Van 3rd, 3rd, Compo, 3rd, Van 3rd.	works 8/15pm Portmadoc-Barmouth	2298		Pwllheli
	2/55	Chester	Pwllheli	6/57	7/00	WR	5	29	Van 3rd, 3rd, Compo, 3rd, Van 3rd.	works 8.45am Birkenhead Monday	6371		Portmadoc
	5/39	Bangor	Afonwen	6/59		LMR	3	1316	3 coach set. N.C.	works 7/10pm ECS to Pwllheli	41324		Bangor
		Afonwen	Bangor		7/05	LMR	6	375	stock off 1/30pm Llan. Jn-Penychain	works 3/35pm Llan. Jn. Sunday	42416		Bangor
ECS		Afonwen	Pwllheli		7/10	LMR	3	1316	3 coach set N.C.	to work 7/40pm Pwllheli-Bangor	41324		Bangor
	7/40	Pwllheli	Bangor	7/51	8/13	LMR	3	1316	3 coach set. N.C.	works 6.35am Amlwch Monday	41324		Bangor
	8/15	Pwllheli	Portmadoc	8/27	8/34	WR	5	30	Van 3rd, 3rd, Compo, 3rd, Van 3rd.	works 7.40am Monday	9013		Portmadoc
	8/15	Portmadoc	Pwllheli	8/29	8/33	WR	5	27c	Van 3rd, 3rd, Compo, 3rd, Van 3rd.	works 6.00am Monday	9009		Pwllheli
	7/20	Bangor	Afonwen	8/32		LMR	4	RSD	Br. 3rd, 3rd, Compo, Br. 3rd. BTK+TK+CK+BTK	works 8/50pm to Bangor	42444		Bangor
		Afonwen	Bangor		8/50	LMR	4	RSD	BTK+CK+TK+BTK	works 4.35am Afonwen Monday	42444		Bangor
	6/55	Machynlleth	Pwllheli	9/28	9/29	WR	4	32	Van 3rd, 3rd, Compo, Van 3rd.	works 5.35am Dovey Jn. Monday	2202		Pwllheli

Notes:

Western Region.

Working of through coaches to and from Paddington, Birmingham Snow Hill, and Swansea taken from the 'Programme of Working of Coaches and Vans in Through Trains'.

Working of local services including Chester and Birkenhead, Wrexham and Ruabon to and from Pwllheli taken from the Central Wales District programme of 'Working of Coaches'.

Locomotive and train crew rostering taken from observations and records. Based on Pwllheli, Portmadoc and Machynlleth running sheds.

London Midland Region.

Working of through coaches to and from Liverpool Lime Street, Manchester Exchange, London Euston and Warrington taken from Western Division Passenger Train Marshalling Circular.

Working of special traffic to and from Butlins Camp at Penychain taken from R.S.D. notices and weekly R.S.D. notices of extra and altered traffic movements.

Working of special and extra locomotive workings taken from Western Division special trains notices for week 23rd July to 29th July 1954.

Working of Locomotive and train crew rostering from personal observations.

The working of the London Midland Region train 10.45am Afonwen to Liverpool, locomotive 42444 and the 11.12am Afonwen to Manchester Exchange working, locomotive 42588 were interchanged for this one day by the direction of Traffic Control at Chester. Normally the locomotive and crew of the 9.00am Bangor to Afonwen working would return with the 10.45am Afonwen to Liverpool working whilst the locomotive and crew working the 7.18am LE from Bangor to Afonwen would work the 11.12am Afonwen to Manchester Exchange trip. The reason for this exchange was not known by either of the train crews.

The stock for the 11.12am Afonwen to Manchester Exchange was taken from Llandudno Jn. to Afonwen with an extra ECS working on Friday 23rd July 1954 and left in the Down Side sidings overnight. The time of the working was 3/50pm from Llandudno Jn. arrive Afonwen 7/15pm. The locomotive worked back to Bangor LE departing 7/45pm.

The two ECS workings from Llandudno Jn. to Penychain were worked from there by two sets of locomotives working LE from Bangor to Llandudno Jn. and working through to Penychain. The 1/30pm Llandudno Jn. to Penychain working W467 was also worked from Llandudno Junction by Bangor locomotive and crew. The workings from Manchester, Liverpool and Warrington to Penychain involved changing locomotives and crews at Bangor, and all return workings, both special and ECS involved changing locomotives on their return to Bangor. The 2/20pm from Penychain to Holyhead ECS ran to Bangor and Holyhead crew and locomotive worked from there to Holyhead. The 9.35am Liverpool Lime Street to Penychain was strengthened to 12 coaches and Control decided that the two locomotives that brought the train from Bangor (40130 + 42175) would work back 2xLE from Penychain to Bangor MPD. The locomotives and crew of the W325 8.15am Manchester Exchange to Penychain (42455 + 42233) would work back from Pwllheli East 2xLE to Penychain and work the ECS back to Bangor. The working was not shown in the working timetable but was included in the Weekly Traffic Notices instead.

The Saturday duties at Bangor were prepared according to Traffic requirements on Fridays. Normal scheduled turns were adhered to, wherever possible, although crews were offered overtime. The extra work was covered by passed cleaners, passed firemen etc wherever possible. Only Bangor men worked over the Afonwen line and outsiders were kept to the main line.

The divergence of the Llanberis and Afonwen lines at Seiont Bridge, 1 mile south of Caernarvon. The Llanberis branch is the nearest to the camera in the top view and the left-hand line in the bottom view.

Author & J. M. Dunn

THE
LLANBERIS BRANCH

IN the 1860s three schemes were proposed to link Llanberis with the main line, but the LNWR, who were approached by the slate owners, were unresponsive, and it was left to independent companies to raise the required capital. Two of the proposals were to connect Llanberis with Caernarvon whilst the third was to link the valley with Bangor, but it was the second Bill which received the Royal Assent. The ceremonial cutting of the first sod was conducted on 15th September 1864 at Llanberis. Despite this, there was another attempt to link Llanberis with Bangor in 1865 which failed for technical reasons.

By 1866 the independent undertaking was in financial difficulties and the LNWR offered to purchase and complete the line, with veiled threats to resurrect the line to Bangor direct should the Carnarvon and Llanberis Board prove stubborn. Bickering and argument continued but eventually the Carnarvon and Llanberis line became directly under the control of Euston, on a joint ownership basis, finally being vested in the LNWR by Act of Parliament in July 1870. The branch was inspected in June 1869 and was opened by the LNWR on 1st July that year. The station at the Caernarvon end was initially a temporary structure, known as 'Morfa', located south of the castle, near the quay. The LNWR constructed a line underneath the Castle Square parallel to the Afonwen line, linking the C & L and the Afonwen branch with the LNWR main line at the former Bangor & Carnarvon Railway station site. The Morfa station was removed when permission to run trains through to the B & C station was granted in January 1871.

Details of the early struggles to establish Llanberis on the railway network can be found in Peter E. Baughan's *A Regional History of Railways Volume 11 North & Mid Wales*, published by David & Charles.

The life of the branch was uneventful. The earliest services consisted of five trains each way daily. Seasonal traffic soon built up, especially after the opening of the Snowdon Mountain Railway and, due to the tourist traffic, observation cars were added to trains in the summer months early in the present century. Nevertheless, the general traffic passenger receipts were less than satisfactory and from 1st April 1914 a rail motor operated the service. Further economies were forced on the line during the 1914-18 war, and on 1st January 1917 Pontrûg station was closed for the duration. It re-opened in July 1919, but the days of the regular passenger service on the branch were numbered. Road services had developed in the period after the war to such an extent that the passenger service was withdrawn as from 22nd September 1930. However, the line continued to be used for excursion traffic with some

measure of success. To attract traffic, a halt was erected at a point west of the Llanberis terminal, called Padarn Halt. The intermediate stations of Pontrûg, Pontrhythallt and Cwm y Glo were used occasionally but were not shown in the public timetables. All passenger traffic ceased during the Second World War, although there was an increase of freight due to the establishment of a bomb assembly unit and stores at the Glynrhonwy quarry, between Cwm y Glo and Llanberis. A network of sidings was laid and extensively used until the end of hostilities, when traffic gradually fell away.

After the war, excursion traffic returned in a very limited way, being restricted to through workings from Prestatyn and Rhyl, with one train a day on three days a week. A short return working from Llanberis to Caernarvon allowed crews to be changed and the locomotive to be serviced, an arrangement which persisted until the excursions were withdrawn. Freight traffic was finally withdrawn on 7th September 1964 having run as a single train on three days a week. Track was lifted from Llanberis towards Caernarvon in 1965, using rail hauled wagons throughout.

The trackbed is still largely intact, although some bridges have disappeared, and at Llanberis the route is now part of a by-pass for the village. The station buildings are intact at Llanberis, although the goods shed has been demolished, whilst at Cwm y Glo, the whole station site has been flattened. Pontrhythallt station is now a private house, externally unaltered, while the station house at Pontrûg is also still standing.

ROUTE DESCRIPTION

For the first mile, the line ran parallel to the Afonwen branch, but without any physical connection outside Caernarvon station limits. The two single lines fell away sharply, descending under Turf Square and Castle Square, before levelling off on emerging from Caernarvon tunnel. At one time there was a halt here, a residue from when the line was independent, and before the connecting line to the LNWR station was made. Both lines climbed from here for a half mile to the point where they parted company. The Afonwen line continued to climb, but the Llanberis branch fell away, passing under the Pwllheli road, by Seiont bridge (1¼ miles). Here the line levelled out and swung very sharply left, whilst a siding ran off for the Seiont Mill and the brickworks. Half a mile further on the line crossed the River Seiont and just beyond a siding for Peblig Mill branched off to the left (1¾ miles). Traffic to the Seiont flour mill and Peblig Mill virtually ceased before the war, although when

No. 42617 near Pontrûg returning to Caernarvon with a two coach articulated set after working a morning excursion from Rhyl to Llanberis in 1952.
Author

the Peblig Mill site was developed into a munitions factory during the war, some materials were brought in by rail. These sidings were both serviced by 'up' trains returning from Llanberis.

Between Peblig and Pontrûg the line crossed the River Seiont a further six times, climbing steadily in the process. Pontrûg station, 3½ miles from Caernarvon, was a simple affair, with a short, low platform on the 'up' side. There was a shed of standard LNWR pattern with a booking office and waiting room on the platform for passengers, although it was unlikely that there would have been many due to the sparsity of nearby housing. The station master had a house on site.

The climb continued for a further mile before easing off slightly. At 5½ miles, Jones' Siding branched off on the left hand side to serve a slate products mill. The line crossed the River Seiont yet again at 5¾ miles and ran in to Pont-rhythallt station.

Pontrhythallt was the intermediate block post, and single line tokens were exchanged here. The blue train staff for Caernarvon-Pontrhythallt was exchanged for the red Pontrhythallt-Llanberis staff. Despite the sparsity of traffic, the station buildings were quite substantial, similar in design to Cwm y Glo and Llanberis. There was a single platform face, which could only accommodate four coaches although this was usually sufficient. Freight traffic was also

Between Padarn Lake Halt and Glynrhonwy sidings the line passed under a private footbridge of unusual ornate design. This view was taken looking towards Llanberis. *Author*

rather limited in capacity and, despite the fact that it was a token exchange point, there were specific instructions that trains were *not* to cross in the station.

The gradient evened out still further between Pont-rhythallt and Cwm y Glo, which was a mile further on. The line made a sweeping curve before passing under the Caernarvon-Llanberis road and running into the station. The buildings were on the 'down' side, again served by a short platform of low height. The two sidings, one of which served a goods shed, were serviced by 'down' trains. Traffic here was mainly incoming coal. Despite the closure to regular traffic in 1930, both Cwm y Glo and Pont-rhythallt stations had a thriving business in local excursion traffic especially in the summer months.

Once clear of the station, the line passed through some of the most beautiful countryside in the British Isles. Llyn Padarn was approached, half a mile beyond Cwm y Glo, and on emerging from a short tunnel, the line ran alongside the lake and, passing on a causeway, made its way to a rocky outcrop known as Pen Gilfach, where a cutting was made, before opening out to expose the complex known as Glynrhonwy Sidings. This was situated on the 'up' side 8¼ miles from Caernarvon and before the war served the local slate quarries. However, these closed during the depression and the network remained out of service. During the last war the quarries were adapted to form an underground bomb store and facilities were updated and the track layout rearranged. The complex was a joint civilian and services unit, the civilian side being known as 'Nicaco' whilst the military establishment was designated 'RAF Llanberis'. Traffic reached a peak during the latter days of the war, with two freight trains daily handling traffic. Naturally on cessation of the hostilities the traffic dwindled to nothing, but the quarry was used again, this time to dispose of surplus ammunition which was exploded in the open pits. This process continued for about five years after the war before stocks were exhausted.

When the complex was finally closed, British Railways made use of the sidings for the storage of passenger coaches out of season.

A further half mile towards Llanberis was Padarn Lake Halt, built in 1936 to cater for local and tourist traffic, and 400 yards beyond that was Llanberis station, the terminus of the line. Even the platform at Llanberis was of short length although there was a very narrow extension adjoining the north end. This was in fact the ticket platform, where trains would stop first while the tickets were collected. When this had been done, the train drew up the 100 feet or

Seen from the road above Llanberis tunnel, looking over the causeway to Llanberis, steam in the far distance reveals the approach of the evening excursion to Rhyl, hauled by No. 42617.
Author

LNWR 2—4—2T No. 620 of Llanberis shed on a local working to Caernarvon, crossing the causeway on Llyn Padarn.

Passengers inside the observation car in 1938.   *J. M. Dunn*

so to allow passengers to alight at the station. With longer trains the extension served in the more normal capacity, the only problem being to persuade passengers not to try to climb up to the coaches from the bottom of the ramp.

The station buildings were more extensive than Cwm y Glo or Pontrhythallt, incorporating extra staff accommodation. There was also a substantial goods shed, and at one time an engine shed, water tower and turntable.

OPERATION

Up until 1921, there was always one engine shedded at Llanberis to work most of the turns. Details of the earliest locomotives have not come to light but LNWR No. 620 was based in the village for many years. This was a Webb 2—4—2T which became LMS No. 6702, although it had moved from the district by 1929. A rake of four 6-wheeled coaches made up the usual set and was probably more than sufficient for local needs. As already recorded, a rail motor was drafted in to work the branch from 1914 onwards and, from verbal accounts of drivers who were based at Caernarvon shed before grouping, the unit was worked by Caernarvon men on a complex roster which involved trips to Nantlle and Bethesda as well as Llanberis. The unit was out of the district in 1925, but whether it ever returned has not been established. There is also an unconfirmed report that a petrol railcar was tried very briefly at some date and there is a photograph on page 155 of such a vehicle at Penygroes, working the Nantlle branch.

When Llanberis shed closed, the work passed to Caernarvon and the locomotive diagrams were more intensively rostered. A train crew might work from Caernarvon to Llanberis with a passenger turn, back to Bangor, then on to Bethesda and return, spending some time on 'Bangor station shunt'. They were then relieved by Bangor men who would take the locomotive and stock to Afonwen, and return to Bangor, before being relieved by another crew from Caer-

narvon, who would work through to Llanberis and back to Caernarvon.

This local working was modified when Caernarvon shed closed in 1931 and Bangor took over responsibility for the work. There was a Llanberis link, but this was a very general group and did not last beyond a couple of seasons. As the work contracted, trips on the branch were scattered amongst the links generally, including the No. 1 link that worked 'the Welshman' from Caernarvon to Euston and return. The Second World War cut out many lodging turns as well as many poorly patronized trips, and the two daily turns on the Llanberis line were covered by No. 1 or No. 2 links. Drivers from No. 3 link maintained route knowledge with one trip every ten weeks on a Wednesday.

After the war, the daily freight trip was covered by No. 2 link, except on Wednesdays when No. 1 link worked the turn. With the return of the summer excursions, more men were upgraded from the lower links. The No. 2 link was made up from ten sets to twelve for the summer season. Turn 241 worked the daily goods in 1955 departing Bangor at 6.25 a.m. The excursion from Rhyl to Llanberis and the return working were always Bangor No. 2 link turns. Until 1956 they were extra duties and, un-numbered, expanded the link from ten to twelve sets for the summer season. In 1956 the work was included in the locomotive and carriage working diagrams and allocated turn and circuit numbers. In 1957 the Rhyl to Llanberis working was by turn 61, and the return working by turn 62. The coaching diagram indicates a set of seven coaches including an observation car. The circuit number varied each day, as the working was listed as an RSD notice. The working circuit numbers for the stock was as follows:

Monday	circuit 1499	Thursday	circuit 1719
Tuesday	circuit 1585	Friday	circuit 182
Wednesday	circuit 1659		

On Saturday the stock, less the observation car, worked on circuit 741 together with circuit 742, totalling ten vehicles to Chester. Circuit 741 then worked forward to Leek via Crewe and Stoke, arriving at 2.22 p.m. It returned ECS to Crewe at 2.35 p.m., arriving there at 3.38 p.m. It then formed the 4.25 p.m. to Bangor, arriving at 6.48 p.m. and was then worked empty stock to Rhyl, arriving at 8.20 p.m. The stock was cleaned and serviced on the Sunday.

The crew booked on at 6.40 a.m., working the 7.25 a.m. to Llandudno Junction, then the 8.20 a.m. to Llandudno Town. From there they worked the 8.40 a.m. to Rhyl, and picked up the stock for the excursion, which they worked with the same engine, right through to Llanberis, arriving there at 11.18 a.m. At one time, the crew brought the locomotive and the observation car back to Caernarvon where they cleaned the fire, and were relieved by Bangor men on turn 62. The fresh crew returned with the locomotive and coach to Llanberis at 3.00 p.m. After watering and trimming the coal, they departed for Rhyl at 5.20 p.m. and, having stabled the stock, worked back light engine to Bangor.

LLANBERIS BRANCH—(Single Line).

Train Staff Stations—Carnarvon, Pontrhythallt, and Llanberis.

A Passenger Train cannot cross another Passenger Train on this Branch.

Miles.	WEEK DAYS—DOWN.	1	2	3	4	5	6	7	8	9	10	11	12	13	14
		Goods See Note.	Mixed	Seas'n Excursion.	Goods 9	Pass.	Pass.	Eng. and Van.	Pass.	Pass.	Pass.				
		a.m.	a.m.	a.m.	a.m.	a.m.	p.m.	p.m.	p.m.	p.m.	p.m.				
...	CARNARVON ...dep.	7 0	9 25	9 50	10 50	11 25	12 35	...	4 35	6 35	8 31	...	...	...	...
1¼	Glan Morfa Siding......	7 15	..	...	X	...	...	...	...	...	...	...	...	...	...
1¾	Peblig Siding	...	...	...	...	...	...	...	...	...	...	...	...	...	...
3½	Pont Rug............	...	9 36	...	...	...	12 46	...	4 46	6 46	8 41	...	...	...	...
5¾	Pontrhythallt ... arr.	7 30	9 44	10 §2	11 10	11 37	12 54	...	4 54	6 54	8 49	...	...	...	...
	dep	...	9 45	10 §2	12 10	11 38	12 55	...	4 55	6 55	8 50	...	...	...	...
6¾	Cwm-y-Glo	C	9 50	Collect Carnarvon	12 20	...	1 0	...	5 0	7 0	8 55	...	...	...	...
8¼	Glynrhonwy Siding ...		...		X	...	...	1 30	...	...	...	...	...	...	...
	Ticket Stage ...... arr.	...	9 56		...	11 44	1 4	...	5 4	7 4	8 59	...	...	...	...
	dep.	...	9 57		...	11 45	1 5	...	5 5	7 5	9 0	...	...	...	...
9	LLANBERIS(forS)arr	...	9 58	10 13	12 30	11 46	1 6	1 35	5 6	7 6	9 1	...	...	...	...

No. 2—The Engine of this Train to perform any shunting required at Llanberis.

No. 4—To call at Glynrhonwy Siding when required to detach, and No. 21 when required to attach.

No. 4 to make a trip to Glynrhonwy Siding after arrival of the 12.35 p.m. Passenger Train from Carnarvon (see Nos. 7 and 19).

Miles.	WEEK DAYS—UP.	15	16	17	18	19	20	21	22	23	24	25	26	27	28
		Pass.	Goods See note	Pass.	Pass.	Goods	Pass.	Goods 9	Pass.	Seas'n Excur	Pass.	Pass.			
		a.m.	a.m.	a.m.	p.m.	p.m.	p.m.	p.m.	p.m.	p.m.	p.m.	p.m.			
...	LLANBERIS (for Snowdon) dep.	7 45	C	10 20	11 55	1 10	2 20	2 35	4 0	5 50	6 0	7 50			
¾	Glynrhonwy Siding ..	...		...	...	1 15	...	X	...	C	...	...			
2¼	Cwm-y-Glo...............	7 50	...	10 25	12 0	...	2 25	3 0	4 5		6 5	7 55			
3¼	Pontrhythallt ... arr.	7 54	...	10 29	12 4	...	2 29	3 5	4 9	5§57	6 9	7 59			
	dep.	7 55	8 10	10 30	12 5	...	2 30	3 20	4 10	5§57	6 10	8 0			
3⅝	Jones Siding	...	...	...	...	...	...	X	...	...	...	...			
5½	Pont Rug.................	8 2	...	10 37	12 12	...	2 37	...	4 17	...	6 17	8 7			
7¼	Peblig Siding	...	X	...	...	...	...	X	...	...	...	...			
7¾	Seiont Mill Siding......	...	X	...	...	...	...	X	...	...	...	...			
9	CARNARVON ...arr.	8 10	8 50	10 46	12 20	...	2 45	3 50	4 28	6 9	6 25	8 15			

No. 21 to stop at Cwm-y-Glo for Tranship purposes

Nos. 1 & 16 are regular on Mondays, Tuesdays, Wednesdays, and Fridays.

Extract from LNWR service timetable – July, August & September 1904

Carnarvon and Llanberis—Single Line.

Train Staff Stations—Carnarvon, Pontrhythallt and Llanberis.

A Passenger Train cannot cross another Passenger Train on this Branch.

Miles.	WEEK DAYS—Down.	1	2	3	4	5	6	7	8	9	10	11	12	13	14
		Motor	Motor	Motor	G Goods			Motor	Motor	Motor	Motor		Motor		Motor
		a.m.	a.m	a.m.	a.m.			p.m.	p.m.	p.m.	p.m.		p.m.		p.m.
	CARNARVON ...dep.	6 55	8 2	9 23	9 45	...	...	12 50	2 30	4 0	6 15	...	8 10	...	10 0
1⅜	Glan Morfa Siding....	...	...	H C	X	...	...	...	...	...	H C	...	...	...	SO
1¾	Peblig Siding	...	...	...	...	...	...	...	...	...	...	...	...	...	...
3½	Pont Rug............	7 7	...	9 35	...	...	...	1 2	2 42	4 12	6 27	...	8 22	...	10 12
5¾	Pontrhythallt ... arr.	7 13	8 15	9 41	10 5	...	...	1 8	2 48	4 18	6 33	...	8 28	...	10 18
	dep	7 14	8 16	9 42	10 15	...	...	1 9	2 49	4 19	6 34	...	8 29	...	10 19
6⅞	Cwm-y-Glo	7 19	8 21	9 47	10 35	...	...	1 14	2 54	4 24	6 39	...	8 34	...	10 24
8¼	Glynrhonwy Siding ...	...	...	...	...	...	...	...	...	...	...	...	...	...	..
8½	Hickmans Siding	...	...	...	...	...	...	...	...	...	...	...	...	...	
	Ticket Stage ... arr.	7 23	8 25	9 51	...	...	...	1 18	2 58	4 28	6 43	...	8 38	...	10 28
	dep.	7 24	8 26	9 52	...	...	...	1 19	2 59	4 29	6 44	...	8 39	...	10 29
9	LLANBERIS(forS)arr	7 25	8 27	9 53	10 45	...	...	1 20	3 0	4 30	6 45	...	8 40	...	10 30

Miles.	WEEK DAYS—Up.	15	16	17	18	19	20	21	22	23	24	25	26	27	28
		Motor	Motor		Motor	G Goods	X—Calls at Cwm-y-Glo to attach Live Stock only.	Motor	Motor	Motor		Motor		Motor	Motor
	LLANBERIS (for Snowdon) dep.	a.m. 7 30	a.m. 8 30	...	a.m. 11 0	a.m. 11 25		p.m. 1 35	p.m. 3 5	p.m. 4 35	...	p.m. 6 50	...	p.m 8 45	p.m. 10 35
½	Hickmans Siding	H C	...	...	H C	...		...	...	...	...	...	...	...	SO
¾	Glynrhonwy Siding ..	...	...	...	...	11 59		...	...	...	...	...	...	...	...
2⅛	Cwm-y-Glo...............	7 35	8 35	...	11 5	X		1 40	3 10	4 40	...	6 55	...	8 52	10 42
3¼	Pontrhythallt ... arr.	7 39	8 39	...	11 10	12 0		1 44	3 14	4 44	...	6 59	...	8 57	10 47
	dep.	7 40	8 40	...	11 11	12 10		1 45	3 15	4 45	...	7 0	...	8 58	10 48
3⅜	Jones Siding	...	...	...	...	X		...	...	...	...	...	...	...	...
5½	Pont Rug.................	7 46	8 46	...	11 17	...		1 51	3 21	4 51	...	7 6	...	9 7	10 57
7¼	Peblig Siding	...	...	...	...	X		...	...	...	...	...	...	...	...
7⅜	Seiont Mill Siding......	...	...	...	...	X		...	...	...	...	...	...	...	...
9	CARNARVON ...arr.	7 55	8 55	...	11 26	12 45		2 0	3 30	5 0	...	7 15	...	9 17	11 7

Extract from LNWR service timetable for 1922

Towards the end of the branch's days, men on turn 61 worked through at 1.05 p.m. to Bangor, and were relieved on shed by those on turn 62, who signed on at 2.15 and departed off shed at 2.40 p.m.

For the excursions, Stanier class '4' tanks were used, usually Nos. 42460, 42588 or 42628 in 1952-4, and latterly No. 42444 or 42544.

By 1957, many of the Stanier engines were replaced by the standard British Railways class '4MT', the batch at Bangor being numbered 80088-92. On several occasions in that period, however, the solitary Fowler 2–6 4T No. 42415 was rostered. Despite having cab doors, it was preferred to the standard classes, and was certainly a stronger engine.

The goods workings were usually covered with one of the two Fowler 0–6–0 locomotives, either No. 44445 or 44305. On odd occasions it would be a class '4MT' and, if the crew were in luck, a class '5' 4–6–0. On two occasions

No. 45144 was scheduled and made very short work of the job. The 'goods' spent some time shunting at Caernarvon, before ambling on, spending half an hour in Pontrhythallt and another half an hour at Cwm y Glo, before reaching Llanberis at 10.10 a.m. The usual procedure was to clear all work in the yard before cleaning the fire and having 'a cup and a bite'. The return working left Llanberis at 11.05 a.m. and, after waiting time at Cwm y Glo again and more time at Pontrhythallt, would arrive at Cacrnarvon at 12.50 p.m. After a half hour wait to clear the yard and park the wagons, the crew would work light engine back to Bangor.

The only unconfirmed reports of a DMU working on the branch are of three Sunday afternoon excursions in 1956 which were unadvertised and consequently poorly patronized. Even the demolition trains were steam hauled right up to the end. Ironically, it was Llandudno Junction men and locomotives that worked these.

No. 42444 of Bangor shed heels over on the sharp curve by Seiont Mill sidings with the morning excursion from Rhyl to Llanberis. The locomotive was based at Bangor and worked to Rhyl each morning before returning on this trip.   *Author*

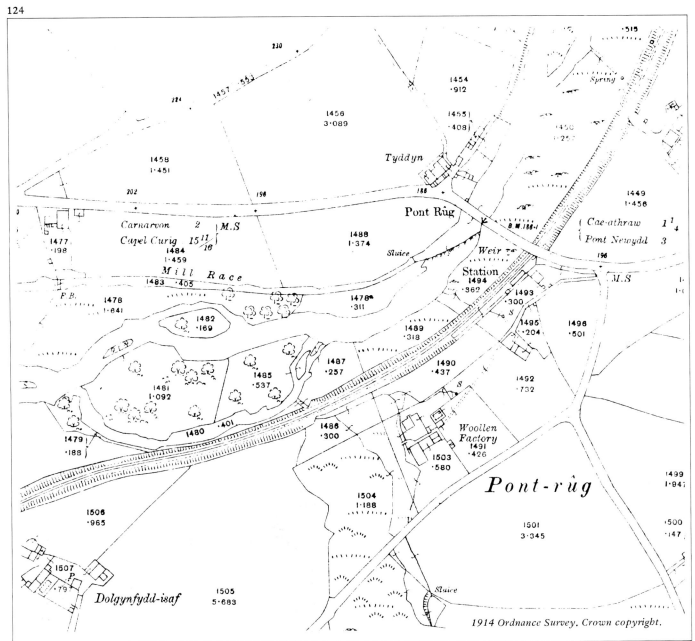

230

1457 531

234

1456
3·089

1458
1·451

202

196

186

1454
·912

1455
·408

Tyddyn

·515

Spring

1450
·252

1449
1·456

Pont Rûg

Carnarvon 2 M.S
Capel Curig 15 11/16

1477
·198

1484
1·459

1488
1·374

8 M.186·1

Sluice

Weir

Cae-athraw 1 1/4
Pont Newydd 3

196

Mill Race

1483
·405

F.B.

1478
1·641

1482
·169

1478a
·311

Station
1494
·362

M.S

1493
·300

S

1489
·318

1495
·204

1496
·501

1481
1·092

1485
·537

1487
·257

1490
·437

S

1492
·732

1479
·188

1480 ·401

1486
·300

Woollen
Factory
1491
·426

1503
·580

Pont-rûg

1499
1·947

1506
·965

1504
1·188

1501
3·345

·500
·147

1507
P
·79

Dolgynfydd-isaf

1505
5·683

Sluice

1914 Ordnance Survey. Crown copyright.

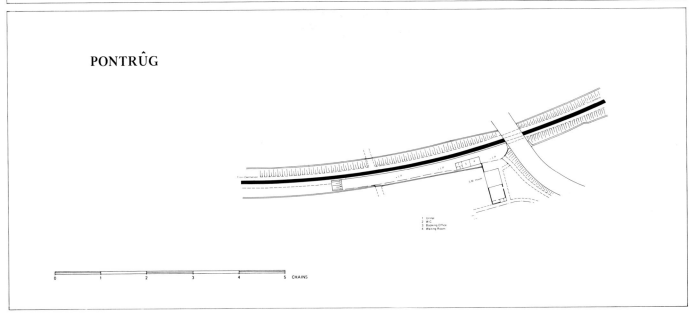

PONTRÛG

From Carnarvon

8 M. House

1. Urinal
2. W.C.
3. Booking Office
4. Waiting Room

0   1   2   3   4   5   CHAINS

Although poor in quality, this photograph has been included as it is the only known view of Pontrûg station. It shows a typical train, probably hauled by locomotive No. 620, which was based at Llanberis for many years.
Collection Author

Pontrûg

Pontrûg opened on 1st June 1880 about eleven months after the opening of the branch. It was located at a convenient meeting point for various hamlets but at the time of the opening, there was no settlement at Pontrûg. Consequently traffic was almost non-existent.

The station, such as it was, consisted of a single timber platform on the 'up' side, 250 feet long, with a single wooden hut containing a booking office and waiting room and a station master's house. As it was located in a cutting, crossed at the Llanberis end by the Caernarvon to Llanberis road, the station was apparently difficult to sight from the footplate, and its short length could have provided problems for long trains. Perhaps, fortunately for the drivers, long trains were uncommon on the branch so the problem rarely arose.

Due to poor support, the station closed temporarily from 1st January 1917 until July 1919. It finally closed in 1930 when regular passenger traffic ceased on the branch. There was no demand for excursion traffic to stop here, and the station had been demolished by 1938.

There were no freight facilities at Pontrûg.

Distance from Caernarvon:	3 miles 900 yds up direction; next token point
Distance from Pontrhythallt:	2 miles 320 yds down direction; next token point

Running time from Pontrûg:
up direction
    passenger trains — 8 minutes to Caernarvon
down direction
    passenger trains — 5 minutes to Pontrhythallt

Gradient leaving station:	*up direction*	1:57 falling
	down direction	1:57 rising

Intermediate sidings:
up direction	Peblig Mill siding
	Seiont Mill siding
	Glan Morfa siding
down direction	Jones' siding

Token for Caernarvon-Pontrhythallt section — coloured blue, Large staff.

126

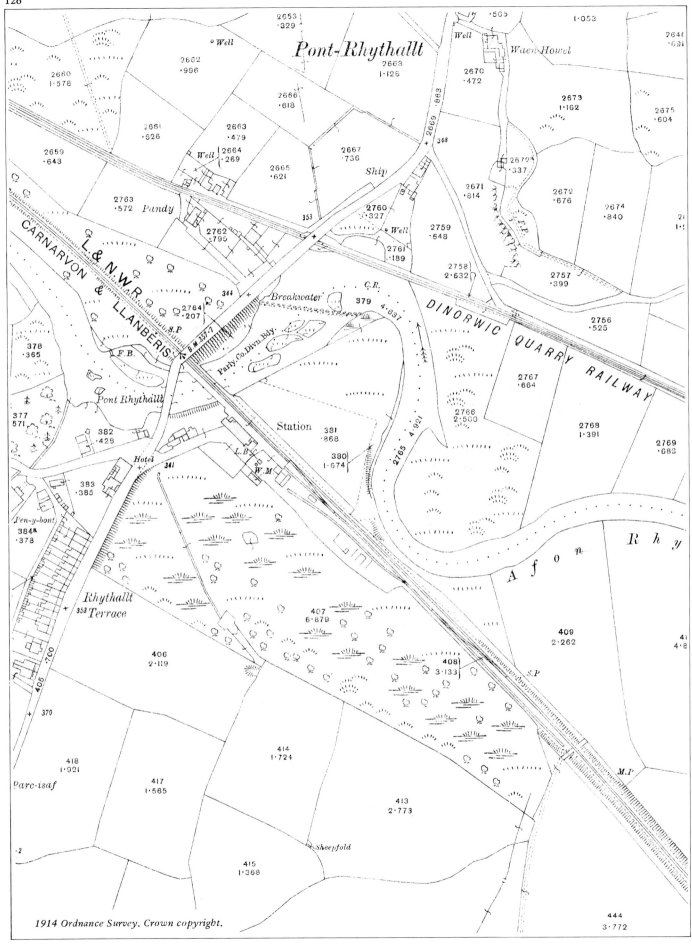

Pontrhythallt station in 1952, taken from the Penisarwaen road bridge, looking towards Llanberis. The shortened platform can be clearly seen, as can the wide bridge abutments, which formerly held the wooden platform extension.   *Author*

Pontrhythallt

Brought into use just after the line opened, Pontrhythallt was first listed in October 1869. It was the intermediate token exchange point between Caernarvon and Llanberis, but, despite this, there were no facilities for passenger trains to cross here, although it is on record that a freight train was once shunted into the yard to enable an excursion to pass.

The station platform was originally 320 feet in length and was carried across the river on the support piers for the railway bridge. The wooden extension was cut back just after the second war to 180 feet which caused minor complications when four coach excursions were picking up or setting down passengers.

The station building, of similar design to Cwm y Glo and Llanberis, incorporated a station master's house, and was constructed of the same dressed granite blocks.

The six lever frame was mounted on the platform at the Caernarvon end, whilst the token instruments were to be found in the office. The levers controlled signals only, points to the goods yard being controlled by two lever frames mounted by the points and locked by a key on the train staff. The goods yard was small, and never very busy. Coal was the main import, with some livestock being

Distance from Pontrûg:	2 miles 420 yards up direction; next station
Distance from Caernarvon:	5 miles 1299 yards up direction; next token point
Distance from Cwm y Glo:	1 mile 69 yards down direction; next station
Distance from Llanberis:	3 miles 364 down direction; next token point

Running time:
up direction
    passenger trains — 5 minutes to Pontrûg
    freight trains — 40 minutes to Caernarvon
down direction
    passenger trains — 4 minutes to Cwm y Glo
    freight trains — 5 minutes to Cwm y Glo
Intermediate siding: Jones' siding 487 yards
Gradient leaving station: *up direction*   1:358 falling
                                                  down direction   1:358 rising
Single Line Tokens
    Pontrhythallt-Caernarvon No. 2 — Large staff coloured blue
    Pontrhythallt-Llanberis — Large staff coloured red

handled from time to time, and there was a very small goods shed, but this was removed some time before 1952. There was also a small fixed crane in use in the goods yard, although this too had fallen into disrepair by 1952.

128

Taken from the road overbridge at Pontrhythallt, looking back to Caernarvon, showing the track that was relaid shortly before closure.
Author

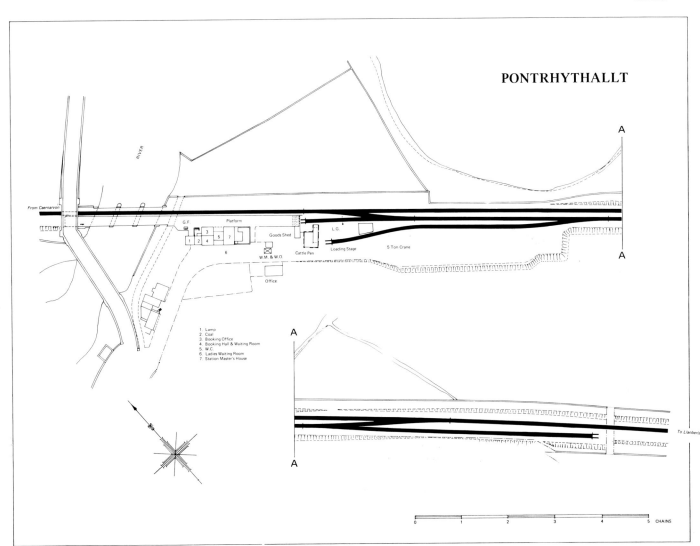

PONTRHYTHALLT

1. Lamp
2. Coal
3. Booking Office
4. Booking Hall & Waiting Room
5. W.C.
6. Ladies Waiting Room
7. Station Master's House

Pontrhythallt station, taken from the road bridge over the Padarn Railway.

Author

Pontrhythallt station, taken from the platform and looking towards Caernarvon.

D. Thompson

The goods yard at Pontrhythallt, taken from the coal stack and looking towards Caernarvon. *Author*

The south yard access, looking towards Llanberis. *Author*

Looking towards Caernarvon with the last freight train unloading at Pontrhythallt on 3rd September 1964. The locomotive is No. 42489 of Bangor shed.

Author's collection

In happier times, No. 42260 of Bangor shed leans into the curve as it takes the broad sweep under the road bridge and past Cwm y Glo station on its way to Llanberis in 1952.   *Author*

Cwm y Glo station viewed from the road overbridge, looking towards Llanberis in 1952.   *Author*

Cwm y Glo

Cwm y Glo opened for traffic on 1st July 1869 and served several surrounding villages including Cwm y Glo itself. It was situated partly in a cutting, access being made through a rocky outcrop, which was also bridged by the Caernarvon to Llanberis road. It was similar in design to Pontrhythallt, but with the living accommodation centrally located and without the platform canopy. The platform was fairly short, being approximately 320 feet in length. Like all stations on the line, the platform height was low, and portable steps were available. However, there was always much more passenger traffic here than at the other intermediate stations, and a public house was built close by, as was a small shop at the entrance to the station.

The goods yard, serviced by down trains, had two sidings serving a large stone goods shed and coal wharves.

There were no signals, and points were controlled by a ground frame unlocked by a key on the train staff for the Pontrhythallt to Llanberis section.

After the Second World War, the excursion traffic generated locally declined and few trains called at the station other than the 'goods'.

The site was cleared a few years ago for road improvements and the track bed is now incorporated in the main Caernarvon to Llanberis road.

Distance from Pontrhythallt: 1 mile 69 yards up direction; next token point

Distance from Padarn Lake Halt: 1 mile 1581 yards down direction; next station

Running time from Cwm y Glo:
up direction
passenger trains – 3 minutes to Pontrhythallt
freight trains – 5 minutes to Pontrhythallt
down direction
passenger trains – 4 minutes to Padarn Lake Halt
freight trains – 10 minutes to Llanberis

Intermediate sidings:
down direction Glynrhonwy siding 1 mile 1100 yards
Hickman's siding as above

Gradient leaving station: *up direction* 1:144 rising
down direction 1:144 falling

Intermediate station in Pontrhythallt to Llanberis token section.

No. **75009** of Llandudno Junction shed stands at Cwm y Glo platform with a demolition train before returning to Caernarvon with a 'Junction' train crew in charge.

E. N. Kneale

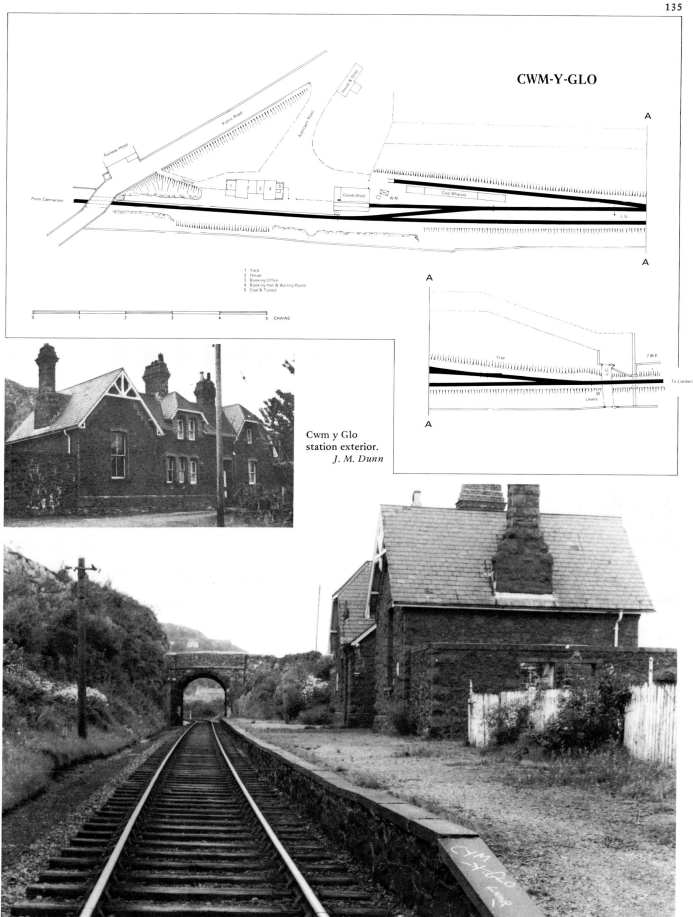

CWM-Y-GLO

Public Road

House & Shed

Approach Road

Incline

Railway Hotel

From Caernarvon

1 2 3 4 5

Goods Shed

W.M.

Coal Wharves

L.G.

A

A

1 Yard
2 House
3 Booking Office
4 Booking Hall & Waiting Room
5 Coal & Toilets

0   1   2   3   4   5   CHAINS

A

Trap

7 M.P.

To Llanberis

Levers

A

Cwm y Glo
station exterior.
J. M. Dunn

The platform and road overbridge at Cwm y Glo, looking back towards Caernarvon.

Lens of Sutton

Another view of the station and goods shed taken from rocks overlooking the station.   *J. M. Dunn*

The entrance to the goods yard, taken from the main line, looking towards Caernarvon in 1966. The gradient changes just before the platform. The wagons in front of the shed are for the demolition squad, and the Railway Hotel can be seen in the background.   *Author*

The evening return excursion from Llanberis to Rhyl and Prestatyn passes the entrance to Cwm y Glo yard with locomotive No. 42461 of Bangor and driver Hugh Caulfield at the controls in 1952.
Author

Taken from the rocky outcrop overlooking the station, this photograph shows the goods shed and yard and the single line curving away towards Llanberis in 1966. The tunnel mouth can just be seen in the distance, and beyond are the Dinorwic Quarry slate tips. *Author*

The afternoon train from Caernarvon to Llanberis crossing the causeway near Llanberis, with the observation coach in 1952. *Author*

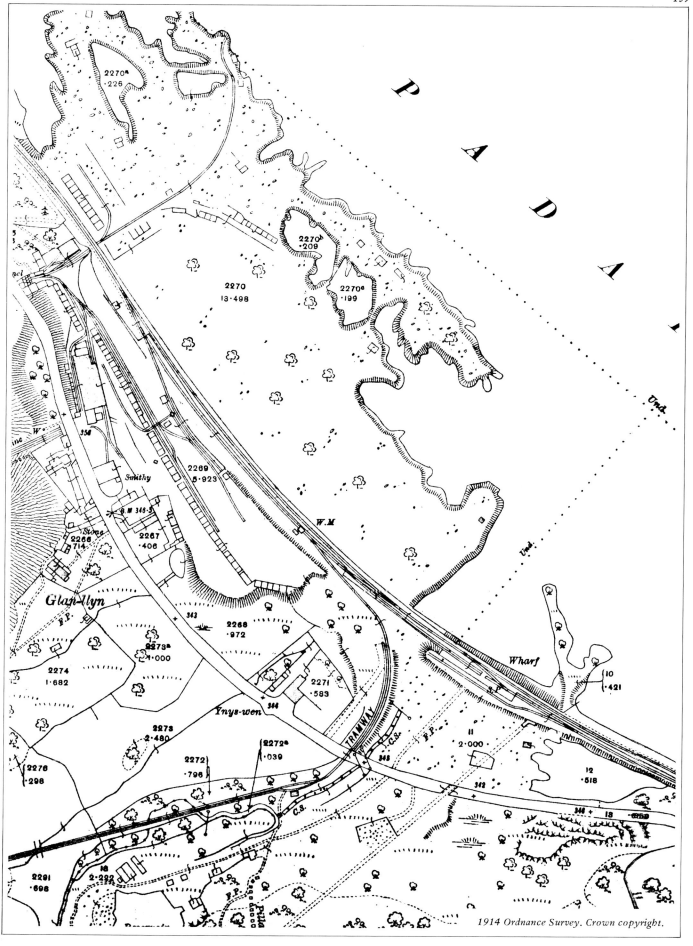

1914 Ordnance Survey. Crown copyright.

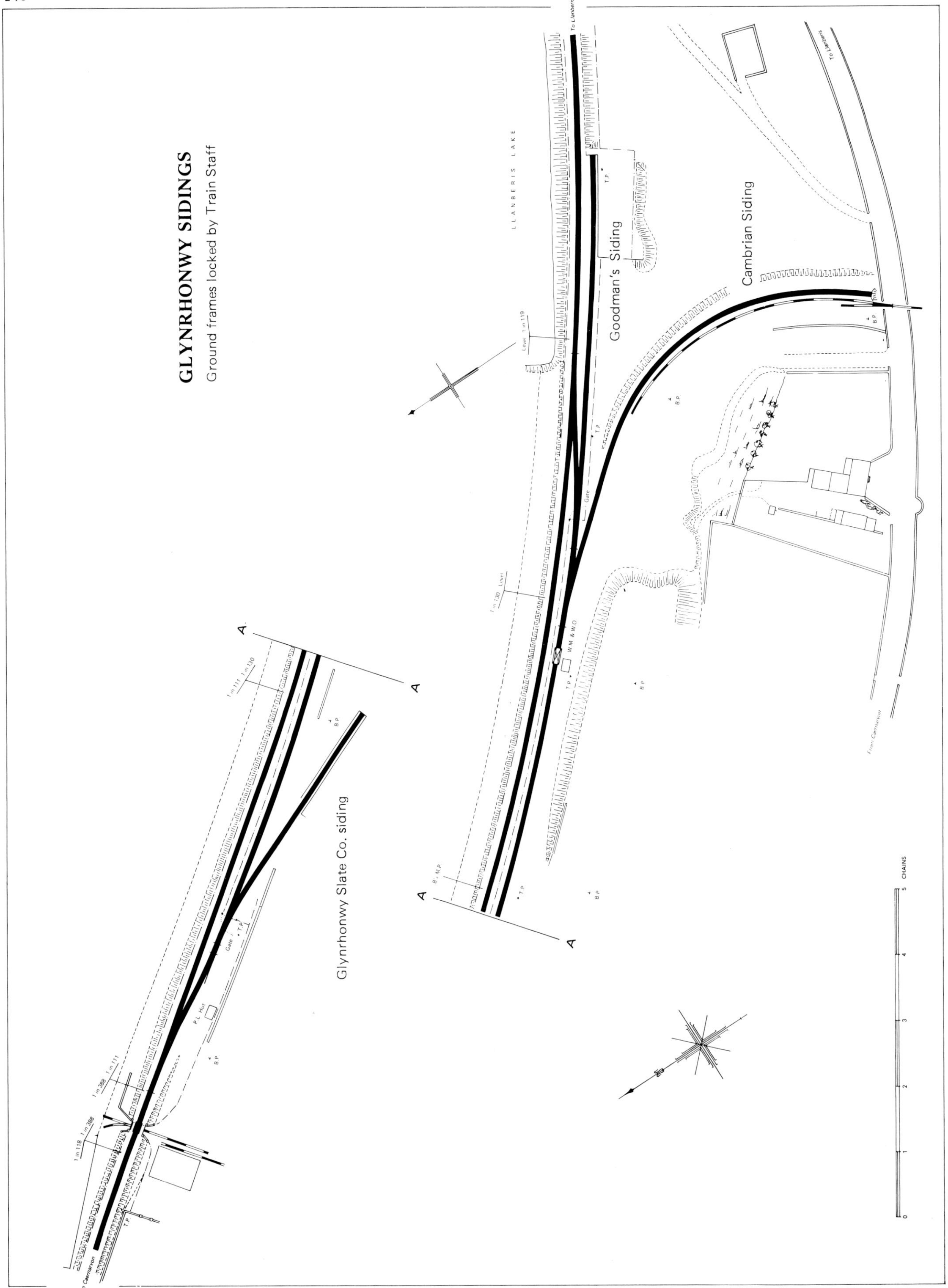

GLYNRHONWY SIDINGS
Ground frames locked by Train Staff

Glynrhonwy Slate Co. siding

Goodman's Siding

Cambrian Siding

LLANBERIS LAKE

To Llanberis

To Llanberis

From Caernarvon

From Caernarvon

Level 1 in 119

1 in 120 Level

W.M. M & W.O.

A

A

A

A

1 in 111   1 in 120

1 in 111

1 in 386

1 in 386

1 in 119

P.L. Hut

Gate

0   1   2   3   4   5 CHAINS

An aerial view of the Glynrhonwy complex in 1951, showing the extent of the quarry workings. Of special interest is the collection of coaches parked in the sidings for the winter. The practice was repeated for two winter seasons before storage was found elsewhere.   *Airviews (Mcr) Ltd.*

The only known photograph of Padarn Halt, taken on 27th June 1956 after several years of disuse. The construction of the platform is clearly seen as well as the proximity of Llanberis terminus, whose home and advanced starting signals are visible. *H. C. Casserley*

Padarn Halt

Padarn Halt, opened to cater for tourist traffic on 21st November 1936, was also used by local folk as a convenient picking up point on excursion trains. It was more central to the village than the terminal station and could be reached off the main street very quickly. Had it been built earlier it may possibly have staved off withdrawal of regular passenger trains.

It was 130 ft long, constructed of timber, with a small hut which served as an office, and was staffed as required by someone from Llanberis. After the war, the local excursion traffic failed to reappear and the halt was rarely used. It disappeared some time before the line closed finally, and photographs of the halt are extremely rare. There were no signals.

Distance from Cwm y Glo:	1 mile 1581 yards up direction; next station
Distance from Llanberis:	474 yards down direction; next token point

Running time:
   up direction
      passenger trains — 4 minutes to Cwm y Glo
   down direction
      passenger trains — 1 minute to Llanberis

Intermediate sidings:
up direction	Hickman's siding	481 yards
	Glynrhonwy siding	550 yards

Gradient leaving station:	*up direction*	1:456 falling
	down direction	1:456 rising

Intermediate station in Pontrhythallt to Llanberis token section.

A return excursion train in the platform awaiting departure one evening in 1952. Notice the camping coach in the siding on the left. *Author*

Llanberis

The terminus opened on 1st July 1869. It was situated on the edge of the village, but convenient for some traffic from Dinorwic quarry, carried over the causeway between Llyn Padarn and Llyn Peris. The line was not a financial success and was closed to regular passenger traffic on 22nd September 1930, although frequent excursions both inward and outward continued until the Second World War intervened. After the war, local excursions all but ceased but the freight traffic persisted until the final train on 3rd September 1964.

The single platform was 400 feet in length and supplemented by a ticket platform extending towards Caernarvon for a further 300 feet. This was an extremely narrow wooden structure, 3 feet wide, with a ramp at the Llanberis end. It was built to deter fare dodgers who might be tempted to jump out of the train without a ticket, local trains halting alongside before moving up to the main platform.

The main building bore a resemblance to Cwm y Glo and Pontrhythallt, although here there was more office accommodation and a central canopy. The station master's house was at the Caernarvon end and, in addition to the booking

Distance from Padarn Halt:	474 yards up direction; next station
Distance from Pontrhythallt:	3 miles 364 yards up direction; next token point

Running time:
up direction
    passenger trains – 1 minutes to Padarn Halt
    passenger trains – 5 minutes to Cwm y Glo
    passenger trains – 8 minutes to Pontrhythallt
    freight trains – 15 minutes to Pontrhythallt (minimum)
Gradient leaving station: *up direction*   level
Single Line Token
    Llanberis-Pontrhythallt – Large staff coloured red

hall and office, there was a ladies waiting room, porters room, lamp room and toilets. A footbridge spanning the platform and tracks led from the lake shore to the area outside the station. It was a standard design mounted on stone pillars with a loading gauge hanging from its centre.

The single line staff instruments were located in the office, whilst a small lever frame controlled signals from the platform. Points were worked from four 2-lever ground frames unlocked by a key on the train staff, whilst single lever points were the order in the goods yard.

A 1920s view of the station with the observation car and another standby carriage stabled in the run-round. *J. M. Dunn*

The goods shed was constructed of granite, similar to the station building, and housed a small crane. Freight traffic was the mainstay of the line, but apart from slate sent out from the smaller quarries, the main traffic, coal and general merchandise, was incoming.

The locomotive shed here had closed and the staff moved to Caernarvon by 1922. However, the building remained intact until 1939 or 1940 before being demolished. The large water tower was left standing until the line was lifted to serve a water column alongside. A 42 ft turntable had also been provided but this was little used after the shed closed and gradually fell into a dangerous state. It was removed and the pit filled in before the line closed. Despite the continued decline, the station was

The width of the ticket platform is particularly evident in this 1956 view.

J. H. Moss

Another view along the platform showing the small canopy over the entrance to the booking hall. The sidings are devoid of stock in this 1947 view, but this was rather unusual.

L & GRP, courtesy David & Charles

Driver Moi Edwards brings No. 42460 to a halt with empty stock for a Sunday Schools special excursion on the morning of 4th October 1952. The camping coach was still in use even this late in the season.

Author

The exterior of the station in 1954 after the grey stone had been painted cream all over. *J. J. Davis*

always clean and tidy and the permanent way staff regularly won prizes for the best length of track.

For some years, camping coaches were based here. One was located in the carriage landing road and one beyond the crossover of the centre release road.

There was sufficient road traffic to justify a railway lorry being based here and this was parked by the goods shed each night. Despite the sparse traffic the station was sufficiently busy to command Class 2 status for its staff.

When the line closed, the site was cleared, but the station building survived to become an arts and craft centre. The canopy and its support brackets remain but the appearance of the building is largely altered, particularly by the installation of new windows and the removal of the small canopy from the forecourt elevation.

The lever frame outside the station building on 20th October 1963 with an SLS special pulling into Llanberis headed by Nos. 41200 and 41324.
B. Cowlishaw

A general view of the platform as seen from the coal siding in 1948.

L & GRP, courtesy David & Charles

An unidentified 'Cauliflower' with a train of six-wheeled stock in the coal siding clear of the run-round loop.

Author

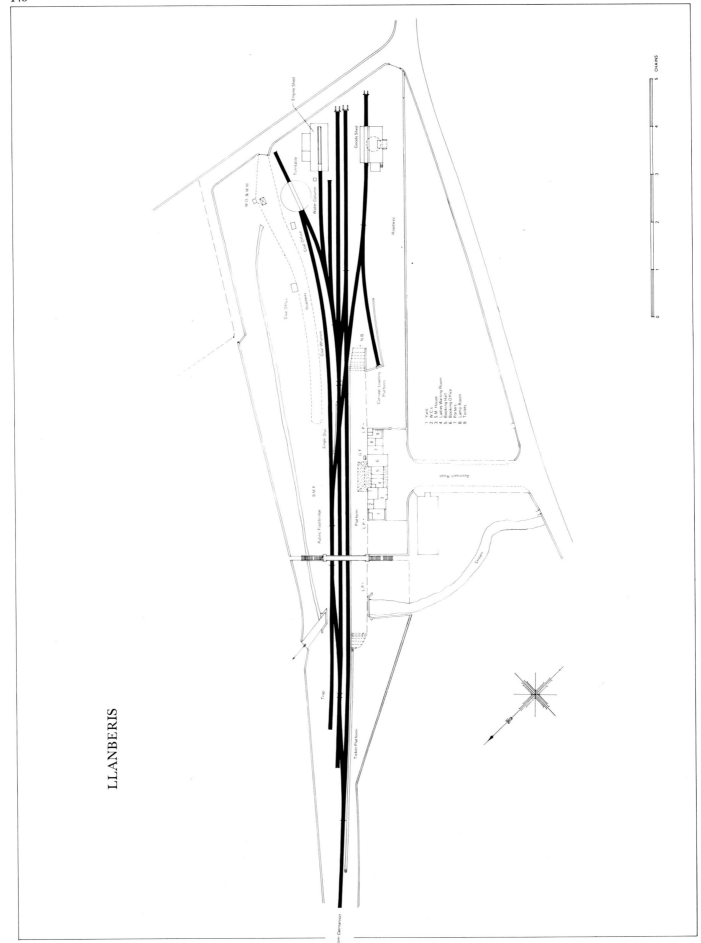

LLANBERIS

1 Yard
2 W C s
3 S M House
4 Ladies Waiting Room
5 Booking Hall
6 Booking Office
7 Porters
8 Lamp Room
9 Toilets

CHAINS

0 1 2 3 4 5

A general view of the goods yard and other sidings in 1952. The vehicle in the carriage landing is a camping coach.

Author

The goods shed in 1965. *Author*

An earlier view of the goods shed taken in 1932. *G. H. Platt*

A general view of the yard on 2nd May 1937 showing the goods shed, loco shed, turntable, weigh office and weighbridge. Note the carriage landing in the foreground and the private owner wagon in the coal road.

W. A. Camwell

LNWR 0–6–0 'Cauliflower' No. 666, shortly to be renumbered 8371 in the LMS renumbering scheme, stands outside Llanberis shed on 12th June 1925. This locomotive was transferred out of the district shortly afterwards and was allocated to Swansea in 1926.

Collection J. W. T. House

The engine shed at Llanberis in 1937, showing the tank incorporated into the structure, the column outside and the corner of the turntable pit.

Author's collection

152

Nantlle in its heyday with a passenger train of four-wheeled stock at the platform and narrow gauge wagons spread out over the yard. This is the only view so far discovered showing the elusive signal cabin and signals.

National Library of Wales

THE NANTLLE BRANCH

The Nantlle Railway was incorporated in 1825 and opened in 1828 as a horse-drawn 3′ 6″ narrow gauge line conveying copper and slate to Caernarvon. Its course ran on much the same formation as the Carnarvonshire Railway as far as Coed Helen on the outskirts of Caernarvon. There it entered a short tunnel under an unclassified road, before winding down and crossing the Afon Seiont to terminate at the harbour. At the southern end, the line failed to reach Nantlle, but disappeared into quarries at Talysarn, about two miles short of Nantlle village.

The line opened in 1828 and by 1857 the Nantlle Railway was operating four passenger trains daily, hauled by eight horses, between Talysarn and Caernarvon, with a further four horses performing other duties, including the working of a Penygroes to Portmadoc omnibus. Several other schemes were mooted before the Nantlle Railway was eventually absorbed by the Carnarvonshire concern and

these have been described by Peter E. Baughan in his book *A Regional History of Railways Vol. 11 — North & Mid Wales* published by David & Charles.

Traffic remained under horse power throughout the Nantlle Railway's existence, and parts of the system remained 3′ 6″ gauge until the branch closed to freight traffic on 2nd December 1963.

Immediately after change of ownership, the line was converted to standard gauge, initially between Penygroes and Pant, with the sections at either end remaining narrow gauge. This caused problems with transhipping twice, although the practice of loading narrow gauge wagons onto standard gauge wagons, similar to the Padarn Railway, was used. The whole state of affairs was unsatisfactory and traffic was reverting to the roads, such as they were.

In 1870, a new junction was authorised at Penygroes, and the remainder of the Nantlle line was converted to

LNWR 0—6—2T number 2457 at Nantlle station with a train of six-wheeled coaches for Penygroes at the turn of the century. Eventually the working of passenger trains was reduced to 'motor' trains or railcars.

Ifor Jones (GCC)

153

standard gauge. By December 1871 a single platformed station had been built at Talysarn, together with a goods shed, and a turntable. Through traffic for minerals commenced on 1st August 1872, with passenger traffic officially starting on 1st October the same year. There were six trains each way during the week, with two extra trains on Saturdays and Caernarvon fair days. There was one intermediate siding, Tanrallt siding, about 550 yards from Nantlle station.

It is listed in the working timetable for 1904 and shown on maps dated 1914. It is included in the working timetable for 1922 but not in the freight timetable for 1935 so presumably it had ceased to be in use by this time.

The turntable at Nantlle was removed in 1901. It is also probable that the signal box was disconnected at this time.

Later rail motor trains were introduced on the branch, the most likely date being 1st April 1914. However, traffic

NANTLLE BRANCH—(SINGLE LINE.)
Train Staff Stations—Penygroes and Nantlle.

Miles.	WEEK DAYS. DOWN.	1	2	3	4	5	6	7	8	9	10	11	12	13	14	15	16	17
		Goods 3	Mixed 3	Pass. 3	Pass 3	SO Goods	Pass. 3	Pass. 3	Pass 3	Empt. Coach	G'ds. 4	Pass. 4	Mix'd 4	SO Pass 4	Pass. 4	Eng. 4	Pass. 4	Pass 4
		a.m.	a.m.	a.m.	a.m.	a.m.	p.m.	p.m.	p.m.	p.m.	p.m.	p.m	p.m.	p.m.	p.m.	p.m.	p.m	p.m.
	PEN'YES dp	7 25	8 0	9 17	9 40	10 0	11 25	1 0	1 35	1 55	2 30	3 27	5 20	5 50	6 30	7 20	7 55	8 50
3/4	T'hallt Sid..	X	...	...	...	...	...	...	SO	X	...	...	...	...	...	...	...	...
1 1/4	N'TLLE ar	7 35	8 5	9 22	9 45	10 5	11 30	1 5	1 40	2 0	2 40	3 32	5 25	5 55	6 35	7 25	8 0	8 55

All Engines working on the Nantlle Branch to do what Shunting is required at Nantlle and Penygroes throughout the day.

Miles.	WEEK DAYS. UP.	18	19	20	21	22	23	24	25	26	27	28	29	30	31	32	33	34	35
		Mixd 3	Pass. 3	Pass 3	SO Light Eng.	SO Pass 3	Pass 3	Pass. 3	ass 3	SO Rlf. Train	Gds. 3	Pass. 4	Mix. 4	Emp Co'b 4	Pass. 4	Goods 4	Pass 4	Pass 4	Eng. 4
		a.m.	a.m.	a.m.	a.m.	a.m.	a.m.	p.m.	p.m.	p.m	p.m.	p.m.	p.m.	p.m	p.m	p.m	p.m	p.m	p.m
	N'TLE dp.	7 45	9 5	9 39	9 50	10 40	11 10	12 45	1 20	1 50	2 10	3 12	5 5	5 39	6 15	6 40	7 40	8 35	9 0
3/4	T'hallt Sid.	...	...	...	C	...	...	...	...	...	...	...	SO	...	C on	...	...	...	...
1 1/4	PEN'YES ar	7 50	9 10	9 35	9 55	10 45	11 15	12 50	1 25	1 55	2 20	3 17	5 10	5 35	6 20	6 45	7 45	8 40	9 5
															Sats.				

No. 8—to be worked on Saturdays by Market Stock to form No. 25. Engine and Coaches of 25 to return empty to Nantlle at 1.55 p.m. Engine to then work out No 27.

Extract from LNWR service timetable – July, August & September 1904

Pen-y-groes and Nantlle—Single Line—One class only.
Train Staff Stations—Penygroes and Nantlle.

Miles.	WEEK DAYS. Down.	31	32	33	34	35	36	37	38	39	40	41	42	43	44	45	46	47	48	49
		6.10 a.m. G Goods from Car'n'rvn	Pas	Pas from Car'n'rvn	Pas	Pas	Pas		Pas	Ety. Ches S	Pas S		Pas		Pas	Light Eng.	Pas	Pas	Pas	Pas SO
		a.m.	a.m.	a.m.	a.m.	a.m.	a.m.		p.m.	p.m.	p.m.		p.m.		p.m	p.m	p.m.	p.m.	p.m.	
...	PEN-Y-GROES ...dep.	7 5	7 40	9 13	10 0	10 35	11 45	...	12 57	1 15	1 55	...	3 10	...	4 0	4 45	5 35	6 20	10 23	
	Taurhallt Siding	X	...	...	...	...	...	...	...	...	...		...		...	...	...	...	...	
1 1/4	NANTLLE ...... arr.	7 10	7 45	9 18	10 5	10 40	11 50	...	1 2	1 20	2 0	...	3 15	...	4 5	4 50	5 40	6 25	10 28	

Miles.	WEEK DAYS. Up.	50	51	52	53	54	55	56	57	58	59	60	61	62	63	64	65	66	67	68
		Pas	Pas for Car'n'rvn	Pas	Pas	Pas		Pas	Pas	Pas S		G Min'l for Car'n'rvn S	G Mfn'l for Car'n'rvn SO	Pas	Pas	Pas	Pas		Light Eng. for Car'n'rvn SO	
		a.m.	a.m.	a.m.	a.m.	a.m.		p.m.	p.m.	p.m.		p.m	p.m	p.m.	p.m	p.m.	p.m		p.m	
...	NANTLLE ...dep.	7 25	8 10	9 40	10 15	11 25	...	12 40	1 7	1 35	...	2 10	3 30	4 25	5 15	6 0	6 30	10 35	...	
	Tanrhallt Siding	...	...	...	...	...		...	...	...		...	...	...	...	...	...		...	
1 1/4	PEN-Y-GROES ...arr.	7 30	8 15	9 45	10 20	11 30	...	12 45	1 12	1 40	...	2 20	3 40	4 30	5 20	6 5	6 35	10 40	...	

Extract from LNWR service timetable for 1922

Stock for the Nanttle branch train stands in the bay platform at Penygroes before the advent of the 'motor' trains.   *Author's collection*

During the First World War a petrol electric railcar was tried on the Nantlle branch. It did not stay long, but fortunately someone took this view of it standing in the Nantlle bay at Penygroes.   *Author's collection*

The site of Tanrallt sidings taken from a footbridge over the branch looking towards Nantlle.   *J. M. Dunn*

was poor, and wartime economies forced the LNWR to withdraw passenger services from 1st January 1917 until July 1919.

The branch locomotive worked out from Caernarvon each day, assisting an early trip to Afonwen from Caernarvon (Mondays excepted, when it worked the stock outward), and throughout the rest of the day worked to and from Penygroes, shunting in between trains. The relieving crew travelled out as passengers, the early turn men returning the same way, and when work on the branch was finished for the day, the loco and crew would return to Caernarvon with any mineral wagons remaining at Penygroes. The pattern remained unchanged until passenger traffic ceased on the branch on 8th August 1932.

With the loss of passenger traffic and decline in demand for slate, there was no longer any need for a branch loco-motive as one trip daily sufficed, working out from Bangor to Menai Bridge, then on to Caernarvon, where some shunt-ing took place before working forward to Nantlle and shunting there for a further hour. At one period, a short trip to Penygroes with minerals took place, the wagons working forward with the returning freight from Afonwen. The Nantlle trip worked light engine back to Nantlle and shunted for a further hour before making its way back to

Menai Bridge yard. This pattern lasted for about three years, after which the intermediate trip to Penygroes was cut out and the trip became a straight 'out and home' working. This remained the routine from about 1937 until 1956 when traffic only justified running the trip on alternate days.

And so it remained until 3rd December 1963, when the line passed into history. It was visited on rare occasions by special excursion trains, but by and large was unrecorded, and not missed by the local population, who had accepted the withdrawal of services as inevitable.

The station building was a large slate-clad stone structure incorporating a house which remained occupied well after the line was dismantled. There was also a water tower and separate water column beyond the platform face, but no buffer stops, only an old permanent way chair on top of the rail giving indication of the end of the track. Tranship-ment of slates from the narrow gauge took place on a wharf which brought the narrow gauge level with the standard gauge wagon floors. There were three flimsy looking slate company offices on the wharf and a 5 ton yard crane for the transhipment from the standard gauge to narrow gauge wagons. A wooden goods shed catered for other railway traffic and there was the usual wharf for coal which always remained the main inward traffic.

An undated view of Nantlle station showing the transhipment and yard sidings.

Author's collection

The station staff at Nantlle.

W. J. Williams (GCC)

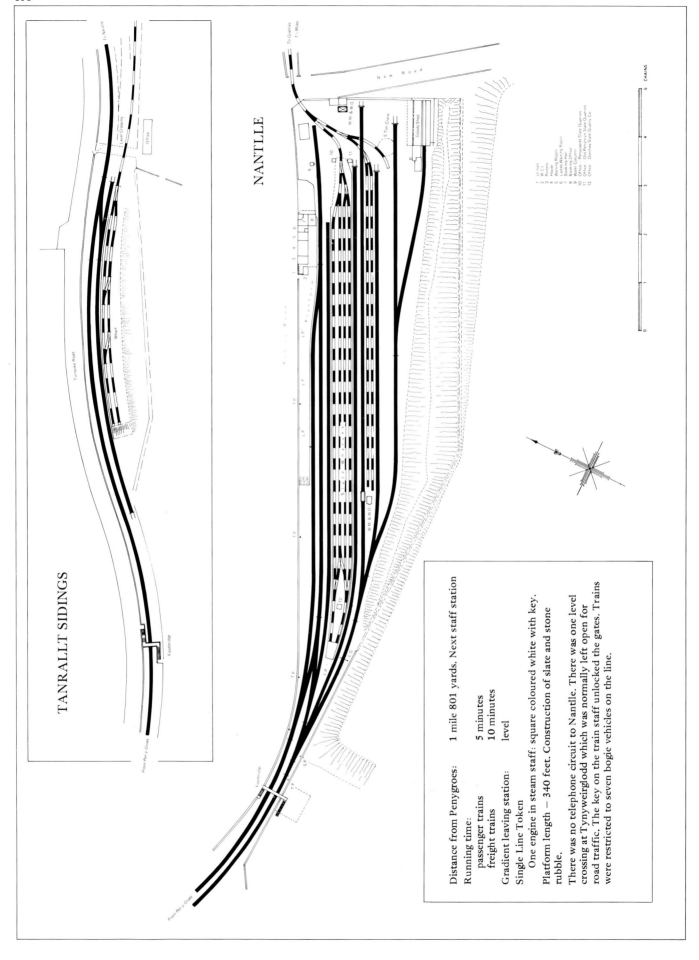

TANRALLT SIDINGS

NANTLLE

Distance from Penygroes: 1 mile 801 yards. Next staff station
Running time:
    passenger trains   5 minutes
    freight trains   10 minutes
Gradient leaving station: level
Single Line Token
    One engine in steam staff: square coloured white with key.
Platform length — 340 feet. Construction of slate and stone rubble.

There was no telephone circuit to Nantlle. There was one level crossing at Tynyweirglodd which was normally left open for road traffic. The key on the train staff unlocked the gates. Trains were restricted to seven bogie vehicles on the line.

1   Urinals
2   W.C.s
3   Porters
4   House
5   Waiting Room
6   Ladies Waiting Room
7   Booking Hall
8   Booking Office
9   Water Column
10   Office   Penygroes Slate Quarries
11   Office   Old Penyfrn Slate Quarries
12   Office   Dorthea Slate Quarry Co

0   1   2   3   4   5 CHAINS

This 1924 view shows a variety of wagons from all companies awaiting loading in the tranship sidings.
C. L. Mowat

The transhipment siding clearly showing some of the narrow gauge trackwork. *W. A. Camwell*

Fowler 0—6—0 No. 44445 at the tranship platform with Ritchie Thomas at the controls. Horses, hired from a contractor, were still being used to haul the narrow gauge wagons from the slate quarries when this photograph was taken on 20th April 1957. *W. A. Camwell*

Stanier 2–6–4T No. 42599 waits at Nantlle station with the return freight to Caernarvon on 30th August 1961.

T. J. Edgington

The goods shed at Nantlle, constructed of timber with a slate roof, viewed from the tranship sidings in 1964. *Author*

Another view of the horse team. The yard is full of stock, but the sidings, as seen here, were sometimes used as a crippled wagon store.

W. A. Camwell

Looking north along the narrow gauge transhipment siding from the Nantlle end towards Penygroes, showing more of the simple pointwork. The narrow gauge trackbed belonged to British Railways as proclaimed by a maroon coloured plaque on a telephone post alongside the public road into the village centre.   *W. A. Camwell*

The water column and the station building, looking towards Penygroes. Inverted rail chairs provided a crude buffer stop whilst in the foreground can be seen the narrow gauge tracks with the swivel crossing.

H. C. Casserley

The water tower, water column and end of the standard gauge tracks at Nantlle in 1964 with the course of the former tramway still visible beyond.

Author

MENAI BRIDGE

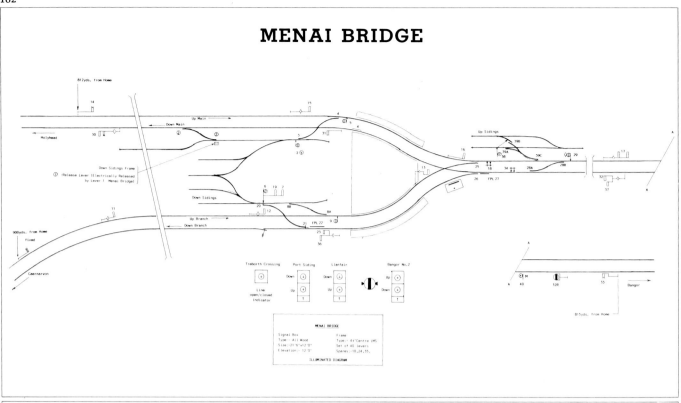

TREBORTH

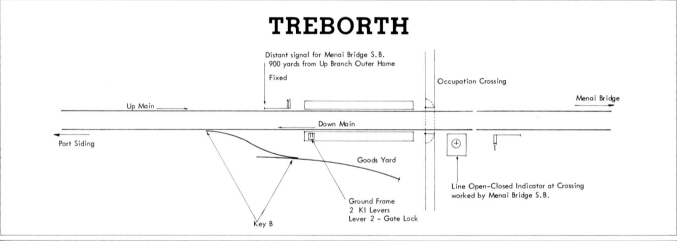

PORT SIDING

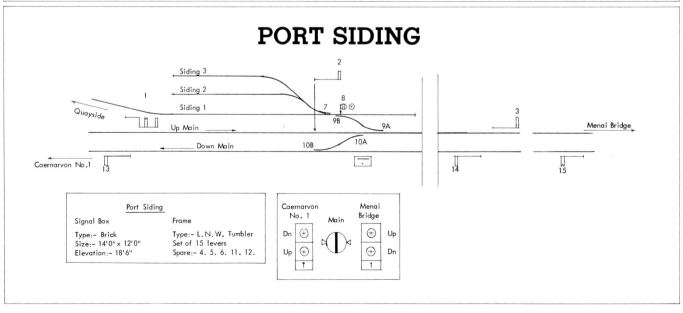

PORT DINORWIC

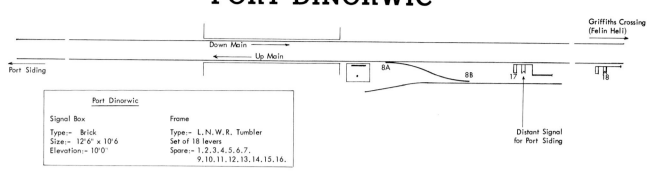

Griffiths Crossing
(Felin Heli)

Down Main

Up Main

Port Siding

8A

8B

17

18

Distant Signal
for Port Siding

Port Dinorwic

Signal Box

Type:- Brick
Size:- 12'6" x 10'6
Elevation:- 10'0"

Frame

Type:- L.N.W.R. Tumbler
Set of 18 levers
Spare:- 1.2.3.4.5.6.7.
9.10.11.12.13.14.15.16.

FELIN HELI

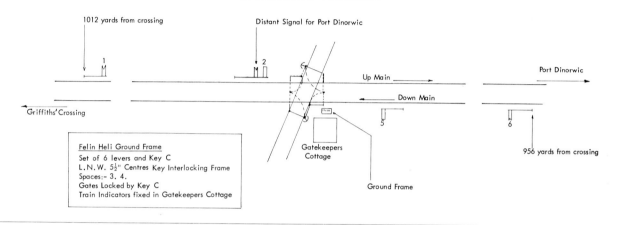

1012 yards from crossing

Distant Signal for Port Dinorwic

1

2

Up Main

Port Dinorwic

Griffiths' Crossing

Down Main

5

6

Gatekeepers
Cottage

Ground Frame

956 yards from crossing

Felin Heli Ground Frame

Set of 6 levers and Key C
L.N.W. 5½" Centres Key Interlocking Frame
Spaces:- 3. 4.
Gates Locked by Key C
Train Indicators fixed in Gatekeepers Cottage

GRIFFITHS' CROSSING

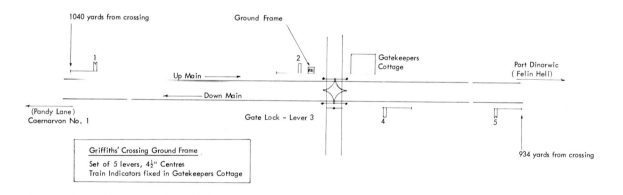

1040 yards from crossing

Ground Frame

1

2

Gatekeepers
Cottage

Up Main

Port Dinorwic
(Felin Heli)

Down Main

(Pandy Lane)
Caernarvon No. 1

Gate Lock - Lever 3

4

5

934 yards from crossing

Griffiths' Crossing Ground Frame

Set of 5 levers, 4½" Centres
Train Indicators fixed in Gatekeepers Cottage

PANDY LANE

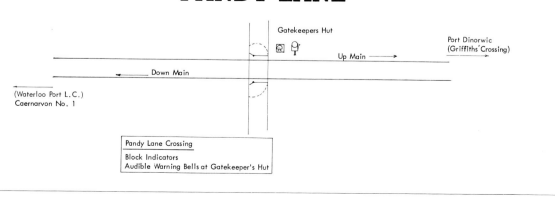

Gatekeepers Hut

Port Dinorwic
(Griffiths' Crossing)

Up Main

Down Main

(Waterloo Port L.C.)
Caernarvon No. 1

Pandy Lane Crossing

Block Indicators
Audible Warning Bells at Gatekeeper's Hut

WATERLOO PORT

Lever 1-slot on Caernarvon No. 1 Up Starter
400 yards from crossing

Ground Frame

Gatekeepers Cottage

Port Dinorwic (Pandy Lane)

Up Main →

← Down Main

1   2

→ Caernarvon No. 1

3   4

1085 yards from crossing

Distant Signal for Caernarvon No. 1

Waterloo Port Crossing Ground Frame

Set of 4 levers. 4½" centres
All Working
Uncontrolled Gates :- Padlocked
Train Indicators fixed in Gatekeepers Cottage Porch.

CAERNARVON NO.1

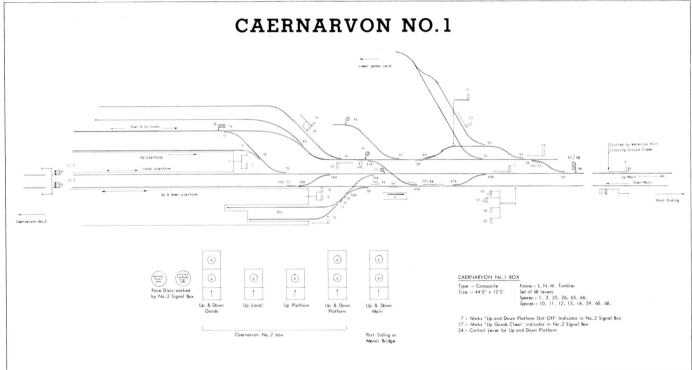

Lower goods yard

Slotted by Waterloo Port Crossing Ground Frame

Caernarvon No. 2

Down & Up Goods

Up platform

Local platform

Up & Down platform

Bay

Up Main

Down Main

Port Siding

Face Discs worked by No. 2 Signal Box

Up & Down Goods   Up Local   Up Platform   Up & Down Platform   Up & Down Main

Caernarvon No. 2 box

Port Siding or Menai Bridge

CAERNARVON No.1 BOX

Type - Composite   Frame :- L. N. W. Tumbler
Size :- 44'0" x 12'0"   Set of 68 levers
        Spares :- 1, 3, 25, 26, 65, 66.
        Spaces :- 10, 11, 12, 13, 14, 59, 60, 68.

7 - Works "Up and Down Platform Slot Off" Indicator in No.2 Signal Box
17 - Works "Up Goods Clear" indicator in No.2 Signal Box
24 - Control Lever for Up and Down Platform

CAERNARVON NO.2

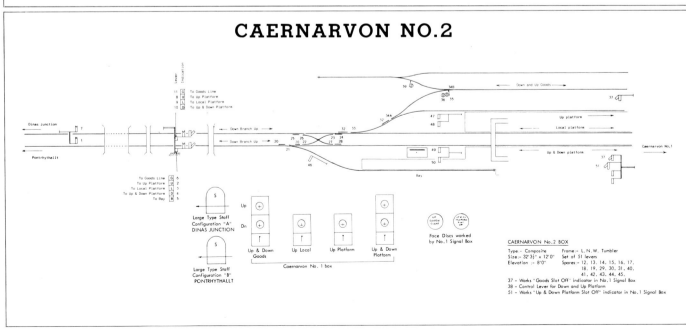

Lever Indication

11 G   To Goods Line
8 U   To Up Platform
9 L   To Local Platform
10 D   To Up & Down Platform

Dinas Junction

Pontrhythallt

Down Branch Up

Down Branch Up

Down and Up Goods

Up platform

Local platform

Up & Down platform

Bay

Caernarvon No. 1

To Goods Line G 6
To Up Platform U 2
To Local Platform L 3
To Up & Down Platform D 4
To Bay B 5

Large Type Staff Configuration "A" DINAS JUNCTION

Large Type Staff Configuration "B" PONTRHYTHALLT

Up

Dn

Up & Down Goods   Up Local   Up Platform   Up & Down Platform

Caernarvon No. 1 box

Face Discs worked by No. 1 Signal Box

CAERNARVON No.2 BOX

Type - Composite   Frame :- L. N. W. Tumbler
Size :- 32'3½" x 12'0"   Set of 51 levers
Elevation :- 8'0"   Spares :- 12, 13, 14, 15, 16, 17,
                18, 19, 29, 30, 31, 40,
                41, 42, 43, 44, 45.

37 - Works "Goods Slot Off" indicator in No.1 Signal Box
38 - Control Lever for Down and Up Platform
51 - Works "Up & Down Platform Slot Off" indicator in No.1 Signal Box

QUAY SIDING

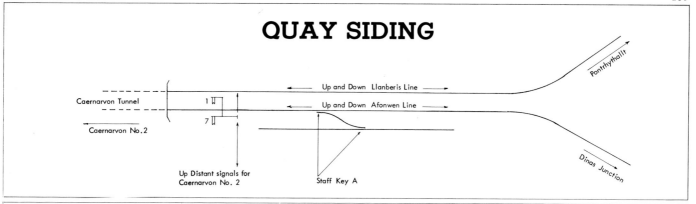

Caernarvon Tunnel

Caernarvon No. 2

1

7

Up and Down Llanberis Line

Up and Down Afonwen Line

Ponthythallt

Dinas Junction

Up Distant signals for
Caernarvon No. 2

Staff Key A

PANT CROSSING

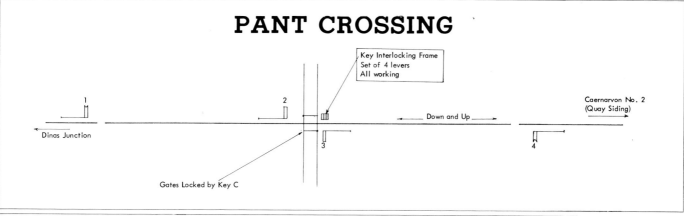

Key Interlocking Frame
Set of 4 levers
All working

1

2

3

4

Dinas Junction

Down and Up

Caernarvon No. 2
(Quay Siding)

Gates Locked by Key C

DINAS JUNCTION

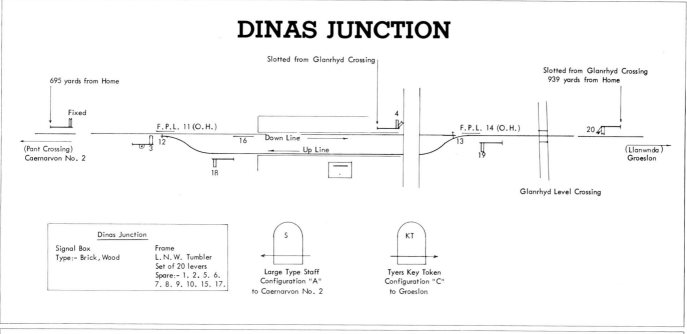

Slotted from Glanrhyd Crossing

Slotted from Glanrhyd Crossing
939 yards from Home

695 yards from Home

Fixed

F.P.L. 11 (O.H.)

4

F.P.L. 14 (O.H.)

20

12

16

Down Line

13

(Pant Crossing)
Caernarvon No. 2

3

Up Line

19

(Llanwnda)
Groeslon

18

Glanrhyd Level Crossing

Dinas Junction	
Signal Box	Frame
Type:- Brick, Wood	L. N. W. Tumbler
	Set of 20 levers
	Spare:- 1. 2. 5. 6.
	7. 8. 9. 10. 15. 17.

S

Large Type Staff
Configuration "A"
to Caernarvon No. 2

KT

Tyers Key Token
Configuration "C"
to Groeslon

LLANWNDA

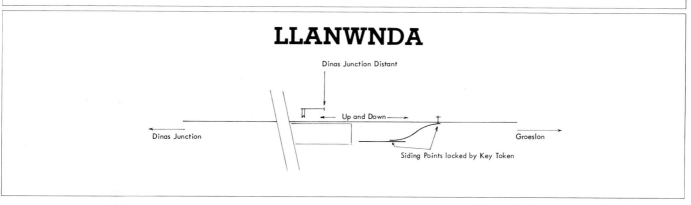

Dinas Junction Distant

Dinas Junction

Up and Down

Groeslon

Siding Points locked by Key Token

GROESLON

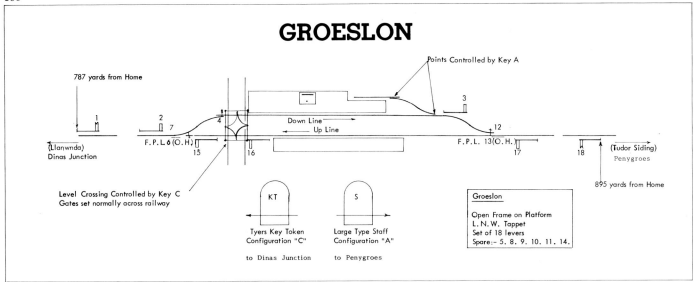

Points Controlled by Key A

787 yards from Home

1
2
7
4
3
12
15
16
17
18

F.P.L 6 (O.H.)

Down Line
Up Line

F.P.L. 13 (O.H.)

(Llanwnda)
Dinas Junction

(Tudor Siding)
Penygroes

895 yards from Home

Level Crossing Controlled by Key C
Gates set normally across railway

KT

Tyers Key Token
Configuration "C"

to Dinas Junction

S

Large Type Staff
Configuration "A"

to Penygroes

Groeslon

Open Frame on Platform
L. N. W. Tappet
Set of 18 levers
Spare:- 5. 8. 9. 10. 11. 14.

TUDOR SIDING

Siding Points locked by Key Token

Groeslon

Penygroes

PENYGROES

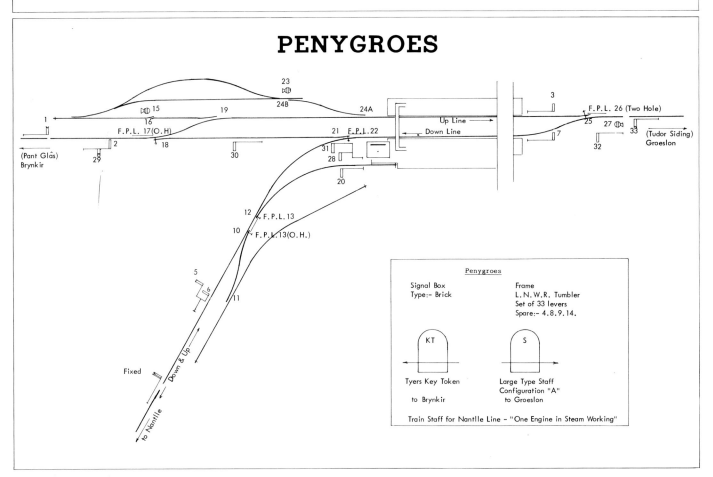

23
24B
24A
3
F.P.L. 26 (Two Hole)
15
19
16
25
27
33
1
F.P.L. 17 (O.H.)
21
F.P.L. 22
Up Line
Down Line
7
32
(Tudor Siding)
Groeslon
2
18
30
31
28
29
20

(Pant Glâs)
Brynkir

12
F.P.L. 13
10
F.P.L. 13 (O.H.)

5
6
11

Fixed

Down & Up

to Nantlle

Penygroes

Signal Box
Type:- Brick

Frame
L. N. W. R. Tumbler
Set of 33 levers
Spare:- 4.8.9.14.

KT

Tyers Key Token

to Brynkir

S

Large Type Staff
Configuration "A"
to Groeslon

Train Staff for Nantlle Line - "One Engine in Steam Working"

PANT GLÂS

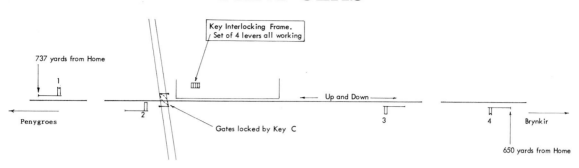

Key Interlocking Frame.
Set of 4 levers all working

737 yards from Home

1

← Up and Down →

Penygroes

2

Gates locked by Key C

3

4

Brynkir

650 yards from Home

BRYNKIR

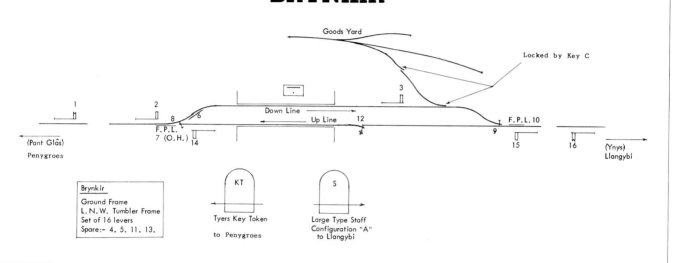

Goods Yard

Locked by Key C

1

2

8   6

Down Line

3

Up Line   12

F.P.L. 10

F.P.L.
7 (O.H.)   14

9

15

16

(Pant Glâs)
Penygroes

(Ynys)
Llangybi

Brynkir

Ground Frame
L. N. W. Tumbler Frame
Set of 16 levers
Spare:- 4. 5. 11. 13.

KT

Tyers Key Token

to Penygroes

S

Large Type Staff
Configuration "A"
to Llangybi

YNYS

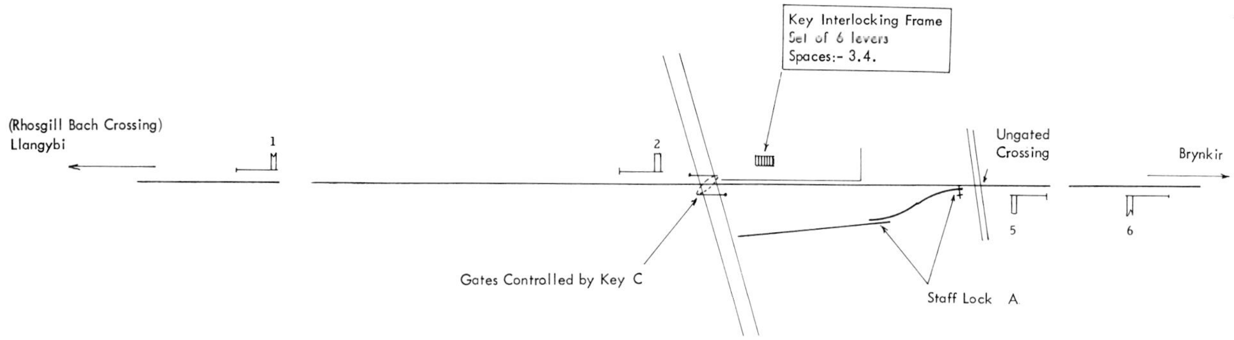

Key Interlocking Frame
Set of 6 levers
Spaces:- 3. 4.

(Rhosgill Bach Crossing)
Llangybi

1

2

Ungated
Crossing

Brynkir

Gates Controlled by Key C

5

6

Staff Lock   A

RHOSGILL BACH CROSSING

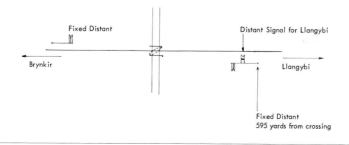

Fixed Distant

Distant Signal for Llangybi

Brynkir

Llangybi

Fixed Distant
595 yards from crossing

LLANGYBI

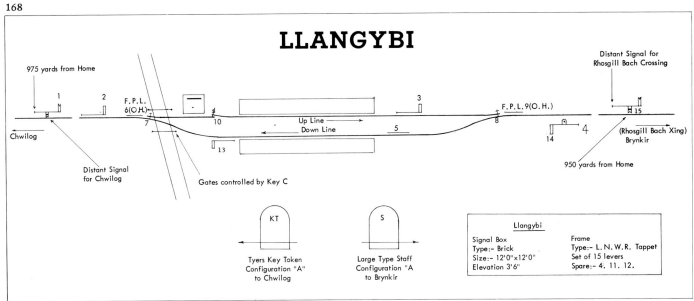

Distant Signal for
Rhosgill Bach Crossing

975 yards from Home

1   2
F.P.L.
6(O.H.)   F.P.L.9(O.H.)   15

Chwilog   7   10   8   4

Up Line
Down Line   5   14   (Rhosgill Bach Xing)
13   Brynkir

950 yards from Home

Distant Signal
for Chwilog

Gates controlled by Key C

KT   S

Tyers Key Token   Large Type Staff
Configuration "A"   Configuration "A"
to Chwilog   to Brynkir

Llangybi	
Signal Box	Frame
Type:- Brick	Type:- L.N.W.R. Tappet
Size:- 12'0"x12'0"	Set of 15 levers
Elevation 3'6"	Spare:- 4. 11. 12.

CHWILOG

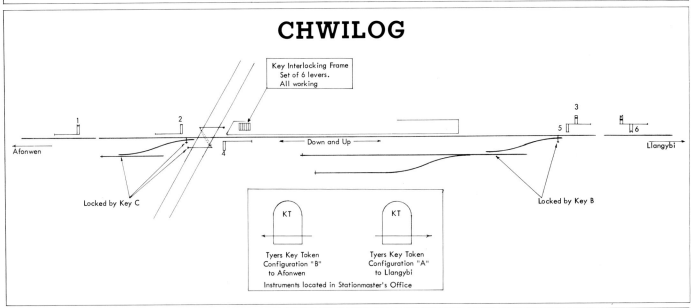

Key Interlocking Frame
Set of 6 levers.
All working

1   2   3
5   6

Afonwen   4   Llangybi

Down and Up

Locked by Key C   Locked by Key B

KT   KT

Tyers Key Token   Tyers Key Token
Configuration "B"   Configuration "A"
to Afonwen   to Llangybi

Instruments located in Stationmaster's Office

AFONWEN

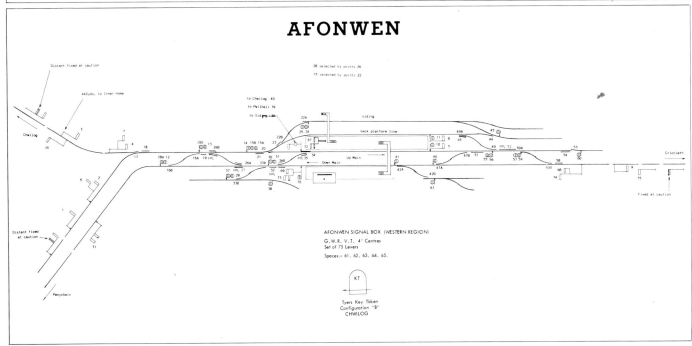

Distant fixed at caution

440yds. to Inner Home

2B selected by points 26
1S selected by points 22

to Chwilog 40
to Pwllheli 39
to Sidings 38

Chwilog

Criccieth

Fixed at caution

Distant fixed
at caution

Penychain

AFONWEN SIGNAL BOX (WESTERN REGION)
G.W.R. V.T. 4" Centres
Set of 75 levers
Spaces:- 61. 62. 63. 64. 65.

KT

Tyers Key Token
Configuration "B"
CHWILOG

SEIONT MILL SIDING

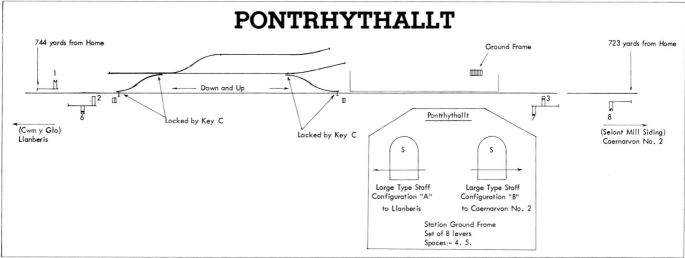

Pontrhythallt

Caernarvon No. 2

Siding Points locked by Key on Train Staff

PONTRHYTHALLT

744 yards from Home

1

2

6

(Cwm y Glo)
Llanberis

Locked by Key C

Down and Up

Locked by Key C

Ground Frame

723 yards from Home

3

8

(Seiont Mill Siding)
Caernarvon No. 2

Pontrhythallt

S

S

Large Type Staff
Configuration "A"
to Llanberis

Large Type Staff
Configuration "B"
to Caernarvon No. 2

Station Ground Frame
Set of 8 levers
Spaces:- 4. 5.

CWM Y GLO

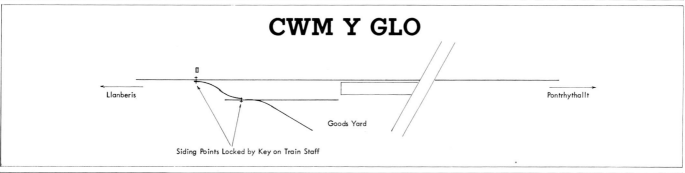

Llanberis

Pontrhythallt

Goods Yard

Siding Points Locked by Key on Train Staff

LLANBERIS

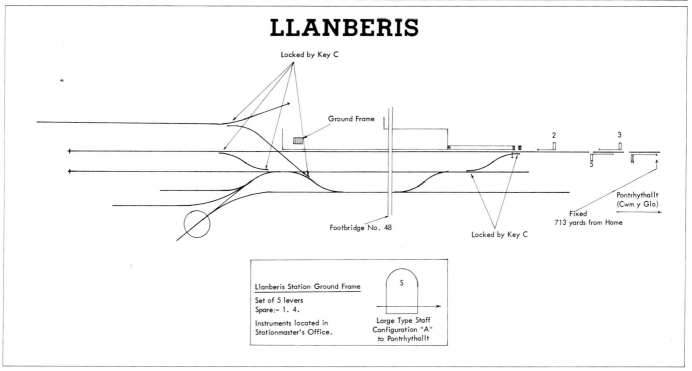

Locked by Key C

Ground Frame

2

3

5

Pontrhythallt
(Cwm y Glo)

Footbridge No. 48

Locked by Key C

Fixed
713 yards from Home

Llanberis Station Ground Frame

Set of 5 levers
Spare:- 1. 4.

Instruments located in
Stationmaster's Office.

S

Large Type Staff
Configuration "A"
to Pontrhythallt

NANTLLE

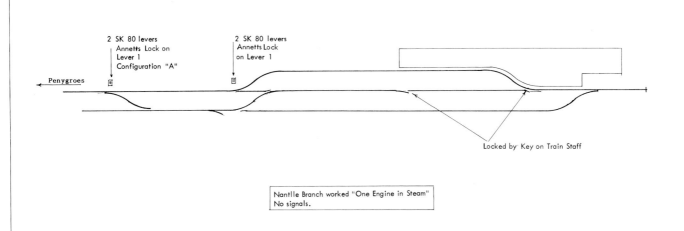

2 SK 80 levers
Annetts Lock on
Lever 1
Configuration "A"

2 SK 80 levers
Annetts Lock
on Lever 1

← Penygroes

Locked by Key on Train Staff

Nantlle Branch worked "One Engine in Steam"
No signals.

ACKNOWLEDGEMENTS

This work would have been much the poorer but for the help and encouragement given by all who were approached. Obviously thanks are due to those who supplied photographs from their collections, including the following: H. C. & R. M. Casserley, D. Chaplin, V. R. Anderson, B. Cowlishaw, W. A. Camwell, J. J. Davis, T. J. Edgington, F. M. Gates, J. S. Gilks, J. W. T. House, E. N. Kneale, R. Gulliver for supplying and permitting the use of the Mowat collection, Joe Moss, Mrs K. Platt who made the late G. H. Platt's negatives available for this work, L& GRP by permission of David & Charles Holdings Ltd., Lens of Sutton, British Railways, D. Thompson, Clwyd County Council Archives Services at Hawarden and Ruthin, Gwynedd County Council Archives Services at Caernarfon, Llangefni and Dolgellau, John Wood, Mrs. June Ward for permission to use her late husband Gordon's photograph, and Vic Bradley of the Llanberis Lake Railway.

The following have provided assistance and to them go thanks also: Greg Fox; Roy Anderson; Eric Lynn; C. J. Preston; R. Paddison; W. Jones (Wil Bach Bob Shunt); H. G. Wilson of the North West HMRS); Roger Carpenter; Steven Goodhall; Vernon & Bill Griffiths of Llandudno Junction shed; Bernard Mathews; Vic Roberts of British Rail, Chester; Vic Thomas, former driver of Rhyl; Ivor Vaughan; Peter Webber; R. J. Dean for facilities afforded; Owen Hughes, Headmaster of Grango School, Rhos, for providing facilities and encouragement; The National Library of Wales, Aberystwyth; The Royal Commission on Ancient and Historical Monuments in Wales; and Miss Hilary Sherrington.

Thanks must be extended to my wife Norma, who puts up with the upheaval, to Nicola for assistance when needed, and general encouragement, and to Paul Karau and the staff of Wild Swan Publications.

Finally, special thanks are due to Richard Foster for devoting so much of his time to correcting the manuscript and signalling plans.

I hope this volume will serve as a permanent tribute to the men of Bangor shed.

Bill Rear
Johnstown
Wrexham